Aug. 2019

W9-BPJ-918

Philadelphia

MAP INCLUDED

day BY day ®

3rd Edition

by Reid Bramblett

FrommerMedia LLC

Contents

Published by:

Frommer Media LLC

ISBN 978-1-628-87450-1 (paper), 978-1-628-87451-8 (ebk)

Editorial Director: Pauline Frommer
Development Editor: Holly Hughes
Production Editor: Lindsay Conner
Photo Editor: Meghan Lamb
Assistant Photo Editor: Phil Vinke
Cartographer: Roberta Stockwell
Indexer: Maro Riofrancos

Front cover photos, left to right: Reading Terminal Market © Sean Pavone / Shutterstock.com; Liberty Bell and Independence Hall © Songquan Deng; Eakins Oval © Pabkov / Shutterstock.com
Back cover photo: Bike Rider at Philadelphia Museum of Art © Fotos593 / Shutterstock.com

For information on our other products or services, see www.frommers.com.

Frommer Media LLC also publishes its books in a variety of electronic formats. Some content that appears in print may not be available in electronic formats.

Manufactured in China

5 4 3 2 1

About This Guide

Organizing your time. That's what this guide is all about.

Other guides give you long lists of things to see and do and then expect you to fit the pieces together. The Day by Day guides are different. These guides tell you the best of everything, and then they show you how to see it in the smartest, most time-efficient way. Our authors have designed detailed itineraries organized by time, neighborhood, or special interest. And each tour comes with a bulleted map that takes you from stop to stop.

Hoping to visit the birthplace of American democracy or gaze upon the Liberty Bell? Planning to graze for lunch at Philly's famous Reading Terminal Market? Hoping to catch a Phillies home game at Citizens Bank Park? Whatever your interest or schedule, the Day by Days give you the smartest routes to follow. Not only do we take you to the top attractions, hotels, and restaurants, but we also help you access those special moments that locals get to experience—those "finds" that turn tourists into travelers.

The Day by Days are also your top choice if you're looking for one complete guide for all your travel needs. The best hotels and restaurants for every budget, the greatest shopping values, the wildest nightlife—it's all here.

Why should you trust our judgment? Because our authors personally visit each place they write about. They're an independent lot who say what they think and would never include places they wouldn't recommend to their best friends. They're also open to suggestions from readers. If you'd like to contact them, please send your comments our way at feedback@frommers.com, and we'll pass them on.

Enjoy your Day by Day guide—the most helpful travel companion you can buy. And have the trip of a lifetime.

About the Author

Reid Bramblett is thrilled that, after authoring or contributing to dozens of Frommer's guidebooks over more than 20 years, he is finally getting to write one about his hometown. He grew up in Cheltenham, on the border of Philadelphia (though he did live at 2nd and Vine in Old City as a child). He has written about travel for everyone from *Newsweek,* the *Miami Herald,* and *Modern Bride* to MSNBC.com and Travelandleisure.com; served as Associate Editor at *Budget Travel* magazine; and started his own award-winning ReidsGuides.com family of travel sites. After long stints in New York City, Missouri, and Europe, he has returned to the Philly exurbs of Montgomery County to raise his kids.

An Additional Note

Please be advised that travel information is subject to change at any time—and this is especially true of prices. We therefore suggest that you write or call ahead for confirmation when making your travel plans. The authors, editors, and publisher cannot be held responsible for the experiences of readers while traveling. Your safety is important to us, however, so we encourage you to stay alert and be aware of your surroundings.

Star Ratings, Icons & Abbreviations

Every hotel, restaurant, and attraction listing in this guide has been ranked for quality, value, service, amenities, and special features using a **star-rating system.** Hotels, restaurants, attractions, shopping, and nightlife are rated on a scale of zero stars (recommended) to three stars (exceptional). In addition to the star-rating system, we also use a **kids icon** to point out the best bets for families. Within each tour, we recommend cafes, bars, or restaurants where you can take a break. Each of these stops appears in a shaded box marked with a coffee-cup-shaped bullet ☕.

The following **abbreviations** are used for credit cards:

AE	American Express	DISC	Discover	V	Visa
DC	Diners Club	MC	MasterCard		

Frommers.com

Now that you have this guidebook to help you plan a great trip, visit our website at **www.frommers.com** for additional travel information on more than 4,000 destinations. We update features regularly to give you instant access to the most current trip-planning information available. At Frommers.com, you'll find scoops on the best airfares, lodging rates, and car rental bargains. You can even book your travel online through our reliable travel booking partners. Other popular features include:

- Online updates of our most popular guidebooks
- Vacation sweepstakes and contest giveaways
- Newsletters highlighting the hottest travel trends
- Online travel message boards with featured travel discussions

A Note on Prices

In the "Take a Break" (☕) and "Best Bets" sections of this book, we have used a system of dollar signs to show a range of costs for 1 night in a hotel (the price of a double-occupancy room) or the cost of an entree at a restaurant. Use the following table to decipher the dollar signs:

Cost	Hotels	Restaurants
$	under $100	under $10
$$	$100–$200	$10–$20
$$$	$200–$300	$20–$30
$$$$	$300–$400	$30–$40
$$$$$	over $400	over $40

How to Contact Us

In researching this book, we discovered many wonderful places—hotels, restaurants, shops, and more. We're sure you'll find others. Please tell us about them, so we can share the information with your fellow travelers in upcoming editions. If you were disappointed with a recommendation, we'd love to know that, too. Please write to: Contact@FrommerMedia.com.

16 Favorite
Moments

16 Favorite Moments

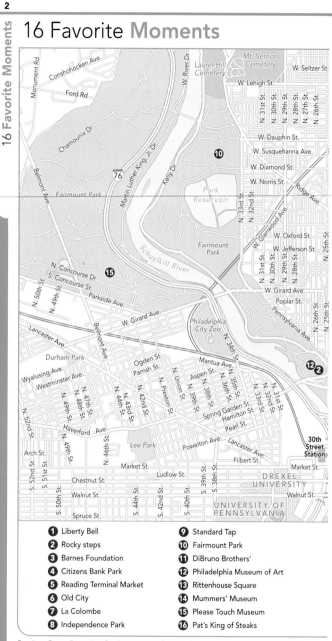

1 Liberty Bell
2 Rocky steps
3 Barnes Foundation
4 Citizens Bank Park
5 Reading Terminal Market
6 Old City
7 La Colombe
8 Independence Park
9 Standard Tap
10 Fairmount Park
11 DiBruno Brothers'
12 Philadelphia Museum of Art
13 Rittenhouse Square
14 Mummers' Museum
15 Please Touch Museum
16 Pat's King of Steaks

Previous Page: Browsing the Barnes Foundation's delightfully eclectic art collection.

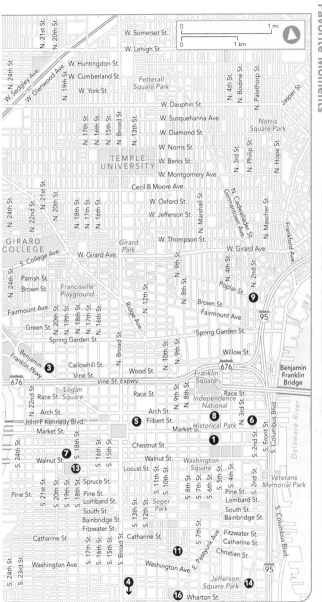

etting a true feeling for all that is Philadelphia means being willing to embrace extremes. One minute you're immersed in American history, the next you're elbow-to-elbow in a crowd of modern-day foodies. You'll be able to embrace nature at the largest city park in the U.S., glimpse Philly's unique brand of chic at Rittenhouse Square, see cutting-edge art in Old City—and, of course, have your fill of that special sandwich which many Philadelphians think is as important as Benjamin Franklin (well, almost).

The iconic Liberty Bell, a Philly must-see.

❶ **Visit the Liberty Bell.** The cracked bell that no longer tolls seems to top every tourist's to-do list. Go see it early, but also walk by it again after dusk, when its bronze cast seems to glow inside its modern glass-and-steel house. *See p 9.*

❷ **Run like Rocky up the steps of the Philadelphia Museum of Art.** When you get to the top, turn around, pump your fists in the air, and belt out a few bars of "Gonna Fly Now" (or just play it in your head). Then, get your photo taken with the boxer's statue at the foot of the steps. *See p 45.*

❸ **Soak in Albert Barnes' amazingly eclectic collection.** You'll find an amazing array of work from

Matisse (1869–1954), Renoir (1841–1919), Picasso (1881–1973) and Cézanne (1839–1906), plus African sculpture, Pennsylvania Dutch furniture, architectural oddments, and more in this museum's hip new home on the Parkway. *See p 33.*

❹ **Take in a Phillies game.** Don't tell, but the Phillies are my favorite of all of the local pro teams, and not just because they brought home the Series in 2008 and went all the way in 2009. The Phils have a special vibe that's spirited and modest. Go catch a game at Citizens Bank Park, and when that ball soars "outta here," watch—and hear—the ballpark's giant Liberty Bell ring. *See p 168.*

⑤ Get a taste—literally—of Reading Terminal Market. You'll find dozens of local vendors here, boasting every sort of fare Philadelphia has to offer, from tandoori and cheesesteaks to cannoli and shoofly pie. Even though it's crazy-packed on Saturday mornings, that's when I like to go, to soak in the hustle and bustle—and see what everyone else is buying. *See p 110.*

⑥ Gallery hop Old City on First Friday. Go on the first Friday of the month, and you'll be treated to edgy art, welcoming crowds, and free wine and beer—if you can snag it—mostly along North 2nd and 3rd streets. *See p 32.*

⑦ Order a "cappuccino for here" at La Colombe. For less than $3, you can enjoy a silky foamed coffee in a handsome Deruta cup and discover why *Food and Wine* rated this spot the best cafe in the country. *See p 63.*

⑧ Meet the Colonials. Go ahead. Strike up a chat with the 18th-century characters roaming Independence Park and Old City. Each tricorn-hatted soldier, full-skirted seamstress, fresh-faced page, and dead-ringer for Ben Franklin has an engaging personal story to tell about the birth of the nation. (Plus, they give the best directions.) *See p 26.*

⑨ Drink a pint of hand-pumped ale at Northern Liberties' Standard Tap. You'll be participating in an age-old tradition. Before Prohibition, Philadelphia was the beer-brewing capital of the Western Hemisphere. Today, local micro-breweries such as the Philadelphia Brewing Company, Yards, and Victory are reviving that legacy via delicious stouts, lagers, ambers, pilsners, and more. *See p 122.*

⑩ Walk or bike in Fairmount Park. It's the country's largest city park; my favorite part of it to roam is called Valley Green, with wide pathways, historic bridges, and WPA-era buildings. The area is especially pretty in fall when the leaves change colors and in winter when you can just imagine the horse-and-carriages of yesteryear jingle-belling through the snow. *See p 87.*

⑪ Cram yourself into DiBruno Bros. Dubbed "the House of Cheese," this impossibly narrow space in the Italian Market is full of charming cheesemongers who talk you into blowing all your money on

The Philadelphia Phillies always attract an energetic crowd to Citizens Bank Park.

an herb-coated raw sheep's milk concoction from the wilds of Provence, or an extra-sharp Provolone aged for 2 years in Italy. *See p 82.*

⑫ Tour the Art Museum. For every 50 folks who jog up the Rocky Steps, maybe one bothers going inside the Philadelphia Museum of Art itself. Don't lose out on 200 rooms of exquisite works from Old Masters to Impressionists, recreated medieval cloisters to contemporary installations. Come see why this is one of the premier art galleries in North America. *See p 13.*

⑬ Go high-brow along Rittenhouse Square. The time to go is late afternoon to late evening, when a seat at a sidewalk table at one of the seen-and-be-seen watering holes will ensure you a view of the most stylish impromptu parade in town. *See p 93.*

⑭ Catch the Mummers. What Mardi Gras is to New Orleans, this oddly engaging, entirely debauched New Year's Day parade is to Philadelphia, only much chillier

Don't just jog up the steps a la Rocky— go inside the Philadelphia Museum of Art to enjoy its many masterpieces.

A costumed interpreter playing Betsy Ross engages young visitors to Independence Park.

and much less organized, if you can picture that. (Imagine a bunch of burly contractors dressed in sequins, feathers, and face paint, stopping along Broad Street to dance and strut to loud pop tunes, and you've got an idea of Mummery.) *See p 20.*

⑮ Let the kids go nuts at Memorial Hall. It may look like an imposing venue, but ever since the Please Touch Museum moved in, it's as welcoming as a playground. Besides reversing the "no touching" rule, it has hundreds of exhibits encouraging kids to play and explore, ride and create, and play some more. *See p 9.*

⑯ Eat a cheesesteak. Preferably at a red picnic table beneath the neon lights at Pat's King of Steaks in South Philly. At 2:30am, just after the bars have all let out. (You didn't think I'd leave this off the list, did you?) *See p 109.* ●

The Best **in One Day**

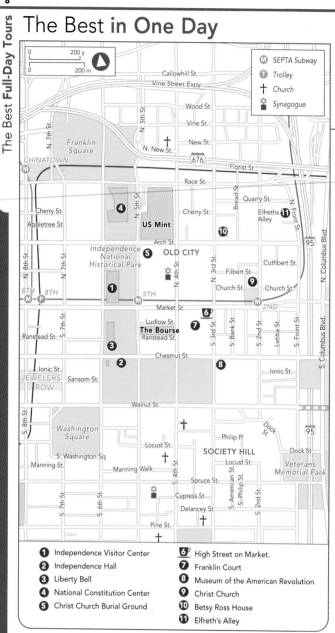

	SEPTA Subway
Ⓜ	SEPTA Subway
Ⓣ	Trolley
†	Church
✡	Synagogue

1 Independence Visitor Center
2 Independence Hall
3 Liberty Bell
4 National Constitution Center
5 Christ Church Burial Ground
6 High Street on Market.
7 Franklin Court
8 Museum of the American Revolution
9 Christ Church
10 Betsy Ross House
11 Elfreth's Alley

Previous Page: A horse-and-carriage ride is a fitting way to visit historic Independence Hall.

With only a day, focus on the founding of the United States. Philadelphia preserves an astounding number of the buildings, monuments, and even entire streets dating back to the Revolution and beyond. Today the country's "most historic square mile" will be your stomping grounds: Wear comfortable shoes, leave pocket knives at home (security checks), and don't be afraid to chat up the costumed "Colonials." START: **Independence Visitor Center, 6th & Market sts.**

❶ ★★ Independence Visitor Center. With its self-service kiosks, concierge services, umpteen maps and brochures, and box office for tickets to Independence Hall and historic homes, this welcome center isn't just a great first stop for a tour of historic Philadelphia, it's a great first stop for *any* tour of Philadelphia. ⏱ *½ hr. 6th & Market sts.* ☎ *800/537-7676. www.phlvisitor center.com. Daily 8:30am–7pm.*

❷ ★★★ Independence Hall. Where it all went down: the Declaration of Independence, the Articles of Confederation, and the U.S. Constitution. Squeeze into the stately spaces where George Washington (1732–1799), Thomas Jefferson (1743–1826), John Adams (1735–1826), Benjamin Franklin (1706–1790), and their Colonial brethren conceived of a country affording its citizens "life, liberty and the pursuit of happiness."

Don't miss Washington's "Rising Sun Chair," rare maps of the 13 colonies, and the tipstaff (a wooden and brass instrument used to subdue rowdy onlookers in the courtroom). Half-hour tours are guided. ⏱ *1 hr.; includes wait in line. Chestnut St., btw. 5th & 6th sts.* ☎ *215/965-2305. www.nps.gov/ inde. Mar 1–Dec 31, tickets are required (free at Visitor Center or $1.50 in advance online: pick up at least 1 hour before tour). Daily 9am– 5pm (to 7pm in summer).*

❸ ★★★ Liberty Bell. The cracked, 1-ton symbol of American independence and equality resides in a $12.6-million glass gazebo across Chestnut Street from Independence Hall, preceded by a hall exhaustively documenting it and its role in the Revolution. ⏱ *½ hr. Free admission (tickets not required; mandatory security check). Daily 9am–5pm (to 7pm in summer).*

The iconic Liberty Bell glows within its modern glass-and-steel canopy.

❹ ★★ kids National Constitution Center. The world's only museum devoted to the U.S. Constitution is way more fun than it sounds. A performance in the round explains the document's history, and interactive exhibits let you take the Presidential Oath of Office, don a Supreme Court robe, stand next to a Declaration signer, and examine hanging chads from the 2000 election. ⏱ 1½ hr. *525 Arch St.* ☎ *215/409-6600. www.constitutioncenter.org. Admission $14.50 adults; $13 seniors & students; $11 ages 6–18. Buy tickets in advance; arrive 20 minutes early for timed theater show. Mon–Sat 9:30am–5pm, Sun noon–5pm.*

❺ ★ Christ Church Burial Ground. The 1719 expansion of Christ Church (bullet ❾) included the graves of five signers of the Declaration of Independence, one of them Benjamin Franklin. Join the throngs who have tossed a penny on his grave for good luck. ⏱ ¼ hr. *SE corner of 5th & Arch sts.* ☎ *215/922-1695. www.christchurch phila.org. Mon–Sat 9am–5pm, Sun 12:30–5pm.*

☕ ★★ High Street on Market. Step back, momentarily, into modern times for a tasty salad, sandwich, natural soda, cappuccino, and the day's papers at this gourmet cafe. For a longer lunch, try the more formal sister restaurant, Fork, next door (see p 106). *308 Market St.* ☎ *215/625-0988. http://high streetonmarket.com. $–$$.*

❼ ★★ kids Franklin Court. In a brick courtyard off Market St., the outline of Ben Franklin's long-since demolished home is traced by steel girders. Surrounding it is a museum that pays tribute to the many careers (printer, postmaster, publisher, fireman, scientist, politician) of America's favorite Renaissance Man. Highlights include a replica of Franklin's printing press, a post office that hand-stamps postcards, and a newer underground museum (which charges $5 admission). ⏱ 1 hr. *314–322 Market St.* ☎ *215/965-2305. www.nps.gov/ inde. Free admission. Daily 9am–5pm (printing office opens 10am). Post office closed Sun.*

❽ ★★ kids Museum of the American Revolution. The newest addition to Independence Park, this marvelous museum traces the American Revolution from the Sons of Liberty to the messy beginnings of the new country. Its highlight is George Washington's actual campaign tent, his wartime home-from-home. Intriguing exhibits contextualize relics from the era, like—a room dedicated to the "shot heard round the world," for example, contains a fragment of the Old North Bridge at Concord, MA, flanked by rifles and equipment that belonging to soldiers from both sides of the battle. ⏱ 1½ hr. *101 S. Third St.*

In the Colonial era, Christ Church's congregation was full of the political elite.

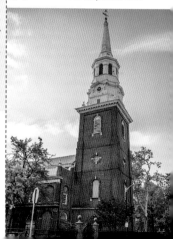

Elfreth's Alley is the oldest continually inhabited street in the United States.

877/740-1776. www.amrev museum.org. Admission $19 adults; $17 seniors & students, $12 children 6–17. Daily 10am–5pm (Jul–Aug 9:30am–6pm)

⑨ ★★ Christ Church. This English Palladian landmark is perhaps the neighborhood's most important Colonial building. George Washington had his own pew here; its baptismal font, a gift from London's All Hallows' Church, was the one in which William Penn (1644–1718) was baptized. The tiny churchyard holds the tomb of Andrew Hamilton, the Philadelphia lawyer who helped establish freedom of the press. 🕐 ½ hr. *2nd & Market sts.* 📞 *215/922-1695. www.christchurch phila.org. Free admission. Mon–Sat 9am–5pm; Sun 12:30–5pm. Closed Mon–Tues in Jan–Feb.*

⑩ ★ kids Betsy Ross House. The jury's out on whether Betsy Ross (1752–1836), the seamstress of the Stars and Stripes, actually lived in this teensy abode (or, for that matter, if she really sewed the first flag). No matter: This restored dwelling remains a classic Philly sight, from cellar kitchen to wee bedrooms to flag-filled gift shop. 🕐 ½ hr. *See p 40.*

⑪ ★★★ Elfreth's Alley. The oldest continuously inhabited street in the U.S.A., this narrow cobblestone lane is lined with small two-story row houses—now, as then, home to tradesmen, artisans, and urbanites of varied religions and ethnicities. Number 124–6, the Mantua Maker's House (cape maker), is the alley's museum, complete with 18th-century garden and dressmaker's shop. 🕐 ¾ hr. *See p 51.*

The Best in **Two Days**

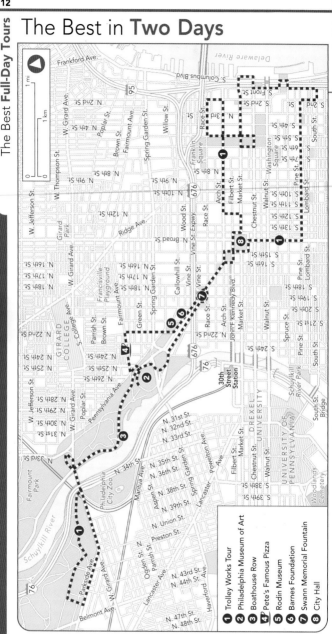

1 Trolley Works Tour
2 Philadelphia Museum of Art
3 Boathouse Row
4 Pete's Famous Pizza
5 Rodin Museum
6 Barnes Foundation
7 Swann Memorial Fountain
8 City Hall

You've done enough walking. On day two, it's time to take a load off and get the lay of the land (and visit some top sights) with a ride around Old City, Center City, Museum Mile, Penn's Landing, and Fairmount Park aboard a Victorian-style trolley. START: 5th & Market sts, or any of the 21 stops along the trolley's route.

❶ ★★ kids Trolley Works Tour. A 24-hour pass for the surprisingly speedy rail-less trolleys and double-decker buses gets you the most comprehensive tour of downtown. On-and-off privileges and unlimited rides mean if Junior wants to see **Eastern State Penitentiary** (see p 68) again, or if you regret not grabbing those vintage earrings on Antique Row, a second chance is just a short ride away. ⏱ 1½ hr. 5th & Market sts.; 26 more stops along route, plus shuttles from hotels and other prime spots. ☎ 215/389-8687. www. phillytour.com. 24-hour pass: $35 adults, $32 seniors, $12 children 4–12. Apr–Nov daily 9:30am–5pm (to 6pm Sat); Dec–Mar daily 10am–4pm.

❷ ★★★ Philadelphia Museum of Art. Hop off at this Greco-Roman temple on a hill, jog up the steps à la Rocky, and get lost in 200 galleries of art and objets, medieval cloisters, and blockbuster special exhibitions. Among the more than quarter-million works are Cézanne's (1839–1906) monumental Bathers, paintings by native Philadelphian Thomas Eakins (1844–1916), and classics from Van Gogh (1853–1890), Poussin (1594–1665), Rubens (1577–1640), Duchamp (1887–1968), and Monet (1840–1926). Head across the street to the new Perelman Building, housing more than 180,000 prints, drawings, photographs, and textiles. ⏱ 2 hrs. 26th St. & Ben Franklin Pkwy. ☎ 215/763-1000. www.philamuseum.org. Admission $20 adults, $18 seniors, $14 students and children 13–18 (does not include special exhibits); first Sun of the month (and Wed after 5pm), pay what you wish. Admission also covers Perelman Building and Rodin Museum. Tues–Sun 10am–5pm (Wed & Fri until 8:45pm).

Victorian-style Trolley Works buses visit most major sites in the Center City and beyond.

Philadelphia Museum of Art

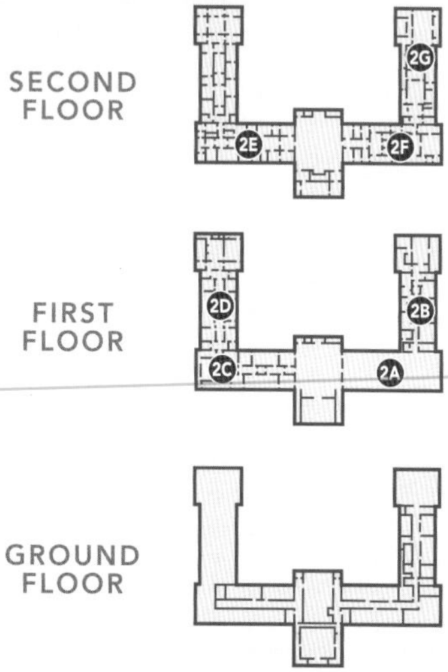

SECOND
FLOOR

2E 2G 2F

FIRST
FLOOR

2D 2B
2C 2A

GROUND
FLOOR

You'll spend most of your time on the first and second floors of this U-shaped museum. Begin where your interests lie—especially at **2A Special Exhibitions,** which are almost always world-class, usually require advance reservations, and charge additional admission. Next, explore works by Thomas Eakins, as well as Shaker and Pennsylvania Dutch furnishings in the **2B American Collection.** Cross the grand stairs (looking up to see Alexander Calder's [1898–1976] *Ghost* mobile) to **2C European Art** 1850–1900, packed with works representative of the Impressionist, Symbolist, Naturalist, and Art Nouveau styles including works by Cézanne, Cassatt (1844–1926),

Monet, Van Gogh, and amazing period objets. Before you head upstairs, take a quick spin through **2D Modern and Contemporary Art** for iconoclastic pieces by Jasper Johns (b. 1930), Cy Twombly (b. 1928), Constantin Brancusi (1876–1957), and Marcel Duchamp. The second floor shows earlier pieces from Europe: **2E 1500–1850 French and English period rooms,** with works by Poussin and Rubens; **2F 1100–1500: Renaissance works** including a 15th-century Venetian bedroom, a French Gothic chapel; and an **2G Asian gallery** that includes an interesting mix: a Japanese teahouse, Persian carpets, and a 16th-century Indian temple hall.

3 ★★ Boathouse Row. From the restaurant, head toward the river, along Kelly Drive, to this iconic row of 10 antique (circa 1850s–1870s) clubhouses belonging to collegiate and other amateur

crew groups and teams. You'll likely glimpse some oarsmen sculling along the river. Come back, if you can, after dark to see the houses lit up. ⏲ ½ hr. See p 69.

☕ ★ Pete's Famous Pizza.
The Parkway lacks for dining
options, but the Art Museum
guards swear by this Fairmont classic, which has served delicious pizzas, cheesesteaks, hoagies, and
burgers since 1980. *2328 Fairmount
Ave.* ☎ 215/765-3040. www.petes
famouspizza.com. $–$$.

⑤ ★★★ Rodin Museum. Far-
ther down the Parkway, stop by this
Paul Cret–designed mini-museum
where *The Thinker* and the *Gates
of Hell* greet you to the largest collection of Rodin's (1840–1917) works
outside of Paris. It's a lovely spot,
replete with major sculptures, plaster models, and original sketchbooks. ⏱ 1 hr. See p 34.

⑥ ★★★ Barnes Foundation.
Moved here (contentiously) from its
original suburban home in 2012,
this world-renowned museum is
stuffed with some 8,000 largely
Impressionist and Post-Impressionist works (Renoir, Cézanne, Matisse,
Picasso, Van Gogh) fussily arranged
by collector Albert Barnes himself
alongside antique everyday objects
(think: iron hinges) and primitive
sculptures. ⏱ 2 hrs. See p 32.

**⑦ ★ Swann Memorial Foun-
tain.** A few more blocks and you'll
run into Logan Circle and its classical centerpiece fountain. Also
known as "The Fountain of the
Three Rivers," the aquatic sculpture
represents the region's three major
waterways: the Schuylkill, Delaware,
and Wissahickon. It was created by
Alexander Stirling Calder (1870–
1945), father of Alexander Calder
(he of the giant mobile in the Art
Museum) and son of City Hall

*Philadelphia's Rodin Museum has the
largest collection of the sculptor's work
outside of Paris.*

sculptor Alexander Milne Calder.
⏱ 20 min. See p 32.

⑧ ★★ City Hall. Until 1987, the
37-foot, 27-ton bronze statue of
Philly founder William Penn—created by Alexander Milne Calder
(1846–1923), as was all the statuary
on this building—was the highest
point in Philadelphia, at 548 feet. In
fact, City Hall briefly reigned as the
world's tallest building from 1901 to
1908, and it's still the largest municipal building in the U.S. Worth it:
Views from the tower observation
deck. Interesting: A 2-hour behind-
the-scenes tour ($15; Mon–Fri at
12:30pm). Surrounding City Hall,
Dilworth Plaza has a concert
lawn, cafe, and fountain that doubles as a winter ice rink. ⏱ 20–120
min. Broad & Market sts.
☎ 267/514-4757. Tower admission
$8 adults, $6 seniors, $4 students.
Tower tours every 15 min. Mon–Fri,
9:30am–4:15pm and some Sat
11am–4pm.

The Best in **Three Days**

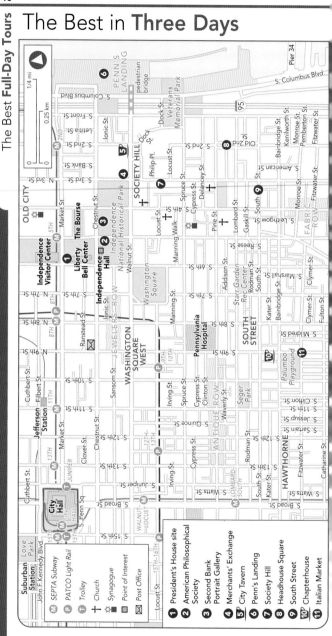

Pier 34

S. Columbus Blvd.

PENN'S LANDING

pedestrian bridge

S. Columbus Blvd

S. Front St.

Letitia St.

S. 2nd St.

N. 2nd St.

S. Bank St.

N. 3rd St.

S. 3rd St.

Dock St.

Ionic St.

Dock St.

Veterans Memorial Park

OLD CITY

Market St.

5TH

The Bourse

Chestnut St.

Independence Visitor Center

N. 7th St.

N. 8th St.

8TH

Liberty Bell Center

Ionic St.

Independence National Historical Park

Independence Hall

Walnut St.

Washington Square

Ranstead St.

JEWELERS ROW

N. 9th St.

Cuthbert St.

Filbert St.

11TH

Jefferson Station

Market St.

Chestnut St.

WASHINGTON SQUARE WEST

Sansom St.

S. 10th St.

S. 11th St.

Clover St.

S. 12th St.

12TH

13TH

JUNIPER

S. 13th St.

Irving St.

Cuthbert St.

Cypress St.

City Hall

S. Juniper St.

S. Broad St.

S. Penn Sq.

15TH

CITY HALL

15TH–16TH

WALNUT

LOCUST

S. 15th St.

Locust St.

SOCIETY HILL

Philip Pl.

Locust St.

Spruce St.

Cypress St.

Delancey St.

4th St.

Manning Walk

Pine St.

Lombard St.

Gaskill St.

Reese St.

Leithgow St.

S. 6th St.

Manning St.

Addison St.

S. 7th St.

Starr Garden Rec Center

Rodman St.

Kater St.

Bainbridge St.

S. 8th St.

Pennsylvania Hospital

S. 9th St.

ANTIQUE ROW

Quince St.

Spruce St.

Cypress St.

Clinton St.

Waverly St.

Seger Park

S. Quince St.

Rodman St.

S. 12th St.

HAWTHORNE

Fitzwater St.

S. 13th St.

South St.

Kater St.

Catharine St.

S. Watts St.

SOUTH

LOMBARD

S. Broad St.

Irving St.

SOUTH STREET

S. Mildred St.

Palumbo Playground

S. Clifton St.

Saraiah St.

Jessup St.

S. 11th St.

S. Marshall St.

American St.

Bainbridge St.

Monroe St.

Fitzwater St.

Old 2nd St.

FABRIC ROW

South St.

Monroe St.

Fitzwater St.

Kenilworth St.

Pemberton St.

95

Leithgow St.

Bainbridge St.

Clymer St.

Fulton St.

Clymer St.

1/4 mi

0.25 km

Suburban Station

Love Park

John F. Kennedy Blvd

Ⓜ SEPTA Subway
Ⓟ PATCO Light Rail
Ⓣ Trolley
✝ Church
✡ Synagogue
■ Point of Interest
⊠ Post Office

❶ President's House site
❷ American Philosophical Society
❸ Second Bank Portrait Gallery
❹ Merchants' Exchange
❺ City Tavern
❻ Penn's Landing
❼ Society Hill
❽ Headhouse Square
❾ South Street
❿ Chapterhouse
⓫ Italian Market

It's time to get to know the city's inimitable blend of gorgeous, gritty, and gourmet that makes Philadelphia . . . *Philly.*
START: **Southeast corner of 6th St. & Market St.**

❶ ★ President's House. This open-air mock-up of low walls and hovering windows and door frames replicates America's first "white house," a three-story brick mansion where both George Washington (1790–1797) and John Adams (1797–1800) lived and worked as President. Plaques and videos give insights on everything from Presidential duties to the lives of the slaves who worked here; in a few spots you can peer at excavations of the actual house's remains. ⏱ *20 min. Market St. at S. 6th St. www.nps.gov/inde. Free admission. Always open.*

❷ ★ American Philosophical Society. Founded by Benjamin Franklin in 1743, the United States's oldest learned society has counted among its members George Washington, Thomas Paine, John J. Audubon, Charles Darwin, Thomas Edison, Albert Einstein, Robert Frost, and Marie Curie. Annual exhibits in its small but fascinating museum are culled from 350,000 books and periodicals, 250,000 images, and 3,000 artifacts—items like Thomas Jefferson's handwritten draft of the *Declaration of Independence,* Benjamin Franklin's library chair, or Lewis and Clark's journals. ⏱ *½ hr. 104 S. 5th St. (just south of Chestnut St.)* ☎ *215/440-3400. www.amphilsoc.org. Free admission. Mid-Apr–Dec Thurs–Sun 10am–4pm.*

❸ ★ Second Bank Portrait Gallery. William Strickland designed this imposing Greek Revival structure in 1816 to house the influential Second Bank of the United States. It now displays excellent paintings of famous early Americans, from Ben Franklin and

Patrick Henry to explorers Lewis and Clark. ⏱ *45 min. 420 Chestnut St. (btw. 4th & 5th sts.)* ☎ *215/965-2305. www.nps.gov/inde. Free admission. 11am–5pm (daily in summer, Wed–Sun fall and spring, Sat–Sun winter).*

❹ Merchants' Exchange. Another Greek Revival Strickland gem, the U.S's oldest stock exchange building dates to the 1830s. It's now the offices of Independence Hall National Park. Check out the curved colonnade in back. ⏱ *5 min. Walnut, 3rd & Dock sts.*

❺ ★ City Tavern. A faithful reconstruction of the original pub where the Founding Fathers hashed out the *Declaration* and *Constitution* over tankards of ale still serves many 18th-century dishes, from West Indies pepperpot soup to Colonial turkey pot pie. *138 S. 2nd St. (at Walnut St.).* ☎ *215/413-1443. www.citytavern.com. $$.*

Walk around to the back of the Greek Revival-style Merchants' Exchange to see its lovely curved colonnade.

With its stone-paved streets and Georgian houses, Society Hill is a delightful neighborhood to stroll around.

6 Penn's Landing. No longer a bustling port, the pedestrian-friendly Delaware Riverfront is now a relaxing place to stroll. If you're into seafaring, visit the **Independence Seaport Museum** (see p 57) and some of the historic ships anchored here: the 1892 *USS Olympia* (oldest steel warship afloat); the 1944 *USS Becuna* (a Guppy 1-A sub that served in World War II, Korea, and Vietnam); and the four-masted tall ship *Moshulu*, now a restaurant (see p 96). Afterward, walk south past the Art Deco–inspired Hyatt Regency, then cross back over Columbus Boulevard at Spruce Street. ⏱ *90 min. See p 95.*

7 ★★ Society Hill. Back on the "mainland," shudder briefly at I.M. Pei's hideous skyscraping trio of Society Hill Towers (1963), then turn south into quiet streets lined by brick Colonial, Georgian, and Federal-style townhouses—one of the city's first residential neighborhoods, and still among its finest. For a neighborhood walk, see p 54. ⏱ *½ hr.*

8 Headhouse Square. This all-brick replica of the original "New Market" or "Shambles" is once again (Sun May–Dec) an open-air farmers market under a continuous English-style shed. ⏱ *15 min. See p 57.*

9 South Street. For decades, this colorful strip of sneaker stores, costume jewelers, and cheap eats has been Mecca for Philly's under-21 set. Make sure you cross 10th Street to see the mosaics of Isaiah Zagar's Philadelphia's Magic Gardens at no. 1020 (www.philadelphias magicgardens.org). ⏱ *15 min.*

10 ★★ Chapterhouse. This airy art gallery–cum-cafe serves espressos, smoothies, and pastries to a crowd of med students and neighborhood types. *620 S. 9th St. (btw. South & Bainbridge sts.).* ☎ *215/238-2626. http://chapter housecafe.wordpress.com. $.*

11 ★★ Italian Market. The mix of old-school Italian vendors of meats, cheeses, pastries, and produce—along with Mexican bodegas and taquerías, and junk shops galore—in the "oldest outdoor market in America" is nothing if not vibrant.

Italian/9th Street Market

A **Sarcone's** (758 S. 9th St.) has been turning out crusty sesame-seed loaves, garlicky tomato pies, and pepperoni-stuffed breads since 1918. **B** **Isgro Pastries** (1009 Christian St.) bakes amazing pine-nut cookies and cannoli. **C** **Fiorella's** (817 Christian St.) makes sausage right in front of you. **D** **Anthony's Chocolate House** (905 S. 9th St.) serves chocolates, biscotti, and home-made gelato from the storefront where Tony's grandfather once hawked produce. The **E** **mural of former mayor Frank Rizzo** (just past Salter St. in parking lot on right) is Philly's most defaced public art. Head to **F** **Claudio's** (922–924 S. 9th St.) for olives, char-cuterie, and house-made mozza-rella. **G** **DiBruno Bros.** (930 S.

9th St.) is the market's most vaunted kiosk for amazing cheeses. **H** **Talluto's** (944 S. 9th St.) has been making fresh pasta for 50 years. **I** **Fante's** (1006 S. 9th St.) offers a cookware and bakeware bonanza. **J** **Giordano's** (1041–1043 S. 9th St.) has cheap produce out front, cheap parmesan and provolone in back.

A few blocks south, on oppos-ing corners of S. 9th Street & Passyunk Avenue, is Philly's ulti-mate (most say overrated) chees-esteak smack-down: **K** **Geno's,** the neon half of the duel, versus **L** **Pat's King of Steaks,** which claims original sandwich cred. ⏱ 2–3 hrs. ☎ 215/278-2903. www.italianmarketphilly.org. 9th St. btw. Fitzwater & Federal sts. Tues–Sat 8am–5pm; Sun 8am–3pm.

Keeping Mum

If you thought the Italian Market was gritty, you ain't seen nothing 'til you've seen the **Mummers Museum.** This unintentionally oddball homage to Philly's New Year's Day parade (think Mardi Gras with way more feathers, fewer beads, and far less organization) encapsulates the ineffable local tradition. Every January 1, hundreds of South Philly locals who've spent the previous year rehearsing routines, concocting opulently clownish costumes and over-the-top sets, and spray-painting their shoes gold, strut down Broad Street, "performing" along the way (dancing, sashaying, playing instruments, stumbling while intoxicated). The parade descends, apparently, from an old wassailing-style tradition. This museum, with its strange decor and old memorabilia, feels more eccentric than historic—but in a good way, kinda like the Mummers themselves. ⏱ ½ hr. 1100 2nd St. (at Washington Ave.) ☎ 215/336-3050. www.mummersmuseum.com. Admission $5. Wed–Sat 9:30am–4pm. ●

The Mummers Parade is a wacky but beloved Philadelphia tradition, held every New Year's Day.

Philadelphia Early America

1 Gloria Dei Old Swedes
2 Sparks Shot Tower
3 Hancock Street
4 Milk & Honey
5 Presbyterian Historical Society
6 B'nai Abraham
7 Mother Bethel African Methodist Episcopal Church
8 Old Pine Street Presbyterian
9 St. Peter's Episcopal
10 Thaddeus Kosciuszko National Memorial
11 Hill-Physick House
12 Old St. Joseph's Church
13 Bishop White House
14 Dolley Todd House
15 Independence Park
16 Carpenter's Hall
17 Arch Street Meeting House
18 Old City Coffee
19 Christ Church
20 Betsy Ross House
21 Elfreth's Alley

Previous page: Rittenhouse Square is a prime spot for people-watching.

It can be easy to forget that the quest for religious freedom inspired the founding of the United States. To early Americans, churches were more than places to worship—they were symbols of liberation. This tour includes some of the city's oldest. START: **Gloria Dei Old Swedes, Columbus Blvd. & Christian St.**

1 ★★ Gloria Dei Old Swedes. Established in 1700, this still-active Episcopal parish is the second-oldest church in the U.S., a legacy of the short-lived Delaware Valley colony of New Sweden (1638-1655). It's an 18th-century microcosm, complete with parish hall, rectory, and graveyard. Hanging inside are two models of ships that carried the first Swedish settlers to these shores in 1638. In the vestry is a silver wedding crown that can be worn by any woman married here (as was Betsy Ross). *½ hr. Christian St. at Columbus Blvd. 215/389-1513. www.oldswedes.org. Free admission. Daily 9am–4pm (closed Mon Labor Day–Memorial Day).*

2 Sparks Shot Tower. Towering over a neighborhood park, this 142-foot brick pillar is the oldest shot tower in the U.S., opened on July 4, 1808. It produced ammunition for the War of 1812 and Civil War via a brilliantly simple process: Molten lead, poured through a copper sieve near the top, dripped out in perfect spheres (thanks to surface tension), which were solidified by the rushing air as each drop fell into a water basin at the bottom. *1 min. 129–131 Carpenter St. No entry.*

3 ★ Hancock Street. One of Center City's many pretty tree-lined alleys, this street is bordered by tiny houses called "trinities"—one floor each for Faith, Hope, and Charity. While walking around the city, follow small cobblestone streets like this to escape traffic and feel a tad bit more Colonial. *10 min.*

4 ★ Milk & Honey Cafe. Always busy, this eclectic cafe—formerly Philadelphia Java Co., where Charlie begins stalking The Waitress in It's Always Sunny in Philadelphia—has yummy sandwiches and smoothies. *518 S. 4th St. (btw. South & Lombard sts.). 215/928-1811. http://milkandhoneymarket.com. $.*

Gloria Dei Old Swedes is the oldest church in Pennsylvania (and still active).

5 Presbyterian Historical Society. The oldest denominational archives in the U.S. (est. 1852) are 30,000 cubic feet of documents tracing the history of American Presbyterians. Worth a pause just to admire their existence. ⏱ *5 min. 435 Lombard St.* ☎ *215/627-1852. www.history.pcusa.org. Free admission.*

6 B'nai Abraham. The oldest synagogue in Philly was founded in 1874 by Russian Jews fleeing Tsar Alexander II—though the current building dates to 1910. ⏱ *5 min. 527 Lombard St.* ☎ *215/238-2100. www.phillyshul.com. Free admission.*

7 ★ Mother Bethel African Methodist Episcopal Church. On the oldest piece of American soil continuously owned by African-Americans stands the mother church of African Methodist Episcopalism, a faith practiced by 2.5 million. Dedicated in 1794 by pastor Richard Allen (1760–1831), who bought his own freedom from slavery, the handsome current church was built in 1890. Mother Bethel houses Allen's tomb, his Bible, and his hand-hewn pulpit—all available for view, by appointment only. ⏱ *½ hr. 419 S. 6th St. (btw. Pine & Lombard sts.).* ☎ *215/925-0616. www.motherbethel.org. Free admission.*

8 ★ Old Pine Street Presbyterian. Dubbed "the church of the patriots," the city's oldest standing (circa 1768) Presbyterian church offers a glimpse of Colonial design—the hand-painted stencils are particularly lovely—and an idea of how John Adams (1735–1826) spent his Sundays. In 1774, pastor George Duffield (1732–1790) became chaplain to the First Continental Congress, serving in 1776 and 1777 under George Washington during the harsh winter at

Old Pine Street Presbyterian is known as "the church of the patriots."

Valley Forge. Buried in the church-yard are 50-some Revolutionary War soldiers, a signer of the Constitution, and a ringer of the Liberty Bell. ⏱ *½ hr. 412 Pine St.* ☎ *215/925-8051. www.oldpine.org. Free admission.*

9 ★ St. Peter's Episcopal. West of Old Pine rises the William Strickland–designed steeple of this ornate 1761 church once attended by George Washington (he sat in box pew 41). Buried in the church-yard are Col. John Nixon, who first read the Declaration of Independence to the public on July 8, 1776; Charles Willson Peale (1741–1827), portraitist of George Washington; Vice-President George Mifflin Dallas (1792–1864), for whom Dallas, Texas, was named; and Commodore Stephen Decatur (1779-1820), hero of Tripoli. ⏱ *½ hr. 313 Pine St.* ☎ *215/925-5968. www.stpeters phila.org. Free admission.*

10 ★★ Thaddeus Kosciuszko National Memorial. One of the great foreign heroes of the Revolution, Thaddeus Kosciuszko (1746–1817) came to Philadelphia from Poland in 1776—just in time to read the Declaration, befriend Thomas Jefferson, and fortify the city. Before that glory, he occupied a room in this Georgian-style boardinghouse, a dwelling he'd requested to be "as small, as remote, and as cheap" as possible. ⏱ ½ hr. 310 Pine St. ☎ 215/597-9618. www.nps.gov/thko. Free admission. Apr–Oct: Sat–Sun noon–4pm. Closed Nov–Mar.

⓫ ★ HIll-Physick House. Built in 1786 and inhabited by Philip Syng Physick, "The Father of American Surgery" (and inventor of soda). ⏱ 40 min. See p 56.

⓬ ★ Old St. Joseph's Church. When this Jesuit church was founded in 1733, it was the only place in the English-speaking world where Roman Catholics could celebrate Mass publicly. Among its worshippers was General Lafayette (1757–1834). The building's unassuming facade is intentional: Ben Franklin advised Founding Father John Greaton (1741–1783) to disguise the church for protection against acts of religious intolerance. The interior has been restored to its Colonial glory. ⏱ 20 min. 321 Willings Alley (4th St., near Walnut St.). ☎ 215/923-1733. www.oldstjoseph.org. Free admission.

⓭ ★★ Bishop White House. Dr. William White (1783–1815) was a community pillar in Federal America: rector of St. Peter's and Christ Church; chaplain to the Second Continental Congress; one of the first U.S. bishops of the Episcopal Church; and pal to Franklin, Washington, and Adams. His elegant, circa-1786 house is decidedly upper-class, from its painted cloth floor and its well-stocked second-floor library to its indoor "necessary"—a novelty in the era of outhouses. Get tickets for the required tours (which include the Todd House, below) at the Independence Visitor Center. ⏱ ½ hr. 309 Walnut St. ☎ 215/965-2305. www.nps.gov/inde. Free admission. Closed though July 2019; normal hours: Daily 10am–4pm.

⓮ ★ Dolley Todd House. John Todd, Jr. was a young Quaker lawyer of moderate means. In his circa-1775 Georgian dwelling, the first floor was his office, and his family lived and entertained on the second floor. Todd died in the 1793 yellow fever epidemic. In the large

The Thaddeus Kosciuszko National Memorial pays tribute to a Polish hero of the American Revolution.

The elegant Bishop White House, built around 1786.

upstairs parlor, his widow Dolley (1768–1849) is said to have met James Madison (1751–1836), her future second husband and U.S. President. ⏱ ½ hr. *4th & Walnut sts.* ☎ *215/965-2305. www.nps.gov/ inde. Free admission. Closed through July 2019. Normal hours: Daily 10am–4pm.*

Dolley Todd House was home to a young Quaker lawyer whose widow married President James Madison.

⓯ ★★★ kids **Independence Park.** "America's most historic square mile" is home to Independence Hall and the Liberty Bell. (See p 9.) In summer, actors in 18th-century costumes roam this area, performing as rabble rousers, muster leaders, and storytellers. Some teach kids to march or roll hoops. Check online for scheduling details, or grab a bench and see what happens. ⏱ *1 hr. www.historic philadelphia.org.*

⓰ ★ **Carpenter's Hall.** In 1774, delegates from 12 of the 13 colonies gathered at this neutral meeting spot, home to the trade guild that erected Independence Hall and Christ Church, for the First Continental Congress. They spent 7 weeks drafting 10 resolutions that declared the rights of the Colonies to the British King and Parliament— the precedent to the Declaration of Independence. Carpenter's Hall remains the club for architects, builders, and structural engineers. ⏱ *½ hr. 320 Chestnut St.* ☎ *215/ 925-0167. www.carpentershall.com.*

Free admission. Tues–Sun 10am–4pm (closed Tues Jan–Feb).

⑰ ★ Arch Street Meeting House. This plain 1804 brick building stands on land deeded by William Penn to his Religious Society of Friends—a.k.a. Quakers—in 1693. Quakers believe in a plain and hierarchy-free style of worship referred to as a "meeting." Weekly meetings include much silent meditation until a "Friend" is moved to speak. 🕐 10 min. 320 Arch St. (at 4th St.). 📞 215/625-0627. www.archstreetfriends.org. Free admission.

⑱ ★ Old City Coffee. This charming cafe is the perfect spot to revive with a double espresso, iced green tea, or homemade coffee cake. 221 Church St. 📞 215/629-9292. www.oldcitycoffee.com. $.

⑲ ★★ Christ Church. This landmark Colonial structure—one of the country's finest examples of Georgian architecture—is worth a quick visit, where you'll see the pews of many a Declaration signer. 🕐 20 min. See p 11.

Independence Park features statues (and actors) in colonial garb.

⑳ ★ kids Betsy Ross House. After all, one of these houses ought to be known for its famous female resident. This twee residence *may* have belonged to Betsy Ross (1752–1836), the woman who *may* have designed and sewn the nation's first flag. Still worth a visit. 🕐 ½ hr. See p 40.

㉑ ★★★ Elfreth's Alley. In the shadow of the Ben Franklin Bridge, cobblestone Elfreth's Alley remains the longest continuously inhabited street in America. No. 26 is now a museum. 🕐 ½ hr. See p 51.

The resolutions decided on in 1774 at Carpenter's Hall formed the precedent to the Declaration of Independence.

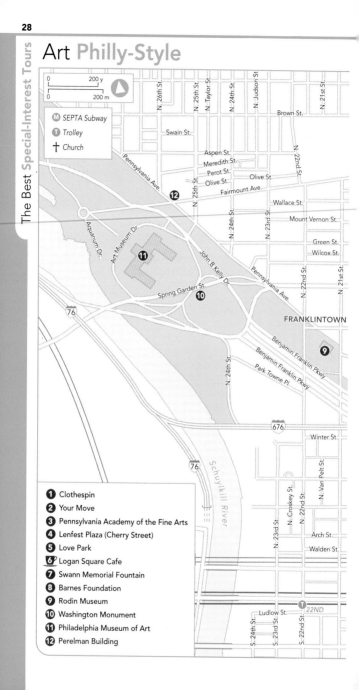

Art Philly-Style

0	200 y
0	200 m

Ⓜ SEPTA Subway
Ⓣ Trolley
✝ Church

N. 26th St.
N. 25th St.
N. Taylor St.
N. 24th St.
N. Judson St.
N. 21st St.

Brown St.

Swain St.

Aspen St.
Meredith St.
Perot St.
Olive St.
Olive St.
Pennsylvania Ave.
N. 25th St.
N. 22nd St.
Fairmount Ave.

Wallace St.

⑫

Mount Vernon St.
N. 24th St.
N. 23rd St.

Green St.
Wilcox St.

Aquarium Dr.
Art Museum Dr.

⑪

John B Kelly Dr.

Pennsylvania Ave.
N. 22nd St.
N. 21st St.

Spring Garden St.
⑩

76

FRANKLINTOWN

Benjamin Franklin Pkwy.
Benjamin Franklin Pkwy.
Park Towne Pl.
⑨

N. 24th St.

676

Winter St.

76

N. Van Pelt St.

Schuylkill River

N. Croskey St.
N. 23rd St.
N. 22nd St.

Arch St.

Walden St.

❶ Clothespin
❷ Your Move
❸ Pennsylvania Academy of the Fine Arts
❹ Lenfest Plaza (Cherry Street)
❺ Love Park
❻ Logan Square Cafe
❼ Swann Memorial Fountain
❽ Barnes Foundation
❾ Rodin Museum
❿ Washington Monument
⓫ Philadelphia Museum of Art
⓬ Perelman Building

Ⓣ 22ND

Ludlow St.

S. 24th St.
S. 23rd St.
S. 22nd St.

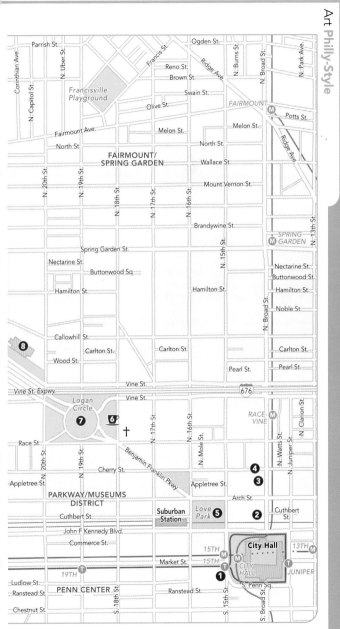

The grand Philadelphia Museum of Art and the rich, eclectic Barnes are the stars of the local art scene. Still, any tour of the city is an art tour, thanks to a 1959 mandate that all new building projects dedicate 1% of construction costs to public art. START: **City Hall, 15th & Market sts.**

Claes Oldenburg's famous "Clothespin" statue.

❶ ★ Clothespin. One of Philadelphia's many public displays of art is Claes Oldenburg's (b. 1929) 10-ton, 45-foot-tall, circa-1976 tribute to, yes, laundry, but also to Brancusi's (1876–1957) *The Kiss.* Across from City Hall (see p 15), this sculpture is a feat of imagination and engineering—notice how the *Clothespin* isn't quite closed—and not without its critics. ⓘ *10 min. 15th & Market sts.*

❷ ★ kids Your Move. It's no coincidence that Daniel Martinez's (b. 1957) colossal game pieces—an iron from Monopoly; dominoes; and "men" from Parcheesi, checkers, and chess—are located directly across from City Hall. The hodgepodge juxtaposes childhood pastimes and adult responsibilities—and offers a nice spot for a photo. ⓘ *10 min. Broad St & JFK Blvd.*

❸ ★★★ Pennsylvania Academy of the Fine Arts. Two blocks north of City Hall, the country's first art museum also happens

Daniel Martinez's "Your Move" is located directly across from City Hall.

The Pennsylvania Academy of the Fine Arts is the country's first art museum and its first arts school.

to be the country's first fine arts school. Known by its acronym, PAFA occupies a beautifully restored, circa-1876 High Victorian Gothic building designed by architects Frank Furness (1839–1912) and George W. Hewitt (1841–1916). Presidential portraitist Charles Willson Peale (1741–1827) and early American sculptor William Rush (1756–1833) founded the Academy in 1805. American realist Thomas Eakins (1844–1916) studied and taught here. All three artists were Philadelphians, and all are well represented among the gallery's thousands of all-American works. Of special note: Furness' splendid red, gold, and blue staircase; an elegant rotunda where Walt Whitman (1819–1892) attended concerts; Benjamin West's (1738–1820) *Penn's Treaty with the Indians*; Peale's paintings of Franklin and Washington; rare works by Rush; and pieces by more modern American artists such as Mark Rothko (1903–1970), Robert Motherwell (1915–1991), Georgia O'Keefe (1887–1986), Edward Hopper (1882–1967), Andrew Wyeth (1917–2009), and Robert Rauschenberg (1925–2008). ⏱ *2 hr. 118 N. Broad St.*

☎ *215/972-2069. www.pafa.org. Admission $15 adults; $12 seniors & students with ID; $8 youth 13–18; 12 and under free. (Free admission to ground-floor gallery). Tues–Fri 10am–5pm, Sat–Sun 11am–5pm. Free tours Wed, Fri & Sat 1pm & 2pm.*

❹ ★ **Lenfest Plaza (Cherry Street).** Claes Oldenburg strikes again! In the summer of 2011, the 51-foot Paint Torch was raised as an exclamation point to this pedestrian-only block of Cherry Street between the two buildings of PAFA. Everyone likes to climb on the dollop of orange paint that "dripped" from the oversized brush to the sidewalk below. Beyond it you may still find an artfully crumpled Grumman Tracker II plane turned into a greenhouse by Jordan Griska; meant to be a temporary installation, at press time it was still standing. ⏱ *10 min. Cherry St. (btw. N. Broad and N. 15th sts.)*

❺ ★★ **Love Park.** Robert Indiana's (1928–2018) bright red, green, and purple font-based work is one of the most iconic monuments in the City of Brotherly Love. Duplicates exist throughout the world, but as the centerpiece of this lovingly planted park (a 2018 renovation added, among other things, a weekday food truck site), it's an enduring reminder of all we need. ⏱ *15 min. 16th St. & JFK Blvd.*

☕ ★ **Logan Square Cafe.** This cafe in Sister Cities Park on the east side of Logan Circle serves gourmet grilled cheeses, classic sandwiches, and 7" pizzas—plus breakfast until 11am. *200 N 18th St. (at Logan Sq.)* ☎ *215/665-8600. www.logansquarecafe.com. $.*

❼ ★★ **kids Swann Memorial Fountain.** Back along Ben Franklin Parkway—occasionally referred to as Philly's Champs-Élysées—are more examples of public artwork, especially sculpture. This grand, classical fountain, with ornate horses and mile-high water, represents the city's three major waterways, the Schuykill, the Delaware, and the Wissahickon rivers. It is the work of Philadelphian Alexander Stirling Calder (1870–1945), son of Alexander Milne Calder (1846–1923)—who did the hundreds of statues festooning City Hall just down the road—and father of Alexander Calder (1898–1976), who

made the mobile in the Art Museum. The fountain serves as a summer splashing spot for local kids. ⏱ *½ hr. Logan Sq. (19th & Race sts).*

❽ ★★★ **Barnes Foundation.** Moved in 2012, amid much brouhaha, from its home in the suburbs to anchor this new Museum Mile

The Swann Memorial Fountain was created by local sculptor Alexander Stirling Calder.

First Fridays: Galleries Galore

Every "First Friday" of the month, the independent art galleries of Old City stay open late to debut exhibits and to serve wine in little plastic cups to enthused, mostly youthful, crowds. If you happen to be in town on a First Friday, get to **Old City** early (galleries usually open 5–9pm for the event; www.oldcityarts.org), start your exploration north of Market Street along 2nd or 3rd, and have at it. Also, if you're planning to dine after you wine, and if you'd like to remain in the neighborhood, be sure to make dinner reservations. On a typical Friday night, Old City is Philly's busiest area. On a First Friday, it's busier still.

Barnes Foundation

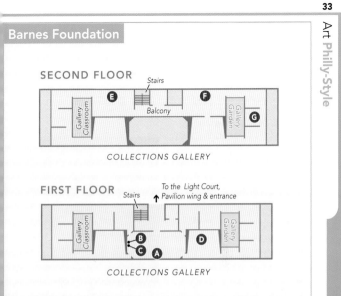

SECOND FLOOR

Stairs

E   **F**

Balcony

Gallery Classroom

Gallery Garden   **G**

COLLECTIONS GALLERY

FIRST FLOOR

Stairs

To the Light Court, Pavilion wing & entrance →

Gallery Classroom

B
C **A**

D

Gallery Garden

COLLECTIONS GALLERY

Surrounded by exhibition spaces and a large atrium, the core of the new building was carefully constructed to mimic precisely the rooms of the original location, a layout in which Barnes had personally arranged his eclectic montages of fine art and everyday objects. Henri Matisse painted the mural **Ⓐ The Dance II** to fit precisely beneath the (reconstructed) arches of the large main room above **Ⓑ Card Players,** one of Paul Cézanne's favorite subjects, and **Ⓒ Models,** Georges Seurat's (1859–1891) study for *Ile de la Grande Jatte.* Among notable works in other rooms: Van Gogh's **Ⓓ Postman,** a portrait of the artist's mailman Joseph Roulin; **Ⓔ Scout Attacked by a Tiger,** one of Rousseau's (1844–1910) signature jungle scenes; and Picasso's paternal, symbolist painting **Ⓕ Harlequins.** Among the objets, don't miss **Ⓖ Seated Couple,** one of Barnes's 200 African sculptures. ⏱ *3 hrs. 2025 Benjamin Franklin Pkwy.* ☎ *215/278-7000. www.barnesfoundation.org. Reservations highly recommended, well in advance. Admission starts at $25 adults, $23 seniors, $5 ages 13–18 and college students; parking $12. Wed–Mon 11am–5pm.*

along the Parkway, this world-renowned museum was the life's work of prescient collector Albert Barnes (1872–1951), a pharmaceutical tycoon who amassed 8,000 works, including 181 Renoirs, 69 Cézannes, 59 Matisses, 46 Picassos (1881–1973), Pennsylvania "Dutch" furniture, primitive sculpture, and forged ironwork.

Mural Capital of the World

Philadelphia is home to more than 3,600 official murals—and untold numbers of non-sanctioned ones as well. When, in 1984, Mayor Wilson Goode hired artist Jane Golden to help purge the city of the graffiti plague, they employed a radical tactic: **The Mural Arts Program** (☎ 215/925-3633; www.muralarts.org).

Rather than hounding graffiti artists and painting over their tags—which would only give them a fresh canvas—Golden enlisted them. Instead of breaking the law to practice their art, graffitists were paid by the city to create; to give their neighborhoods and their struggles a voice; to beautify the city and proudly showcase its diversity. From job skills training to prison programs to an arts education effort serving 1,800 youths annually, Mural Arts has been a wild success. Visit the website for more information and to sign up for highly recommended tours (by trolley, bike, foot, car—or even participatory tours).

Meg Saligman's "Common Threads" is part of the city's Mural Arts program.

9 ★★★ Rodin Museum.

Nearby up the Parkway, this hidden gem of a museum houses the largest collection of works by Pierre Auguste Rodin (1840–1917) other than the Musée Rodin in Paris. You'll recognize the artist's iconic works such as *The Thinker* and the *Gates of Hell*, but don't miss the smaller, more process-oriented exhibits of bronze castings, plaster studies, original sketchbooks, letters, and books. ① *1 hr. 2151 Ben Franklin Pkwy. (at 22nd St.)* ☎ *215/763-8100. Suggested admission $10 adults, $8 seniors, $7 students (or enter on same ticket as*

Philadelphia Art Museum). www.rodinmuseum.org. Wed–Mon 10am–5pm.

10 ★ Washington Monument.

No, this is not DC's famed obelisk, but a statue-festooned fountain (it no longer spouts water) across from the entry to the Philadelphia Museum of Art. Little-known sculptor Rudolf Siemering (1835–1905) completed the work in 1897. Originally set at the entrance to Fairmount Park, its statue of a proud General Washington, in tricorn hat and cape, mounted on a fine steed, now presides over Eakins Oval, named for the beloved Philadelphia painter. ◷ *15 min. Eakins Oval (26th St. & Ben Franklin Pkwy.).*

⓫ ★★ Philadelphia Museum of Art. This Greco-Roman temple on a hill has 227,000 works for your not-so-quick perusal. Among the masterpieces are classics from Rubens, Cézanne, Van Gogh, Duchamp, Eakins, and Monet, plus stunning collections of furniture, jewelry, ceramics, and armor. The permanent installations of a medieval cloister and a Japanese teahouse are especially restful and lovely. ◷ *2 hrs. See p 13.*

⓬ ★★ Perelman Building. This recently opened, thoroughly gorgeous Art Deco building just across the street also belongs to the Philadelphia Museum of Art (above). The Perelman offers marvelously tactile collections in textile and design, along with special exhibits in the same realms. It has a distinguished art reference library, and serves as a satellite for museum exhibits, including Andrew Wyeth (1917–2009), Henri Matisse (1869–1954), and Pierre-Auguste Renoir (1841–1919). Until the planned Frank Gehry–designed tunnel connects this building to the PMA, a shuttle operates between them. ◷ *1 hr. Fairmount & Pennsylvania aves.* ☎ *215/763-8100. www.phila museum.org. Admission on same ticket as Philadelphia Museum of Art. Tues–Sun 10am–5pm.*

The Perelman Building offers collections of textiles and design.

Philly With Kids

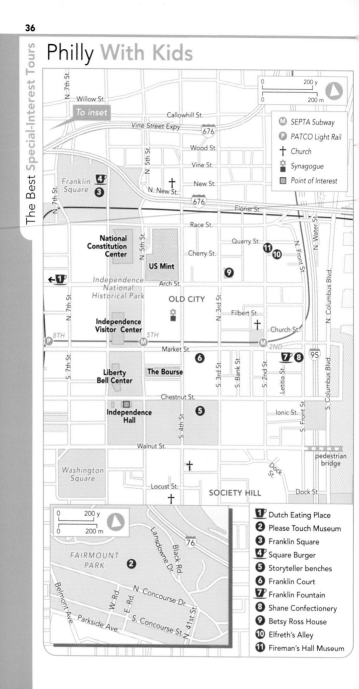

Legend (map key):

- M SEPTA Subway
- P PATCO Light Rail
- † Church
- ☼ Synagogue
- ▢ Point of Interest

Points of Interest:

1. Dutch Eating Place
2. Please Touch Museum
3. Franklin Square
4. Square Burger
5. Storyteller benches
6. Franklin Court
7. Franklin Fountain
8. Shane Confectionery
9. Betsy Ross House
10. Elfreth's Alley
11. Fireman's Hall Museum

In a big city that feels small, small people feel big. A fuss-free kid-centric day calls for frequent breaks, comfortable footwear, and knowing which activities to save for another day, such as the Philadelphia Zoo (p 45), Adventure Aquarium (p 96), and Franklin Institute (see p 48). Even without these three biggies, there's still a great day's worth of fun for little people in the City of Brotherly Love. START: **Please Touch Museum, 4231 Ave. of the Republic.**

The Please Touch Museum encourages a hands-on experience.

1 ★★ Dutch Eating Place.
Want to dig into the biggest, best breakfast in all of Philly? Grab a counter seat at this Mennonite-run luncheonette in bustling Reading Terminal Market and feast on blueberry pancakes, apple toast, and oddly yummy scrapple (PA's meat-scrap specialty). Coffee-loving parents can make a pit-stop at Old City Coffee's nearby kiosk. *12th & Arch sts.* ☎ *215/922-0425. Closed Sun. $.*

2 ★★ Please Touch Museum.
Take the purple PHLASH bus (see p 163) out to Fairmount Park's Memorial Hall. Here, at the serious-looking site of the 1876 Centennial Exhibition (a.k.a. the first World's

Fair) is Philly's least-serious museum, a bright, educational mega-playground for the Gymboree set. As its name suggests, the Please Touch's number-one rule is opposite that of most museums: Climbing, throwing, splashing, honking, jumping, riding, and playing are actively encouraged. Little ones will love the waist-high water tables of River Adventure, the low-shelved supermarket for pretend shopping, a safety-first construction zone, a magically rendered Alice in Wonderland maze, and a mint-condition circa-1824 carousel. You can glimpse local childhoods of yore through exhibits about a beloved former kids' TV show, *Captain Noah*, and the monorail from the old toy department of the historic

Historic Franklin Square has recently added child-friendly attractions like mini-golf.

John Wanamaker store. There's also a busy cafe for juice and pizza. The staff is marvelous, but they are not babysitters—guardians must accompany children at all times.
① *2 hr. 4231 Ave. of the Republic.* ☎ *215/581-3181. www.pleasetouchmuseum.org. Admission $19 (free for children 1 & under). Mon–Sat 9am–5pm; Sun 11am–5pm.*

❸ ★★★ **Franklin Square.** One of William Penn's five original squares, this 7½-acre plot dating to 1682 has recently been reincarnated as a low-key, amusement park–like haven for families. Among the attractions: an 18-hole, Philadelphia-theme mini-golf; a slew of jungle gyms for all ages; a giant sand sculpture; an excellent carousel; an 1838 basin fountain; and benches where "Once Upon A Nation" performers entertain with historical stories (see bullet ❺).
① *1½ hr. Btw. 6th & 7th sts. on Race St. www.historicphiladelphia.org. Carousel: $3. Mini-golf: $9 adults, $7 children 3–12. Apr–Oct daily 10am–7pm (to 9pm Fri–Sat); Nov–Mar daily 10am–5pm.*

❹ ★★ **Square Burger.** You'll find delicious inexpensive hamburgers, salami-wrapped kosher hot dogs, hand-cut fries, and milkshakes made with Tastykake Butterscotch Krimpets (a local, er, delicacy) at this walk-up stand—named, alas, for the location (Franklin Square), not the shape of the burgers. *200 S. 6th St. (btw. 6th & 7th sts. on Race St.)* ☎ *215/629-4026. http://cooperagephilly.com/square-burger.$.*

"Once Upon a Nation" storytellers and re-enactors bring the Colonial era to life throughout Philly.

White girders outline the shape of Benjamin' Franklin's Philadelphia home, which was razed over a century ago.

❺ ★★ Storyteller benches. At benches scattered throughout the Independence Mall—especially between 3rd and 6th streets and Chestnut and Walnut—costumed "Once Upon a Nation" characters engage all ages in tales of Colonial life. ⏱ *30 min. Chestnut St. btw. 3rd & 4th sts. www.historicphiladelphia. org. Free admission. Memorial Day to Labor Day 11am–4pm (days vary).*

❻ ★★ Franklin Court. Past an unassuming brick archway on Market Street is the site, if not the structure, of Ben Franklin's Philadelphia home. (The original dwelling was razed in 1812.) All that's left is an archeological dig around the foundation, along with a modern steel frame "ghost" structure meant to represent the original house. Neither of these may impress the kids, but what they will love is the **Benjamin Franklin Life & Legacy Museum,** which cleverly brings to life Franklin's irrepressible ingenuity and the Colonial times he lived in. In the museum you'll see some of Franklin's lesser-known, more offbeat inventions, such as bowls for a glass armonica (played like water glasses at the dinner table) and swim fins

(Franklin was a champion swimmer). Better yet are the storytellers (even "Ben" appears regularly beneath his beloved mulberry tree) to enliven the court with true tales and craft projects. The gift shop here is especially nice; have the kids buy a postcard and get the instant satisfaction they crave by mailing it at the still-active post office where Franklin served as the nation's first Postmaster General. In the spirit of the times, all mail here is still hand-cancelled, and it's the only post office in the U.S. that does not fly an American flag—since none existed when it first opened in 1775. ⏱ *1½ hr. 314–322 Market St. ☎ 215/965-2305. www.nps.gov/ inde. Museum admission $5 adults, $2 ages 4–16. Daily 9am–5pm. Post office closed Sun.*

❼ ★★★ Franklin Fountain. Homemade ice cream in flavors both familiar (vanilla bean, mint chip, peach) and throwback (teaberry gum, licorice) come by the scoop in parfaits, banana splits, floats, milkshakes, and more at this purposefully old-fashioned soda fountain (est. 2004). *116 Market St. ☎ 215/627-1899. www.franklin fountain.com. $.*

Old-fashioned Franklin Fountain boasts several varieties of homemade ice cream.

❽ ★ Shane Confectionary.
Now that everyone's hopped up on sugar, let's visit the country's oldest candy store, its shelves and display cases crammed with their famous buttercreams, almond butter crunch, cherry bark, and more. After 99 years, the Shane family passed the legacy onto the Berley Brothers, who run Franklin Fountain a few doors up. ⏱ *20 min. 110 Market St.* ☎ *215/922-1048. www.shane candies.com.*

❾ ★ Betsy Ross House. Flag-making lore aside, this tiny house seems just the right fit for pint-sized explorers, who'll marvel at the absolute compactness of life for the average Colonial family. Although Quaker seamstress Elizabeth (Betsy) Ross may not have even lived here, the house's preservers sure have made it look like she did, carefully placing around such handy house-hold items as reusable ivory tablets, pinecones to help start hearth fires, and a handy kitchen hourglass. The courtyard park separating the house from the street isn't just the burial ground for Ross and her last husband—it's the place where you're most likely to meet "Betsy" herself, and to hear her stories. ⏱ *½ hr. 239 Arch St. 215/629-5801.*

www.betsyrosshouse.org. Admission $5 adults, $4 students, seniors; audio tour $7. Daily 10am–5pm (closed Mon Dec–Feb).

❿ ★★★ Elfreth's Alley. No need to do the full tour of the museum at the oldest continuously inhabited street in the United States. It's enough to walk down this narrow cobblestone stretch, look up at the centuries-old row houses, think with your child of your own dwelling, and offer a gentle lesson about getting along with the neighbors. ⏱ *20 min. See p 51.*

Tiny Betsy Ross House recreates the life of an average Colonial family.

Open Sesame

Up I-95 about 27 miles (43.4km), Sesame Place (100 Sesame Rd., Langhorne; ☎ 215/702-ELMO [215/702-3566]; www.sesameplace. com) is theme-park paradise for the post-toddler set. The 14-acre outdoor "neighborhood" of recreation—and nothing but recreation—offers a dizzying array of splashy water park-style rides (bring bathing suits), kiddie coasters, a carousel, and hundreds of ways to experience Elmo and his ilk, including a twice-daily parade and regular staged performances. Admission is steep—$70 adults and children 2 and over, though online that can drop to $49; parking adds another $18. It's open daily Memorial Day–Labor Day (and most weekends out of season); hours vary wildly, from 10am to anywhere from 6 to 9pm. The park is consistently crowded, so arrive early.

⓫ ★ Fireman's Hall Museum.

Benjamin Franklin founded the nation's first volunteer fire company in Philadelphia in 1736. This renovated 1902 fire station has exhibits where you can try on firefighter gear or practice calling 911, and a parking bay crammed with cool fire trucks dating all the way back to horse-drawn wagons from the 1870s. ⏱ ½ hr. See p 52.

Fireman's Hall Museum commemorates America's oldest volunteer fire company, founded by Benjamin Franklin.

What Would Rocky Do?

Fairmount Park

W. Girard Ave.

W. Girard Ave.

E. River Dr.

W. River Dr.

Poplar Dr.

W. Sedgley Dr.

Parrish St.

Pennsylvania Ave.

LOMBARD-SOUTH

South St.

Kater St.

Philadelphia City Zoo

9

N. 34th St.

8

8

Swain St.

Aspen St.

S. Watts St.

Schuylkill River

Zoological St.

76

Mantua Ave.

Brown St.

N. 33rd St.

Art Museum Dr.

Philadelphia Museum of Art

7

Spring Garden St.

0   400 y

0   400 m

Montrose St.   POINT BREEZE

S. Broad St.

To Fairmount Park inset

S. 17th St.

S. 16th St.

S. 15th St.

S. Watts St.

Washington Ave.

Alter St.

Alter St.

Alter St.

Ellsworth St.

S. Mole St.

S. Carlisle St.

Annin St.

Annin St.

Federal St.

ELLSWORTH-FEDERAL

S. Clarion St.

Manton St.

Manton St.

Point Breeze Ave.

Latona St.

Latona St.

Titan St.

Wharton St.

S. Clarion St.

S. Capitol St.

Reed St.

Gerritt St.

Wilder St.

Dickinson St.

S. Bouvier St.

S. Colorado St.

S. Mole St.

S. Hicks St.

S. Carlisle St.

S. Juniper St.

S. Clarion St.

2

S. Capitol St.

S. Opal St.

S. Dorrance St.

S. Cleveland St.

S. Bancroft Ct.

TASKER-MORRIS

Tasker St.

Fernon St.

S. Mole St.

S. Hicks St.

S. Carlisle St.

S. Watts St.

Mountain St.

Morris St.

1

SEPTA Subway

Watkins St.

S. 17th St.

S. 16th St.

S. 15th St.

Castle Ave.

0   200 y

0   200 m

Moore St.

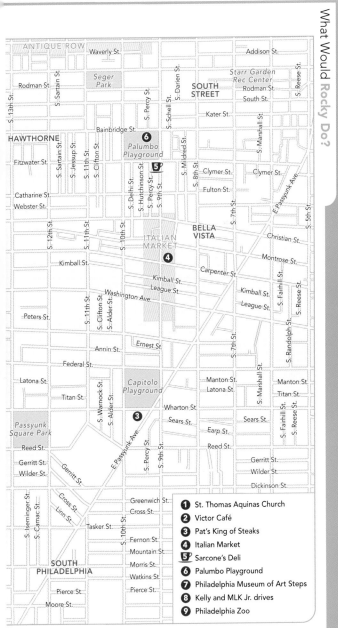

1 St. Thomas Aquinas Church
2 Victor Café
3 Pat's King of Steaks
4 Italian Market
5 Sarcone's Deli
6 Palumbo Playground
7 Philadelphia Museum of Art Steps
8 Kelly and MLK Jr. drives
9 Philadelphia Zoo

In 1976, a rags-to-riches film about a hardscrabble pugilist from Philly's Kensington neighborhood captured America's heart—and, as far as Philadelphians are concerned, never let go. Below are highlights of Rocky Balboa's favorite spots. (One tip: Don't attempt a literal version of the "Rocky Run." You'll be dashing across town for days.) START: **17th & Morris Sts—in South Philly, yo.**

❶ ★ St. Thomas Aquinas Church. The little parish where Rocky and his sweetheart Adrian, plated by Talia Shire, got hitched isn't exactly set up to host tourists, but you can pop in for a look-see. The gilded, chandeliered, Italian baroque-style 1904 St. Thomas has been called the loveliest Catholic Church in South Philadelphia. ⏱ *20 min. 1719 Morris St. (at 17th St.)* ☎ *215/334-2312. www.staquinas.com. Free admission.*

❷ Victor Café. This South Philly restaurant, famous for its opera-singing waiters, served as the retired champ's restaurant, "Adrian's," in 2006's *Rocky Balboa. 1303 Dickinson St. (btw. Broad & 13th sts.).* ☎ *215/468-3040. www.victor cafe.com.*

❸ ★★ Pat's King of Steaks. Balboa started his day with a glass of raw eggs. Only slightly less off-putting is a breakfast of bread-swaddled steak topped "widt" fried onions and "Whiz." But, heck; if you're gonna do it once in your life, do it where, in 1930, a hot-dog seller invented Philly's most famous sandwich—and 46 years later, Rocky ate one. ⏱ *½ hr. 1237 E. Passyunk Ave. (at Wharton St.).* ☎ *215/468-1546. www.patsking ofsteaks.com. Open 24 hrs.*

❹ ★★ Italian Market. America's oldest outdoor market apparently welcomes odd guys in gray sweats who run in traffic. Filmed here: The scene where a vendor—who had no idea a movie was being filmed—tosses Balboa an orange. How the boxer ate the fruit while jogging past flaming 55-gallon drums of trash is anyone's guess. Our advice: Don't run. Stroll. Shop. ⏱ *2 hr. See pp 18–19.*

The Italian Market is America's oldest outdoor market.

5 ★★ **Sarcone's Deli.** Amazing hoagies loaded up with prosciutto, capicola, hard salami, sharp provolone, roasted red peppers, even broccoli rabe, served on Italian bread baked at the family's circa-1918 bakery. *758 S. 9th St. (at Fitzwater St.)* ☎ *215/922-0445. www.sarconesbakery.com. $.*

6 kids **Palumbo Playground.** There's no proof Stallone ever set foot in this South Philly neighborhood park, but it's a great spot for the kids to enjoy the jungle gym and swing set, and for you to engage in a few exercises without having to punch a frozen side of beef. Squat thrusts, anyone? ⓒ *½ hr. Btw. 9th & 10th sts., Fitzwater & Bainbridge sts.*

7 ★★ kids **Philadelphia Museum of Art Steps.** If you don't know what happened here, consider re-renting the movie. The scene of Balboa running up the 72 steps, turning around, and pumping his fists in the air was an instant American film classic (and one of the first scenes filmed with a Steadicam, invented by Philly boy Garrett Brown). Each year, thousands of visitors decide they're "Gonna Fly Now" (many never set foot in the museum itself). At the top of the steps is a bronze imprint of Stallone's Converse sneakers. At the foot of the steps (to the north), there's a Rocky statue—and, usually, a line of folks waiting to pose for a picture with it. ⓒ *½ hr. See p 13.*

8 ★★ **Kelly and MLK Jr. drives.** Stretching from the Art Museum along opposing sides of the Schuylkill River, these winding roads are each paralleled by a wide, sculpture-studded, tree-lined pedestrian path. It's a handsome spot, as crew teams skim along the river. It's also your best bet for attempting a Rocky-like run. A loop from the Art Museum over Strawberry Mansion Bridge and back is 6¼ miles. ⓒ *1½ hr.*

9 ★★ kids **Philadelphia Zoo.** The country's first zoo, dating back to 1874, covers 42 acres on the west side of Fairmount Park. More than 1,300 animals dwell here. A few not-to-be-missed spots: the Primate Reserve; Carnivore Kingdom's snow leopards, red pandas, and family of giant otters; the walk-through jungle habitats of the McNeil Avian Center, with extinct-in-the-wild birds including the Guam Rail and Micronesian Kingfisher; and African Plains for warthogs, antelope, gazelles, giraffes, hippos, and zebras. There's also a petting zoo in the KidZooU area and, for an extra fee, a ride 400 feet above the city via the tiger-striped Zooballoon. Best bet for transportation: Take a PHLASH or SEPTA bus, since parking is sparse and traffic gets heavy. The Rocky connection? In *Rocky II*, our hero proposed to Adrian on a winter's day at what is now Big Cat Falls. ⓒ *2 hrs. 34th St. & Girard Ave.* ☎ *215/243-1100. www.philadelphiazoo.org. Admission $25 adults, $20 children 2–11. Zooballoon additional $12. Mar–Oct daily 9:30am–5pm; Nov–Feb daily 9:30am–4pm.*

The Rocky statue.

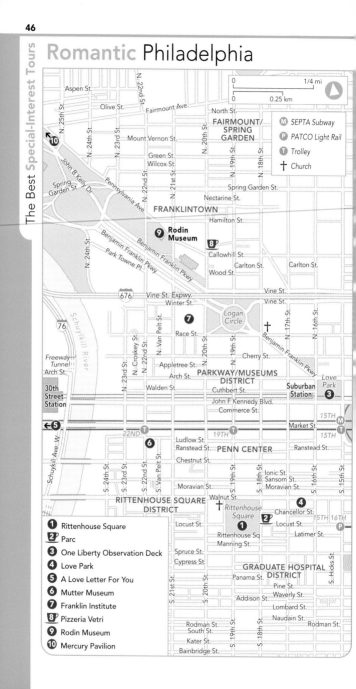

Romantic Philadelphia

0   1/4 mi
0   0.25 km

Ⓜ SEPTA Subway
Ⓟ PATCO Light Rail
Ⓣ Trolley
✝ Church

Aspen St.
Olive St.
Fairmount Ave.
North St.
N. 25th St.
N. 24th St.
N. 22nd St.
N. 20th St.
N. 19th St.
N. 18th St.

FAIRMOUNT/ SPRING GARDEN

Mount Vernon St.
Green St.
Wilcox St.
Spring Garden St.
Nectarine St.

N. 23rd St.
N. 21st St.

John B Kelly Dr.
Spring Garden St.
Pennsylvania Ave.

FRANKLINTOWN

Hamilton St.

❾ **Rodin Museum**

Benjamin Franklin Pkwy.
Park Towne Pl.
N. 24th St.

❽ Callowhill St.
Carlton St.
Carlton St.
Wood St.

Vine St.

676

Vine St. Expwy.
Winter St.
Vine St.

Schuylkill River

76

❼
Logan Circle
Race St.

N. Croskey St.
N. 22nd St.
N. Van Pelt St.
N. 20th St.
N. 19th St.
N. 17th St.
N. 16th St.

Benjamin Franklin Pkwy.

✝
Cherry St.

Freeway Tunnel
Arch St.
Appletree St.
N. 23rd St.
Arch St.

PARKWAY/MUSEUMS DISTRICT

Walden St.
Cuthbert St.

30th Street Station

John F Kennedy Blvd.
Commerce St.

Suburban Station
Love Park
❸

15TH

←❺
Market St

15TH
Ⓜ

Schuylkill Ave. W.

22ND Ⓣ

19TH Ⓣ

15TH
15TH Ⓣ

❻
Ludlow St.
Ranstead St.
PENN CENTER
Ranstead St.
Chestnut St.

S. 24th St.
S. 23rd St.
S. 22nd St.
S. Van Pelt St.
S. 19th St.
S. 18th St.
S. 16th St.
S. 15th St.

Moravian St.
Ionic St.
Sansom St.
Moravian St.
Walnut St.

RITTENHOUSE SQUARE DISTRICT

✝
Rittenhouse Square
❹
Chancellor St.
15TH 16TH

❶
Locust St.
❷ Locust St.
Latimer St.

Ⓟ

Rittenhouse Sq
Manning St.

Spruce St.
Cypress St.

GRADUATE HOSPITAL DISTRICT
Panama St.
Pine St.
Waverly St.
Addison St.
Lombard St.
S. Hicks St.

S. 21st St.
S. 20th St.
S. 19th St.
S. 18th St.

Naudain St.
Rodman St.
Rodman St.
South St.
Kater St.
Bainbridge St.

❶ Rittenhouse Square
❷ Parc
❸ One Liberty Observation Deck
❹ Love Park
❺ A Love Letter For You
❻ Mutter Museum
❼ Franklin Institute
❽ Pizzeria Vetri
❾ Rodin Museum
❿ Mercury Pavilion

Touring Philly à deux can be twice the fun—provided you know where to go. Luckily for couples, Center City's laid-back sidewalks are wide enough for ample hand-holding, and its park benches were custom made for snuggling. (It didn't earn the name "City of Brotherly Love" for nothing.) START: **JFK Plaza, JFK Blvd btw 15th & 16th St.**

❶ ★★ Rittenhouse Square. Designed by French architect Paul Philippe Cret in 1913, this park is the leafy heart of Philly's fanciest neighborhood. Start your day here, when the grass is dewy and everyone else is rushing off to work. ⏱ ½ hr. See p 64.

❷ ★★ Parc. Come nighttime, this glittery Parisian brasserie absolutely bursts with the see-and-be-seen crowd. At breakfast, however, the light is naturally dim and the vibe is delightfully low-key. Order a smoked salmon tartine, polenta and eggs Basquaise, or a pain au chocolat—and linger. *228 S.18th St. (at Locust St.)* ☎ *215/545-2262. www.parc-restaurant.com. $$.*

❸ ★ One Liberty Observation Deck. Share stunning, 360-degree city views and a sky-scraping kiss from the 57th floor in one of Philly's tallest buildings. ⏱ 45 min. 1650 Market St. (btw. 16th and 17th Sts.) ☎ 215-561-3325. http://phillyfrom thetop.com. $14.50 adults, $9.50 ages 3–11. Daily May–Sept 10am– 9pm, Oct–Apr 10am–8pm.

❹ ★★ Love Park. If you haven't felt compelled to say those three little words yet, you'll certainly feel inspired by this charming urban park, where you won't be able to miss Robert Indiana's famous LOVE sculpture. (If that's not a sign, nothing is.) ⏱ ½ hr. 15th St. & JFK Blvd.

Robert Indiana's iconic bright red sculpture is the centerpiece of Love Park.

❺ ★★ A Love Letter For You. Former graffiti artist and Fulbright scholar Steve Power has created a unique love letter in his native West Philly: A series of 50 murals along the El train's Market Street corridor, from 45th to 63rd Streets. Grab a west-bound Market-Frankford Line train, get off at the 63rd Street stop, and ride back to Center City, peering out windows to see the murals as you rumble past. ⏱ ½ hr. ☎ 215/685-0750. www.muralarts. org/artworks/a-love-letter-for-you. Subway tickets: $2.50 each.

❻ ★★ Mutter Museum. You know how, at scary scenes in horror flicks, she will reach over and grab your arm for comfort—even bury her face in your chest so as not to watch? Well, this 19th-century museum of odd and macabre

The elegant, intimate Rodin Museum brings a little bit of Paris to Philadelphia.

medical mishaps is like walking through a Victorian horror movie. It is intensely, fascinatingly creepy, and possibly not suited for every Romantic. Goth couples, on the other hand, frequently rent it out for weddings. Not kidding. ⏱ *1 hr. See p 62.*

❼ ★★★ Franklin Institute. Arguably the weirdest spot in town to steal a kiss: in a giant-but-cramped, continuously beating, walk-through heart. If that doesn't work, there's also the drama of an IMAX theater (additional fee) for a little cuddling; several Escape Room challenges; and interactive exhibits that feel straight out of a one-on-one date on *The Bachelor*, where you get to test the laws of physics through a variety of adrenaline activities. Or come back at night to peer deep into the universe through the rooftop telescopes. ⏱ *2 hr. 20th St. & Ben Franklin Pkwy.* ☎ *215/448-1200. www.fi.edu. Admission $23 adults, $19 children 4–11; IMAX additional $7 adults. Daily 9:30am–5pm (some summer days til 7pm).*

❽ ★★ Pizzeria Vetri. Treat yourselves to some of the country's best Italian-style pizza. *1939 Callowhill St. (at 20th St.)* ☎ *215/600-2629. www.pizzeriavetri.com. $.*

❾ ★★★ Rodin Museum. Is there an artist more romantic than Auguste Rodin (1840–1917)? Perhaps, but there's not a Philadelphia art museum more romantic than this petite space, with its leafy overhangs and serene sculpture. Plus, if you recently bought, say, a circular piece of diamond jewelry, you won't be put off by the admission, a suggested donation of $5. ⏱ *1 hr. See p 34.*

❿ ★★ Mercury Pavilion. Got a ring in your pocket? Keep it there until you reach this cliff-top overlook between the Philadelphia Museum of Art and the Waterworks/Boathouse Row, the prettiest neoclassical gazebo in town for watching a sunset and declaring your undying affection. ⏱ *Whatever it takes. Behind Philadelphia Museum of Art (see p 13).* ●

Old City

SEPTA Subway

† Church

☆ Synagogue

■ Point of Interest

1 Christ Church
2 Larry Becker Contemporary Art
3 Betsy Ross House
4 Elfreth's Alley
5 The Clay Studio
6 Fireman's Hall
7 Pierre's Costumes
8 Wexler Gallery
9 Café Ole
10 Shopping on North 3rd Street
11 Moderne Gallery
12 Shane Confectionery

Previous page: William Penn's statue stands guard outside the Colonial-era Pennsylvania Hospital in Society Hill.

The tree-lined streets of Philadelphia's most landmark-laden neighborhood are perfect for exploring by foot. What's loveliest about Old City is the seamless urban melding of old and new, Colonial and contemporary, classical and artful, and the excellent (and often eccentric) discoveries that pop up where you least expect them. START: **Old City Coffee, 221 Church St.**

❶ ★★ Christ Church. To Old City residents, the gleaming white spire of this most colonial of churches is as iconic to their neighborhood as City Hall's statue of William Penn is to the whole of Philadelphia. A few facts worth noting about this landmark, built in 1727–1754 but still well-attended today: Assigned seating was by pew rather than open benches (note George Washington's prominent pew). The massive Palladian window behind the altar was the inspiration for that of Independence Hall. William Penn was baptized in the font, a gift from All Hallows' Church in London. It's perfectly fine to walk on the floor-level tomb markers in the nave. And the shaded churchyard benches are great places to catch up on people watching. ⏱ ½ hr. *See p 11.*

❷ ★ Larry Becker Contemporary Art. Exemplifying the newer face of Old City, this minimalist, modern gallery displays the mostly spare and always modern work of international artists such as Robert Ryman (b. 1930), Rebecca Salter (b. 1977), and native son Quentin Morris (b. 1945). ⏱ 20 min. *43 N. 2nd St.* ☎ *215/925-5389. Free admission. By appointment only.*

❸ ★ kids Betsy Ross House. Another architectural emblem, this American seamstress' purported dwelling is a brilliant example of the absolute compactness of life for the average Colonial family. Elizabeth (Betsy) Ross (1752–1836) was a Quaker needlewoman who, newly widowed in 1776, worked as a

Mass at the 18th-century Christ Church is still well attended.

seamstress and upholsterer out of the space that is now the gift shop. According to lore, General Washington asked Ross to design the original flag, 13 stars set in a field of 13 red and white stripes. According to recorded history, Ross at the very least sewed such flags for the American fleet. Ross and her last husband are buried In the courtyard park. ⏱ ½ hr. *See p 40.*

❹ ★★ Elfreth's Alley. In 1700, this cobblestone lane was the address of a melting pot of artisans and tradesmen who worked in shipping. Fifty years later, the street was occupied by haberdashers, bakers, printers, and carpenters. In the late 18th through 19th centuries, Jewish, African-American,

Welsh, and German residents lived along Elfreth's Alley. Number 126, the circa-1755 Mantua (cape) Maker's House, belonged to blacksmith Jeremiah Elfreth (1723–1765); it's now the street's museum, with a restored back garden and an interior that includes a dressmaker's shop and bedroom. Best time to visit: The second weekend in June, when most of the alley's houses are open for touring. ⏱ *1 hr. Off 2nd St., toward Front St., btw. Arch & Race sts.* ☎ *215/574-0560. www. elfrethsalley.org. Free admission to visitor center & gift shop; museum $3 adults, $2 children 6–12, free 5 & under (includes 20-minute tour). Tours of museum & alley $8 adults, $2 children. Museum open Fri–Sun noon–5pm. Alley tours Fri at 1pm, Sat–Sun at 1pm & 3pm.*

⑤ ★ The Clay Studio. One of the busiest artist spaces in this always-busy artist community, this center for ceramics started simply as an affordable workspace; it now includes a two-floor gallery for new exhibits by international and up-and-coming ceramicists. Workshops and classrooms offer a behind-the-scenes look. ⏱ *20 min. 137–139 N. 2nd St., btw. Arch & Race sts.* ☎ *215/925-3453. www. theclaystudio.org. Free admission. Mon–Sat 11am–6pm, Sun noon–6pm.*

⑥ kids Fireman's Hall Museum. Run by the Philadelphia Fire Department, this restored 1902 firehouse traces its history back to Ben Franklin (1706–1790), the country's first fire marshal. On display: A circa-1730 hand pumper, the nation's oldest steam fire engine, modern-day fire safety displays, and artifacts from Ground Zero. ⏱ *½ hr. 147 N. 2nd St. at Quarry St.* ☎ *215/923-1438. www.firemanshall museum.org. Free admission. Tues–Sat 10am–4pm.*

⑦ kids Pierre's Costumes. More than a million costumes reside at this spot under the Ben Franklin Bridge. One of the largest costumers in the world, it's a truly fun place to browse—or, if the occasion calls for it, to buy an Uncle Sam top hat, George Washington wig, or just about any Halloween outfit imaginable. ⏱ *20 min. 211 N. 3rd St.* ☎ *215/925-7121. www. costumers.com. Mon–Fri 10am–5:30pm, Sat 10am–4pm.*

⑧ ★ Wexler Gallery. This serene corner space hosts a marvelous variety of cutting-edge art exhibits of fine crafts, exquisite

Antique fire-fighting equipment is on display at the restored 1902 Fireman's Hall.

Wexler Gallery hosts a variety of cutting-edge exhibits.

furniture, art glass, studio jewelry, and more. Like most of the galleries in Old City, Wexler stays open late to welcome art-fueled revelers on the first Friday of each month. ⏱ ½ hr. 201 N. 3rd St. (at Race St.). ☎ 215/923-7030. www.wexler gallery.com. Free admission. Tues–Sat 10am–6pm.

9 Café Ole. Old City earns its nickname, the "Hipstoric District," through places like this laid-back cafe. Stand in line for truly cool fresh-mint iced tea, creative grilled panini, and tasty hummus plates and Mediterranean salads that won't break the bank. *147 N. 3rd St.* ☎ *215/627-2140. $.*

⑩ ★★ Shopping. We may be pointing out the obvious, but this stretch of North 3rd Street between Race and Market streets is studded with great boutiques—plus the occasional bargain. Read more about what's in stores in Chapter 4 (p 73) or just take our word for it and pop into **Lost & Found, My Little Redemption, Sugarcube, Art in the Age, Vagabond**—or whatever vintage or new shop may catch your eye. (We promise you'll come out dressed like you totally belong in the Hipstoric District) ⏱ *Take all the time you need.*

⑪ ★ Moderne Gallery. Among the handful of really great home furnishing shops in this area, Bob Aibel's 20,000-square-foot space is richly stocked with decorative arts from the last century. Look for rare French Art Deco, vintage George Nakashima (1905–1990), Wharton Esherick (1887–1970) pieces, and more artistic gems, all on display and for sale. ⏱ ½ hr. 111 N. 3rd St. ☎ 215/923-8536. www.moderne gallery.com. Free admission.

⑫ ★ kids Shane Confectionery. Want to taste history in the country's oldest candy store? For 99 years, the Shane family stocked their shop with their famous buttercreams, almond butter crunch, cherry bark, and confections galore; a few years ago they passed the legacy on to the Berley brothers (who run Franklin Fountain a few doors up; see p 39). ⏱ 20 min. 110 Market St. ☎ 215/922-1048. www. shanecandies.com.

Society Hill

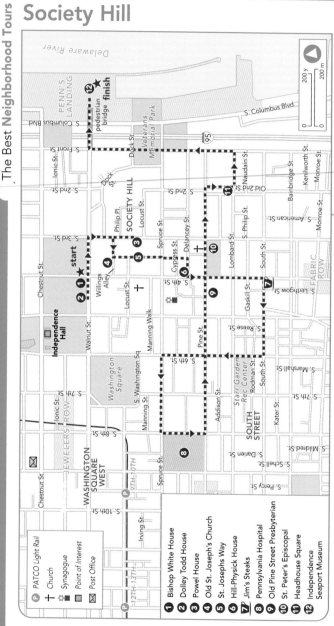

Delaware River

PENN'S LANDING

pedestrian bridge **finish** ⑫

S. Columbus Blvd

SOCIETY HILL

start ★

Independence Hall

Washington Square

WASHINGTON SQUARE WEST

SOUTH STREET

FABRIC ROW

Starr Garden Rec Center

JEWELERS' ROW

❶ Bishop White House
❷ Dolley Todd House
❸ Powel House
❹ Old St. Joseph's Church
❺ St. Josephs Way
❻ Hill-Physick House
❼ Jim's Steaks
❽ Pennsylvania Hospital
❾ Old Pine Street Presbyterian
❿ St. Peter's Episcopal
⓫ Headhouse Square
⓬ Independence Seaport Museum

PATCO Light Rail
✝ Church
✡ Synagogue
■ Point of Interest
✉ Post Office

With the U.S.'s largest concentration of 18th- and early-19th-century architecture, Society Hill also has some of Philly's most modern houses, intended at one era to "improve" the neighborhood. Bounded more or less by Walnut and South streets, the Delaware River, and 8th Street, the neighborhood's posh-sounding name actually refers to the Free Society of Traders, an 18th-century group of Quaker financiers who footed some of William Penn's bills. As you explore, look for details such as wrought-iron boot scrapers; antique hitching posts and marble carriage steps, relics of horse-and-buggy days; and "busybody" mirrors in upper-floor windows, invented by Ben Franklin for residents who wanted to see who's at the door without having to descend the stairs. Go in advance to the Independence Visitor Center (p 9) to pick up the required tour tickets for stops 1 and 2.
START: **3rd & Walnut sts.**

① ★★ Bishop White House. This elegant circa-1786 home exemplifies gracious upper-class life in early America. Owner William White, one of America's first bishops, was a worldly fellow: Notice his library, with Encyclopedia Britannica, Sir Walter Scott's novels, and the Koran. ① ½ hr. See p 25.

② ★ Dolley Todd House. Much more modest (but far from small), this Colonial house belonged to John Todd, Jr., whose widow Dolley (1768–1849) married James Madison (1751–1836), who would later become U.S. President. ① ½ hr. See p 25.

③ ★★ Powel House. Built in 1765 by a wealthy merchant, this gorgeous Colonial Georgian became the home of Philadelphia mayor Samuel Powel (1738–1793) and his wife, Elizabeth Willing (1743–1830), in 1769. The gentle couple were major party throwers: Anyone who was anyone—the Marquis de Lafayette, George Washington, Benjamin Franklin—feasted and danced here. (Future pres and Massachusetts Puritan John Adams dubbed the Powels' parties "sinful dinners.") Note the entryway's

bas-relief plasterwork, mahogany wainscoting, ballroom chandelier, and formal garden. The house is still available for private parties, so call before visiting. ① ½ hr. 244 S. 3rd St. (btw. Walnut & Locust sts). ☎ 215/627-0364. www.philalandmarks.org. Admission $8 adults, $6 seniors & students; $20 families. Tours Apr–Nov Thurs–Sat 11am–3pm; Sun noon–3pm (also Wed 11pm–3pm Memorial Day through Labor Day); Mar & Dec Sat–Sun 11am–3pm; (Jan–Feb by appointment only).

Colonial VIPs partied regularly at handsome Powel House, built in 1765.

④ ★ Old St. Joseph's Church.
Double back up 3rd and turn left down Willings Alley to this church, founded in 1733, which was the only place in the English-speaking world where Roman Catholics—such as Revolutionary hero General Lafayette—could publicly celebrate Mass. ⏱ *15 min. See p 25.*

⑤ St. Josephs Way. Walk between the buildings directly across from Old St. Joe's to enter Bingham Court, a collection of rectilinear brick-and-glass townhouses designed by I. M. Pei as part of a 1960s Society Hill redevelopment initiative (they now go for around $1 million). Continue south along St. Josephs Way, part of a network of narrow alleys between 3rd and 4th streets. Turn right onto Delancey Street (after popping into Delancey Park to pat its iconic three bears). ⏱ *15 min.*

⑥ ★ Hill–Physick House.
Madeira wine importer Henry Hill built this free-standing house in 1786; subsequent owner Philip Syng Physick (1768–1837) added Federal flourishes, an inkstand (with Ben Franklin's fingerprints), and 18th century Italian art. Known as "the father of American surgery," Physick invented the stomach

pump, created new ways to repair fractures, designed needle forceps, pioneered catgut sutures, removed thousands of bladder stones from Supreme Court Chief Justice John Marshall (1755–1835), was doctor to Dolley Madison and President Andrew Jackson—oh, and he helped invent soda, too. ⏱ *40 min. 321 S. 4th St. (at Delancey St.).* ☎ *215/925-7866. www.philaland marks.org. Admission $8 adults, $6 seniors & students. Hourly tours Apr–Nov Thurs–Sat 11am–3pm and Sun noon–3pm (also Wed 11am–3pm Memorial Day–Labor Day); Mar & Dec Sat–Sun 11am–3pm; Jan–Feb by appointment.*

⑦ ★ Jim's Steaks. If it's past 11am, there's a line at this corner stand, a pioneer since 1939 in the field of Philly cheesesteaks. To enjoy the real deal, order "widt (onions) and (Cheez) Whiz" (or, if you must, provolone). Bonus: Unlike its competitors, Jim's serves beer. *4th & South sts.* ☎ *215/928-1911. www.jimssteaks.com. $.*

⑧ ★ Pennsylvania Hospital.
The Colonies' first hospital was founded by—yep, Benjamin Franklin (along with Dr. Thomas Bond) in

Hill–Physick House was home to "the father of American surgery."

The boat shop at Independence Seaport Museum.

1751. Today, the vibrant hospital welcomes visitors to tour its historic sections. The hospital's two wings are connected by a grand Center Building, the highlight of which is a skylit 1804 surgical amphitheater. As you might imagine, the hospital's interiors have much altered since then, but the lovely azalea garden (facing Pine St.) remains, as does a carefully tended apothecary garden. ⏲ ½ hr. 800 Spruce St. (at 8th) ☎ 215/829-3370. www.penn medicine.org. Free admission; tours available if you book 48 hours ahead. Mon–Fri 8:30am–4:30pm.

⑨ ★ Old Pine Street Presbyterian. When John Adams wasn't grumbling about fancy parties, he might have been sitting in a pew inside the city's oldest (circa 1768) Presbyterian church. ⏲ ½ hr. See p 24.

⑩ ★ St. Peter's Episcopal. When Washington wasn't dancing jigs in the Powels' ballroom, he and his wife Martha were participating in more solemn occasions as members of this circa-1761 house of worship. ⏲ 1/2 hr. See p 24.

⑪ Headhouse Square. Although this all-brick, open-air market is only a replica of the 1745 original, the site has recently been reborn as a fantastic local farmers' market, open weekends spring through fall. Flanked by cobblestone streets, the "headhouse" at the top of Pine Street was a firehouse in 1804; it's the nation's oldest surviving firehouse. ⏲ 15 min. 2nd St., btw. Pine & Lombard sts.

⑫ ★ kids Independence Seaport Museum. Just across Columbus Boulevard, this userfriendly attraction celebrates Society Hill's proximity to the Delaware River (after all, the reason the neighborhood was established). Two historic ships lie at anchor: the 1892 USS Olympia (oldest steel warship afloat); and the 1944 USS Becuna (a Guppy 1-A sub who served in World War II, Korea, and Vietnam). Interactive all-ages exhibits include **Workshop on the Water,** where visitors can observe classes in traditional wooden boatbuilding. ⏲ 1 hr. 211 S. Columbus Blvd. (at Walnut St.) ☎ 215/413-8655. www.phillyseaport.org. Admission $17 adults, $12 seniors, children 3–12, students & military ($8 on summer evening hours). Daily 10am–5pm (Memorial Day–Labor Day Historic Ships open Thurs–Sat until 8pm).

City Hall/Midtown

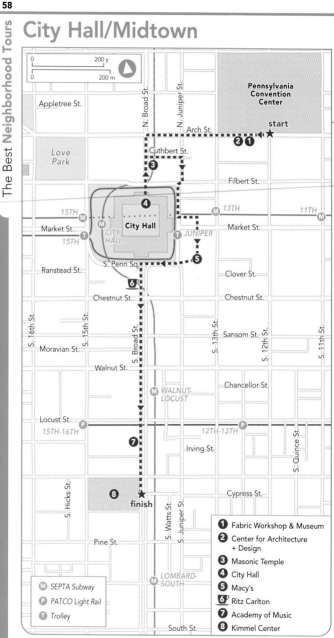

1 Fabric Workshop & Museum
2 Center for Architecture + Design
3 Masonic Temple
4 City Hall
5 Macy's
6 Ritz Carlton
7 Academy of Music
8 Kimmel Center

M SEPTA Subway
P PATCO Light Rail
T Trolley

In the past decade, the heart of Philadelphia has experienced a major renaissance. Broad Street's theaters have grown to become the glittery "Avenue of the Arts;" trendy bistros, shops, and condos transformed a once-dingy corridor of South 13th Street into hip "Midtown Village;" even City Hall has had a facelift and its surrounding Dilworth Plaza turned into a true public space. START: **City Hall, Broad & Market sts.**

1 ★★ **Fabric Workshop & Museum.** A renovated warehouse—a structure familiar to many Philly artists—houses this unique center for the creation, display, and sale of new work in new materials. Three exhibition galleries and a video lounge show off cutting-edge (and often irresistibly tactile) works of local and international artists. In the permanent collection: Robert Morris' nuclear bed linens, a richly embroidered screen by Carrie Mae Weems, and a rubbery rug by Mona Hatoum. Artists' studios tours are available by appointment, and the gift shop is fantastic. ⏱ *1 hr. 1214 Arch St. (btw. 12th & 13th sts).* ☎ *215/561-8888. www.fabricwork shop.org. Free admission. Mon–Fri 10am–6pm; Sat–Sun noon–5pm.*

2 **Center for Architecture + Design.** The Philly chapter of the American Institute of Architects offers pristine design exhibits, such as vintage neon and a 3-D model of Center City. They also offer $15 city architecture tours Tues, Thurs & Sat at 2pm (Sat only Dec–Mar). ⏱ *½ hr. 1218 Arch St.* ☎ *215/569-3186. www.philadelphiacfa.org. Free admission. Mon–Fri 9am–5pm; some Sat 10am–3pm.*

3 ★ **Masonic Temple.** Across from City Hall is a grand lodge of American Freemasonry, a fraternity of obscure, antique origins. A tour of the seven halls offers a crash course in classical architecture— and a glimpse of this fairly secret society where Washington and Franklin were members. ⏱ *1 hr. 1 N. Broad St.* ☎ *215/988-1917. pamasonictemple.org/temple. Admission $15 adults, $10 students with ID & seniors, $5 children 12 & under. Tours Tues–Sat 10am, 11am, 1pm, 2pm & 3pm.*

The Masonic Temple has ornate classical architecture in seven different halls.

The revamped plaza outside of City Hall features a walk-through summertime splash pad.

4 ★★ City Hall. At the center of Center City stands this wedding cake of an all-masonry building, topped off with a 37-foot, 27-ton bronze statue of city "founder" William Penn. Treaty in hand, Penn faces east toward the Delaware River and Penn Treaty Park, where he signed a peace pact with the Native American Leni Lenape (or "Delaware") tribe. City Hall's best parts are its exterior sculptures by Alexander Milne Calder (1846–1923) and its glassed-in observation deck, just below Billy Penn, 500 feet above ground with views clear to New Jersey. An overhaul of surrounding Dilworth Plaza, finished in 2013, provides cafe tables, a park for concerts, and a summer fountain/winter ice rink. ⏱ *1 hr. See p 15.*

5 Macy's. It's a shadow of its former self, but the old John Wanamaker's department store, now a Macy's, still bears traces of its grander days. Back then, proper ladies lunched at the store's Crystal Tearoom, meeting up at a bronze eagle statue from the 1904 World's Fair in a seven-story atrium under the world's largest functional pipe organ (28,604 pipes, still frequently played; www.wanamakerorgan. com). Between Thanksgiving and New Year's, the store's half-hour holiday light show draws crowds. ⏱ *½ hr. 1300 Market St. (at Juniper St.).* ☎ *215/241-9000. www.macys. com. Mon–Sat 10am–8pm, Sun 11am–7pm.*

6 ★ Ritz Carlton. So, it's a little on the fancy side, but it's worth the couple of extra dollars you'll spend to have coffee and warm soft pretzels beneath the grand dome of this Pantheon-like structure, opened as Girard Bank in 1908, converted in 2000 into a, well, ritzy hotel. *See p 141.*

The bronze eagle and famous Wanamaker pipe organ in Macy's atrium.

The Kimmel Center is home to several performing arts venues.

7 ★★★ Academy of Music.
Flickering gas-lit lanterns announce this 19th century opera hall, modeled after Milan's La Scala. Gilded and gorgeous, the Academy is known as the "Grand Old Lady of Locust Street." (Her massive crystal chandelier is to die for.) If possible, catch a performance of the Pennsylvania Ballet, the Opera Company, or a Broadway show. ⏲ *15 min. See p 128.*

8 ★★ Kimmel Center. A few blocks south stands Rafael Viñoly's (b. 1944) dramatic glass-and-steel, accordion-shaped performing arts center. Opened in 2001, the Kimmel encompasses a 2,500-seat, cello-shaped orchestra hall; a 650-seat theater for smaller performances; an interactive education center; and soaring, community-minded Commonwealth Plaza, which often plays host to free performances. Take the elevator to the rooftop garden for a view of Broad Street, also known as the "Avenue of the Arts." (This is the place to get those tickets to the Academy.) Free, 1-hour tours at 1pm daily. ⏲ *½ hr. 300 S. Broad St. (at Spruce St.).* ☎ *215/790-5886. www.kimmel center.org. Free admission. Daily 10am–6pm, or 30 min. past last performance.*

Rittenhouse

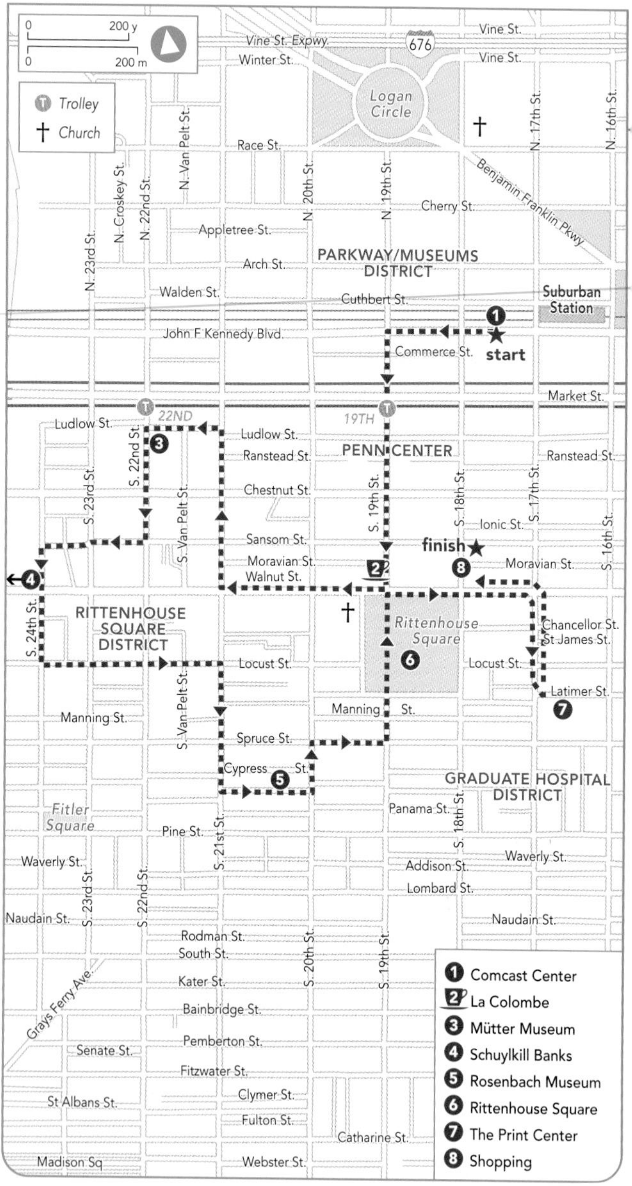

0 — 200 y	
0 — 200 m	

🚋 Trolley
✝ Church

PARKWAY/MUSEUMS DISTRICT

Suburban Station

❶ start

PENN CENTER

finish ★

RITTENHOUSE SQUARE DISTRICT

Rittenhouse Square

GRADUATE HOSPITAL DISTRICT

Fitler Square

Madison Sq

❶ Comcast Center
❷ La Colombe
❸ Mütter Museum
❹ Schuylkill Banks
❺ Rosenbach Museum
❻ Rittenhouse Square
❼ The Print Center
❽ Shopping

Per capita, more people walk to work in Philadelphia than in any other U.S. city. Many of these pedestrians wind up in this exclusive, residential-meets-commercial neighborhood. If it's a sunny spring day, the Square is the perfect spot to have lunch on a park bench. Fashion tip: If you packed something nice, wear it here. (And if not, take shopping breaks!) START: **19th & Walnut sts.**

❶ Comcast Center. Philadelphia's tallest building (975 ft.) comes courtesy of the 25 million people who pay Comcast's cable bills. When the Center debuted in 2009, the *Philadelphia Inquirer* called it "a giant USB memory stick." Stop in the atrium to ogle the people "walking" along the overhead beams, and watch a stunning, 83-foot, 10-million-pixel video display above the elevators. A fun aside: In order to break the "curse of William Penn" (that no Philly pro sports team had won a championship since skyscrapers grew taller than Penn's statue on City Hall), workers attached a figurine of Penn to the Center's final beam. A few months later, the Phillies won the World Series. Coincidence? ⏱ *20 min. 1701 JFK Blvd.* ☎ *215/496-1810. www.comcast.com. Free admission.*

❷ La Colombe. A Rittenhouse resident wouldn't dream of starting the day without a cappuccino and an almond croissant from this chic cafe. Eat in, and your breakfast will be handed to you on pretty Deruta pottery. *130 S. 19th St.* ☎ *215/563-0860. www.lacolombe.com. $.*

❸ ★★ kids Mutter Museum. Visitors—especially kids—will be fascinated, maybe frightened, and definitely grossed out by the huge collection of medical oddities at this dimly lit 19th-century building that feels straight out of Harry Potter—or at least *Young Frankenstein.* A whopping 20,000 strange-to-creepy objects fill the exhibit spaces at the College of Physicians (no longer a college)—including Grover Cleveland's

The 10-million-pixel video display at the Comcast Center.

The Mutter Museum is filled with medical oddities.

"secret tumor," a plaster cast of conjoined twins Chang and Eng (1811–1874), shelves of human skulls, jars of pickled deformed fetuses, John Wilkes Booth's thorax—and horrifying antique surgical instruments. ⏱ 1½ hr. 19 S. 22nd St. (btw. Market & Chestnut sts.). ☎ 215/560-8564. muttermuseum. org. Admission $18 adults, $16 seniors, $13 students, free 5 & under. Daily 10am–5pm.

❹ ★ Schuylkill Banks.
Walk west to the river to explore the recently landscaped park along the riverbank, with some sweeping city panoramas. (There's a handy staircase at 24th and Walnut.) A paved trail runs from here all the way to the Art Museum if you're so inclined—or you can sign up for a kayak tour (www.hiddenriveroutfitters.com). ⏱ 1 hr. 24th and Locust sts. ☎ 215/309-5523. www. schuylkillbanks.org.

❺ ★ Rosenbach Museum.
Although it feels like a library, what with the 30,000 rare books and ten times as many precious documents, this grand repository is, in fact, a museum (affiliated with the Free Library of Philadelphia, p 67). But while you can't leaf through James Joyce's original *Ulysses*, peruse a first-edition Melville, or borrow one of Maurice Sendak's paintings for *Where the Wild Things Are*, selected artifacts and documents are always on display, and you can take a tour of the lovely townhouse's art- and antique-filled rooms, left over from the Rosenbachs' time living here. ⏱ 1 hr. 2008–2010 Delancey Place. ☎ 215/732-1600. www.rosenbach. org. Admission $10 adults, $8 seniors, $5 students, free under 5. Tues & Fri noon–5pm, Wed–Thurs noon–8pm, Sat–Sun noon–6pm.

❻ ★★★ kids Rittenhouse Square.
Nearly a century ago, Paul Philippe Cret (1876–1945), designer of Ben Franklin Parkway, gave this park its rather polished good bones. Today, it's the city's most perfect people-watching spot, with such charming outdoor sculpture as the central plaza's Antoine-Louis Barye's *Lion Crushing a Serpent* (ca. 1832), Paul Manship's *Duck Girl* (ca. 1911) near the reflecting pool,

A paved riverbank trail winds through Schuylkill Banks.

The Rosenbach Museum is home to more than 30,000 rare books.

and Albert Laessle's 2-foot-tall billy goat in the Square's SW corner—since 1919, the preferred climbing toy of the Square's younger set, who've worn poor Billy's head, horns, and spine to a golden shine. 🕐 ½ hr. Btw. 18th & 19th sts., Walnut & Rittenhouse sts.

7 The Print Center. It's worth a detour east of Rittenhouse Square to check out whatever the current exhibition is at this century-old not-for-profit organization, devoted to the arts of photography and print-making, set in a handsome converted carriage house. 🕐 ½ hr. 1614 Latimer St. (btw. 16th & 17th sts.). ☎ 215/735-6090. printcenter. org. Free admission. Tues–Sat 11am–6pm.

8 ★★ Shopping. The streets branching off on either side of 18th Street offer plenty of upscale shopping. There's an **Anthropologie** (1801 Walnut St.) inside the Square's Van Rensselaer mansion. Famous scribes sign their latest works at Philly's premier bookseller,

Joseph Fox (1724 Sansom St.). The display window at **Joan Shepp** (1811 Chestnut St.) is downright museum-quality.

A 1947 bronze sundial by Beatrice Fenton is one of many sculptures adorning Rittenhouse Square.

Fairmount

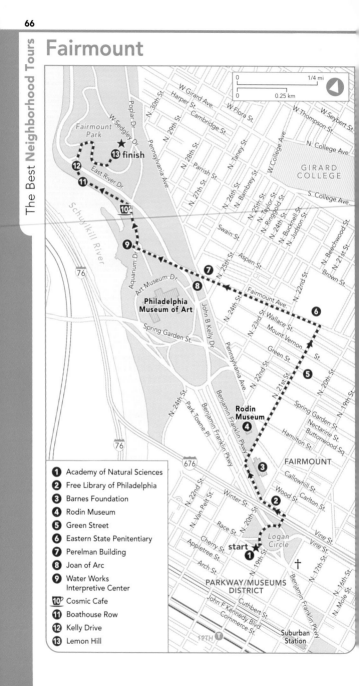

1 Academy of Natural Sciences
2 Free Library of Philadelphia
3 Barnes Foundation
4 Rodin Museum
5 Green Street
6 Eastern State Penitentiary
7 Perelman Building
8 Joan of Arc
9 Water Works Interpretive Center
10 Cosmic Cafe
11 Boathouse Row
12 Kelly Drive
13 Lemon Hill

Bound by Vine and Girard, Broad and the Schuylkill, Fairmount is often called the "Museum District." And, while it's true that the Philadelphia Museum of Art, Franklin Institute, Barnes Foundation, and Academy of Natural Sciences all exist here, so do some marvelous examples of elegant urban living. START: **19th St. & Ben Franklin Pkwy.**

❶ ★★ kids Academy of Natural Sciences. If it's dinosaurs you seek, look no further. More than a dozen impressive specimens, including a massive T-Rex with jaws agape, are on display in the main hall. You'll also find enormous moose, bison, and bears; Asian and African flora and fauna; a tropical butterfly exhibit; and "Outside in" where kids can touch whatever animals happen to stop by that day. ⏲ 1 hr. 19th St. & Ben Franklin Pkwy. ☎ 215/299-1000. www.ansp. org. Admission $20 adults, $16 kids 2–12. Mon–Fri 10am–4:30pm, Sat–Sun 10am–5pm.

❷ Free Library of Philadelphia. Stoic and splendid from its perch at the top of Logan Circle, the central branch of the public library is the best place to delve into writing about local travel and history (second floor). ⏲ ½ hr. 1901 Vine Street. ☎ 215/686-5322. http://freelibrary.org. Free admission.

Mon–Thurs 9am–9pm, Fri 9am–6pm, Sat 9am–5pm, Sun 1–5pm.

❸ ★★★ Barnes Foundation. Moved here from its original suburban home in 2012, this world-renowned museum is stuffed with some 8,000 largely Impressionist and Post-Impressionist works (Renoir, Cézanne, Matisse, Picassos, Van Gogh) intriguingly displayed alongside antique everyday objects and primitive sculpture. ⏲ 2 hrs. 2025 Benjamin Franklin Pkwy. See p 32.

❹ ★★ Rodin Museum. It's the largest collection of the master's statues outside Paris. The sculpture garden—including *Thinker* and *Gates of Hell*—is free. ⏲ ½ hr. See p 34.

❺ Green Street. Stroll this residential thoroughfare to admire beautiful 19th-century townhouses. ⏲ 10 min.

The Academy of Natural Sciences boasts a tropical butterfly exhibit among its many attractions.

The Water Works Interpretive Center features several miniature classical facades.

⑥ ★ Eastern State Penitentiary. This grim medieval-looking former prison was deliberately sited atop the nearest hill to Center City to serve as a warning to criminals. It didn't work: Eastern State stayed in business from 1829 to 1971. An hour-long audio tour offers a glimpse into solitary confinement "rehabilitation" cells and into the lives of its inmates, including robber Willie Sutton, gangster Al Capone, and one very naughty dog. ① *1 hr. 2027 Fairmount Ave. (btw. 21 & 22 sts.).* ☎ *215/236-3300. www.easternstate.org.*

The Joan of Arc monument was originally commissioned by Napoleon III for Paris.

Admission $16 adults, $14 seniors, $12 students and children (not recommended for children under 7). Daily 10am–5pm.

⑦ ★★ Perelman Building. Across the street from the **Philadelphia Museum of Art**—worth a visit when you have a couple of hours (see p 13)—this restored Art Deco office building has textile and design treasures, smaller exhibits, and a lovely cafe. ① *1 hr. See p 35.*

⑧ ★ Joan of Arc. Napoleon III commissioned this gilded equestrian statue of the French heroine in 1874 for Paris. In 1890 the city of Philadelphia asked for a copy, but sculptor Emmanuel Frémiet (1824–1910) gave them the original, sculpting a new version for Paris. (Irony: Valerie Laneau, the 15-year-old model who sat for Joan, herself died in a fire—though at the ripe old age of 77.) ① *10 min.*

⑨ ★★ kids Water Works Interpretive Center. Behind the Art Museum and atop Fairmount Dam, a charming line of miniature classical facades marks the restored location of the country's first municipal water delivery systems. This center aims to teach the importance of clean water via high-tech exhibits—a simulated helicopter ride takes visitors from the Delaware Bay to the headwaters of the Schuylkill River—offering an engaging message of environmental awareness. ⏲ *1 hr. 640 Waterworks Dr.* ☎ *215/685-0723. fairmountwaterworks.org. Free admission. Tues–Sat 10am–5pm, Sun 1–5pm.*

10 **Cosmic Cafe.** This city-operated boathouse cafe serves tasty salads, sandwiches, and pastries. *1 Boathouse Row (Kelly Dr.).* ☎ *215/978-0900. www.cosmic foods.com. $.*

11 ★★ **Boathouse Row.** Although these 10 Victorian-era sculling clubhouses are most famously viewed at night from across the river (their outlines trimmed in tiny white lights), they're great to peek into as you pass by. Together they form the "Schuylkill Navy," most often used by college and high school crew teams. Frank Furness (1839–1912) designed no. 13, Undine Barge Club. ⏲ *½ hr. no. 2–14 Boathouse Row, Kelly Dr.*

12 ★★ **Kelly Drive.** Named for champion Olympian oarsman Jack Kelly (father of actress Grace Kelly), this winding road's adjacent path is popular with cyclists and joggers. Even a short walk here leads to some marvelous sculpture, including one of Kelly himself and, hiding atop a rock, Frederic Remington's (1861–1909) *Cowboy* (ca. 1905). ⏲ *½ hr. See p 87.*

13 ★ **Lemon Hill.** High above Kelly Drive, the Federal-style 19th-century "country" estate of merchant Henry Pratt boasts serene gardens and an impressive trio of stacked oval rooms. ⏲ *½ hr. Sedgeley & Lemon Hill Drive.* ☎ *215/232-4337. parkcharms.com/lemon-hill. Admission $8 adults, $5 seniors & students, free under 12. Apr 13–Dec Thurs–Sun 10am–4pm; Jan–Mar by appt.*

Kelly Drive is popular with cyclists and joggers.

University City

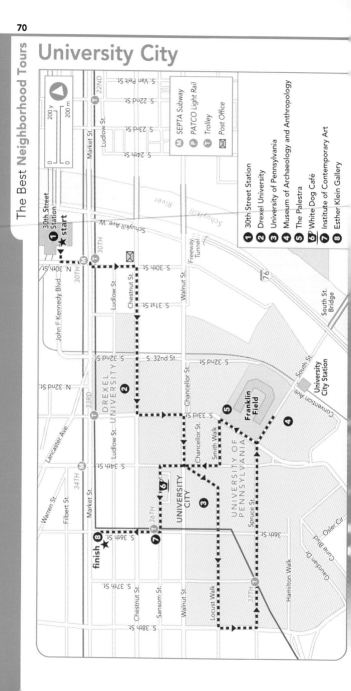

SEPTA Subway
PATCO Light Rail
Trolley
Post Office

1 30th Street Station
2 Drexel University
3 University of Pennsylvania
4 Museum of Archaeology and Anthropology
5 The Palestra
6 White Dog Café
7 Institute of Contemporary Art
8 Esther Klein Gallery

West of the Schuylkill River lies Philly's first suburb, known today as University City. Its centerpiece is the University of Pennsylvania, founded in 1740 by (who else but) Franklin and friends, which boasts the country's first medical, law, and business schools. START: 30th St. Station, btw. 29th & 30th sts. on Market St.

① ★★ 30th Street Station.
Twenty thousand Amtrak, SEPTA, and NJ Transit commuters pass daily through this circa-1933 train station, the roof of which was built to accommodate small aircraft landing. Notice the ornate Art Deco decor, the PA Railroad Workers World War II Memorial featuring the Archangel Michael, and the 1895 Spirit of Transportation relief mural in a side chamber. ① 15 min. 2955 Market St. ☎ 215/580-6500. Daily 24 hr.

② ★★ Drexel University. This high-tech university, founded in 1891, has gone through several name changes, developed a world-class engineering program, and added contemporary architecture, including a dorm by Michael Graves at 33rd and Race sts. ① 1 hr. Btw. 31st & 35th sts, Chestnut & Powelton sts. www.drexel.edu.

Locust Walk is the heart of the University of Pennsylvania.

③ ★★★ University of Pennsylvania. One of the country's oldest universities, "Penn" belongs both to the Ivy League and to the long list of Philadelphia establishments founded by Ben Franklin. The campus is a mix of modern and antique, with a well-heeled and international student body. Penn's heart is "Locust Walk," a vibrant pedestrian thoroughfare passing between ivy-covered 19th-century Gothic buildings; student-populated College Green; giant contemporary sculpture (Claes Oldenburg's Split Button); and the modern, Louis Kahn-designed Fine Arts Library. Look carefully to find Franklin (in bronze) seated on a park bench. ① ½ hr. Woodland Walk to Locust Walk (btw. 34th & 38th sts). ☎ 215/898-5000. www. upenn.edu.

④ ★★★ 🧒 University of Pennsylvania Museum of Archaeology and Anthropology. Since 1887—through 400-some archaeological and anthropological expeditions—Penn's major museum has collected more than 1 million ancient objects. A vast portion of them are displayed (and intelligently explained) within this massive Beaux Arts building's 25 galleries. The Egyptian collection, considered one of the world's finest, includes a colossal Sphinx, enormous columns, and "Mummies, Secrets, and Science," a family favorite. Don't miss the third floor's world-renowned excavation display of Sumerian jewelry and household objects from the royal tombs of Ur. Nearby, ogle

The Museum of Archaeology and Anthropology has collected more than 1 million ancient objects.

giant cloisonné lions from Beijing's Imperial Palace, Chinese court treasures, and tomb figures. Basically, if it's ancient, it's here: Mesopotamia; the Bible Lands; Mesoamerica; the ancient Mediterranean; and native peoples of the Americas, Africa, and Polynesia are all represented. ⏱ *2 hrs. 3260 South St. (a continuation of Spruce St. past 33rd St.).* ☎ *215/898-4000. www.museum. upenn.edu. Admission $15 adults, $13 seniors, $10 students with ID & children 6–17, free 5 & under. Tues–Sun 10am–5pm (to 8pm Wed).*

⑤ ★ The Palestra. If you know college hoops, you know Penn's circa-1927 gymnasium, a.k.a. "The Cathedral of College Basketball." More NCAA men's b-ball games, tournaments, and visiting teams have played here than anywhere else. The tradition continues today, so when you visit, you might catch a St. Joe's, Villanova, Temple, or (of course) Penn game. ⏱ *½ hr. 215 S. 33rd St. (btw. Walnut & Spruce sts.).*

☕ White Dog Cafe. If you're lucky enough to pass 34th & Walnut streets weekdays 11am–3pm, check out the amazing vegetarian/vegan food truck Magic Carpet (www. magiccarpetfoods.com). Otherwise, continue on to this excellent (if pricey) Philly mainstay of eclectic, organic foods. *3420 Sansom St.* ☎ *215/386-9224. www.whitedog. com. $$.*

⑦ ★★ Institute of Contemporary Art. Edgy modern art is always on display at this spare Penn-run gallery, the first museum to show Andy Warhol (1928–1987), Laurie Anderson (b. 1947), and Robert Indiana (b. 1928). ICA installations range from rocketry to music, couture to comics. ⏱ *1 hr. 118 S. 36th St. (at Sansom St.).* ☎ *215/898-7108. www.icaphila.org. Free admission. Wed 11am–8pm, Thurs–Sun 11am–6pm.*

⑧ ★ Esther Klein Art Gallery. At this unique and up-and-coming gallery, contemporary exhibits have a science and technology bent—so that photo you're admiring might have a bio lesson behind it. ⏱ *½ hr. 3600 Market St.* ☎ *215/966-6188. www.kleinartgallery.org. Free admission. Mon–Sat 9am–5pm.* ●

4

The Best Shopping

Center City Shopping

Arader Galleries **8**
Art Star **46**
Benjamin Lovell
  Shoes **15, 36**
Born Yesterday **21**
Boyd's **17**
Bus Stop Boutique **28**
The Clay Studio **43**
DiBruno Brothers **14, 26**
Duross & Langel **7**
Eyes Gallery **30**
The Fabric Workshop
  and Museum **2**
Fleisher/Ollman Gallery **2**

Freeman's **18**
Green Aisle Grocery **27**
Halloween **24**
Head House Books **29**
Hello World **22**
I. Goldberg Army
  & Navy **32**
Joan Shepp **16**
Joseph Fox Bookshop **19**
Lagos **20**
Larry Becker
  Contemporary Art **34**
Locks Gallery **31**
Loop **23**

Lost & Found **40**
M. Finkel & Daughter **25**
Macy's **4**
Material Culture **1**
Minima **37**
Mitchell & Ness
  Nostalgia Co. **5**
Mode Moderne **44**
Moderne Gallery **41**
Momo's Tree House **42**
Newman Galleries **11**
Open House **6**
Philadelphia Runner **12**
Reading Terminal Market **3**

Previous page: Eclectic, funky shops give a youthful vibe to the South Street shopping strip.

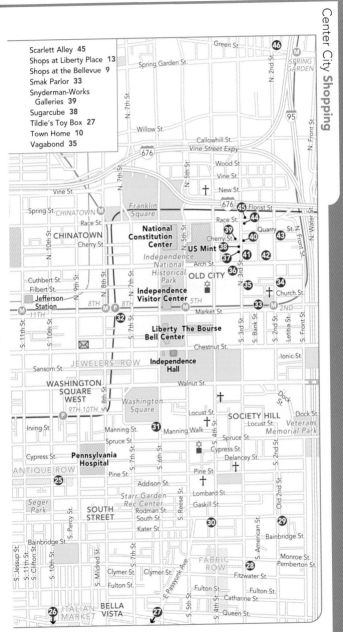

Shopping Best Bests

Best for **Gifts**
★★ Open House, *107 S. 13th St. (p 82)*

Best **Bookshop**
★★ Joseph Fox, *1724 Sansom St. (p 79)*

Best for **Precious Baubles**
★★★ Halloween, *1329 Pine St. (p 83)*

Best for **Antiques with Provenance**
★★ M. Finkel & Daughter, *936 Pine St. (p 77)*

Best for **Emerging Art**
★★ Larry Becker Contemporary Art, *43 N. 2nd St. (p 78)*

Best **Children's Shop**
★★ Momo's Tree House, *205 Arch St. (p 79)*

Best **Edible Souvenirs**
★★★ Reading Terminal Market, *12th & Arch sts. (p 82)*

Best for **Crafters**
★★★ Loop, *1914 South St. (p 80)*

Best **Women's Designer Clothing**
★★★ Joan Shepp, *1616 Walnut St. (p 81)*

Best **Edgy Women's Wear**
★★ Vagabond, *37 N. 3rd St. (p 81)*

Best for **Shoes**
★★ Bus Stop Boutique, *727 S. 4th St. (p 84)*

Best for **Browsing**
★ Macy's, *1300 Market St. (p 80)*

Best for **Foodies**
★★ DiBruno Brothers, *1730 Chestnut St. (p 82)*

Best for **Sports Fanatics**
★★ Mitchell & Ness, *1318 Chestnut St. (p 84)*

Best **Cheap and Chic Clothing**
★★ Lost & Found, *133 N. 3rd St. (p 81)*

M. Finkel & Daughter carries antique furnishings and paintings.

Shopping A to Z

Antiques/Vintage

★★ Arader Galleries CENTER CITY Rare 16th-through 19th-century maps, watercolors, and prints—including some by renowned naturalist John James Audubon (1785–1851)—are the specialty inside Arader's landmark building. *1308 Walnut St.* ☎ *215/735-8811. www.aradergalleries.com. AE, MC, V. Bus: 4, 9, 12, 21, 23, 27, 32, 42, 45. Subway: Walnut-Locust. Map p 74.*

★★ Blendo ANTIQUE ROW It's like grandma's attic, with all the clutter and more of the treasures (plus brand-new finds). Not the cheapest, though. *1002 Pine St. (btw. 10th & 11th sts.)* ☎ *215/351-9260. www.shopblendo.com. AE, DISC, MC, V. Bus: 40, 45, 47M.*

★★ Freeman's RITTENHOUSE The local version of Sotheby's or Christy's, Freeman's has catalogued auctions of art, jewelry, antiques, decorative arts, and fashion. *1808 Chestnut St. (btw. 18th & 19th sts.).* ☎ *215/563-9275. www.freemans auction.com. No credit cards. Bus: 2, 9 17, 21, 31, 32, 33, 33, 38, 42, 44, 48, 62, 78, 124, 125. Map p 74.*

★★★ Material Culture NORTH-WEST PHILADELPHIA Worth the ride north of Fairmount to the Nicetown/Queen's Lane area, this warehouse-sized store is an Aladdin's cave of furnishings, rugs, and one-of-a-kind home decorations—antique, repro, or modern folk items from China, Turkey, South Asia, Africa, and America, Africa, often at amazingly low prices. *4700 Wissahickon Ave. (enter on Roberts Ave.; off Rte. 1 Roosevelt Expwy./Lincoln Hwy.)* ☎ *215/849-8030. www.materialculture.com. AE, MC, V. Bus: H, XH. Train: Queen Lane. Map p 74.*

★★ M. Finkel & Daughter ANTIQUE ROW Known for restored schoolgirl samplers from the 17th- through mid-19th century, this well-appointed shop also stocks American folk art, furnishings, and paintings. *936 Pine St. (at 10th St.)* ☎ *215/627-7797. www.samplings.com. AE, MC, V. Bus: 12, 40, 45, 47M. Map p 74.*

★★ Mode Moderne OLD CITY More vintage than antique, the mint-condition furniture at this two-level shop hails from the dawn of the "atomic" modern era; think Charles and Ray Eames, not Chippendale. *159 N. 3rd St. (btw. Arch and Race sts.)* ☎ *215/627-0299. www.modemoderne.com. AE, DISC, MC, V. Bus: 5, 38, 48, 57. Subway: 2nd St. Map p 74.*

★★ Moderne Gallery OLD CITY Robert Aibel's artful collection includes early Nakashima (1905–1990); French ironwork; and sculpture, furnishings, and woodcuts from the American craft movement. *111 N. 3rd St. (btw. Arch & Race sts.).* ☎ *215/923-8536. www.modernegallery.com. MC, V. Bus: 5, 38, 48, 57. Subway: 2nd St. Map p 74.*

Art

★ Eyes Gallery SOUTH STREET Sometimes religious, often offbeat, and always colorful Latin American folk art bursts from the seams of this long-running multi-floor shop covered in mosaics by local artist Isaiah Zagar. *402 South St. (at 4th St.)* ☎ *215/925-0193. www.eyesgallery.com. AE, DISC, MC, V. Bus: 40, 47, 57. Map p 74.*

★ Fleisher/Ollman Gallery CONVENTION CENTER This storied gallery (which moved in 2013 to the same building as the Fabric

Larry Becker Contemporary Art offers an intimate showcase for modern artists.

Workshop, p 80) carries fine works by emerging contemporary and self-taught American artists. *1216 Arch St. (btw. 12th & 13th sts).* ☎ *215/545-7562. www.fleisher-ollmangallery.com. AE, DISC, MC, V. Bus: 4, 23, 27, 45, 48, 61, 124, 125. Subway: 11th St. Train: Jefferson. Map p 74.*

★★ **Larry Becker Contemporary Art** OLD CITY This intimate space features new, often spare paintings and sculpture from modern artists such as Marcia Hafif (b. 1929) and John Zinsser (b. 1961). *43 N. 2nd St. (btw. Market & Arch sts.)* ☎ *215/925-5389. Exhibits/info on Facebook. No credit cards. Bus: 5, 17, 21, 33, 42, 48, 57. Subway: 2nd St. Map p 74.*

★★★ **Locks Gallery** WASHINGTON SQUARE In a Beaux-Arts building, this powerhouse gallery exhibits big-deal works by de Kooning (1904–1997), Hockney (b. 1937), Rauschenberg (1925–2008), and Louise Nevelson (1899–1988). *600 S. Washington Sq. (at 6th St., btw. Walnut & Spruce sts.).* ☎ *215/629-1000. www.locksgallery. com. No credit cards. Bus: 9, 12, 21, 38, 42, 47, 57, 61. Map p 74.*

★★ **Minima** OLD CITY More "design" than "art," the wares in this glossy white space consist of pristine modern furnishings by Piero Lissoni (b. 1956), Phillippe Starck (b. 1949), Jasper Morrison (b. 1959), and Marcel Wanders (b. 1963). *118 N. 3rd St. (btw. Arch & Race sts.).* ☎ *215/922-2002. www.minima.us. AE, DISC, MC, V. Bus: 5, 38, 48, 57. Subway: 2nd St. Map p 74.*

★ **Newman Galleries** RITTENHOUSE Philadelphia's oldest gallery (ca. 1865) represents Bucks County artists, American sculptors, and traditional painters. *1625 Walnut St. (btw. 16th & 17th sts.).* ☎ *215/563-1779. www.newman galleries.com. AE, DISC, MC, V. Bus: 2, 9, 12, 21, 42. Subway: 15th/16th & Locust St. Map p 74.*

★ **Snyderman-Works Galleries** OLD CITY Since the mid-1960s, the conjoined galleries of Rick & Ruth Snyderman have been at the forefront of fine art ceramics, glass, jewelry, fiber, and furniture, exhibiting everyone from Dale Chihuly, Ettore Sottsass, and William Morris to up-and-comers in contemporary

Joseph Fox Bookshop has hosted readings from the likes of David Sedaris.

Sing-alongs captivate young customers at Momo's Tree House.

studio crafts. *303 Cherry St. (btw. N. 3rd & N. 4th sts.).* ☎ *215/238-9576. www.snyderman-works.com. No credit cards. Bus: 5, 38, 48, 57. Subway: 2nd St. Map p 74.*

Bookstores

★ kids **Head House Books** SOUTH STREET This neat-as-a-pin neighborhood shop stocks classics, bestsellers, and fantastic children's books—and hosts readings by local authors. *619 S. 2nd St. (btw. South & Bainbridge sts.).* ☎ *215/923-9525. www.headhouse books.com. AE, DISC, MC, V. Bus: 40, 57. Map p 74.*

★★ **Joseph Fox Bookshop** RITTENHOUSE Philly's premier book store, set in a tiny walk-up, is cozy and well organized, with a bookish staff who know their stock inside and out. Fox co-sponsors readings/signings by literary heavyweights at the Free Library (p 67) and other venues. *1724 Sansom St. (btw. 17th & 18th sts.).* ☎ *215/563-4184. www. foxbookshop.com. AE, MC, V. Bus: 2, 9, 12, 21, 42. Subway: 15th/16th & Locust St. Map p 74.*

Children's

★ **Born Yesterday** RITTENHOUSE For the Bugaboo stroller set, a haute boutique for hand-knit

sweaters, French onesies, and trendy ensembles for newborns on up. *1901 Walnut St.* ☎ *215/568-6556. www.bornyesterdaykids.com. AE, DISC, MC, V. Bus: 2, 9, 12, 21, 42. Subway: 15th/16th & Locust St. Map p 74.*

★★ **Momo's Tree House** OLD CITY The 2018 Best of Philly winner for Smart Kid Toys specializes in toys that "encourage creative, child-directed play." They even let kids play with the toys before buying. *205 Arch St. (btw. 2nd and Bridge sts.)* ☎ *215/457-2803. www. momostreehouse.com. AE, MC, V. Bus: 5, 38, 48, 57. Subway: 2nd St. Map p 74.*

★ **Tildie's Toy Box** SOUTH PHILLY Penn grads Michelle and Paul Gillen-Doobrajh run this East Passyunk haven for thinking parents who want their kids to be engaged and inspired by gender-neutral toys, games, crafts, and puzzles. *1829 East Passyunk Ave.* ☎ *215/334-9831. www.tildiestoy box.com. AE, MC, V. Bus: 4, 45. Subway: Tasker-Morris. Map p 74.*

Crafts

★★ **Art Star** NORTHERN LIBERTIES If you like Etsy, you'll love this youthful gallery's stock of handmade clothing, accessible art, and sculptural jewelry. *623 N. 2nd St. (btw. Spring Garden St. & Fairmount Ave.).* ☎ *215/238-1557. www.artstar philly.com. MC, V. Bus: 5, 25, 43. Subway: Spring Garden St. Map p 74.*

★★ The Clay Studio OLD CITY
This not-for-profit studio founded in the 1970s by a quintet of Philly artists is the serious, art-focused progenitor to those paint-your-own-pot chain stores. Inspired by their artist-produced pottery? Sign up for a half-day workshop. *137–139 N. 2nd St. (btw. Arch & Race sts.).* ☎ *215/925-3453. www.theclay studio.org. AE, MC, V. Bus: 5, 38, 48, 57. Subway: 2nd St. Map p 74.*

★★ The Fabric Workshop and Museum CENTER CITY
At this not-for-profit center, you can watch noted artists-in-residence work with skilled printmakers and promising apprentices to produce a range of artistic products and printed objects. Bonus: The museum stages buzz-worthy exhibitions (see p 59). *1214 Arch St. (btw. 12th & 13th sts.).* ☎ *215/561-8888. www.fabricwork shopandmuseum.org. MC, V. Bus: 4, 23, 27, 45, 48, 61, 124, 125. Subway: 11th St. Train: Jefferson. Map p 74.*

★★★ Loop RITTENHOUSE
This colorful, gallery-like, always friendly shop offers beautiful yarns, pretty fabrics, and tons of patterns (and advice). *1914 South St. (btw. 19th & 20th sts.).* ☎ *215/893-9939. www. loopyarn.com. DISC, MC, V. Bus: 17, 40. Map p 74.*

Department Stores/Shopping Centers

★ Macy's CENTER CITY
This stalwart stands out for its antique pipe organ, multi-story marble atrium, and holiday light show—carryovers from its days as John Wanamaker's, one of the country's first department stores. See p 60. *Btw. 13th & Juniper sts., Chestnut & Market sts.* ☎ *215/241-9000. www. macys.com. AE, DISC, MC, V. Bus: 4, 17, 27, 31, 32, 33, 38, 44, 48, 62, 78, 124, 125. Subway: City Hall or 13th St. Map p 74.*

Shops at the Bellevue CENTER CITY
On the ground floor of the Park Hyatt you'll find a kick-off to the upscale retail chains along Walnut Street: Nicole Miller, Tiffany & Co., Williams-Sonoma, and Teuscher Chocolates of Switzerland. *200 S. Broad St. (at Walnut St.).* ☎ *215/875-8350. www.bellevue philadelphia.com. Bus: 4, 9, 12, 21, 27, 32, 42. Subway: Walnut-Locust. Map p 74.*

Loop has a wide range of colorful patterns for crafts.

Wanamaker's, one of the first department stores in the country, is now a Macy's.

★ Shops at Liberty Place RITTENHOUSE
On the first few levels of one of the city's tallest buildings, this mini-mall has J. Crew, Express, Jos. A. Bank, Aldo, Victoria's Secret, and about a dozen more stores. *Btw. 16th & 17th sts., Chestnut & Market sts.* ☎ 215/851-9055. *www.shopsatliberty.com. Bus: 2, 9 17, 21, 31, 32, 33, 33, 38, 42, 44, 48, 62, 78, 124, 125. Subway: Walnut-Locust. Map p 74.*

Fashion
★ Boyd's RITTENHOUSE
Selling bespoke suits, $25,000 watches, Dolce & Gabbana frocks, and Manolo Blahniks, this family-run business in a beautiful old building employs a staff of obsessively attentive salespeople and 65 tailors. *1818 Chestnut St. (btw. 18th & 19th sts.).* ☎ 215/564-9000. *www.boydsphila.com. AE, DISC, MC, V. Bus: 2, 9 17, 21, 31, 32, 33, 33, 38, 42, 44, 48, 62, 78, 124, 125. Map p 74.*

★★★ Joan Shepp RITTENHOUSE
The mother-daughter doyennes of the local fashion scene run this industrial-chic boutique, where big-deal designers (Yohji Yamamoto, Stella McCartney, Dries Van Noten, and Pierre Balmain) come to roost. *1811 Chestnut St. (btw. 16th & 17th sts.).* ☎ 215/735-2666. *www.joanshepp.com. AE, DISC, MC, V. Bus: 2, 9 17, 21, 31, 32, 33, 33, 38, 42, 44, 48, 62, 78, 124, 125. Map p 74.*

★★ Lost & Found OLD CITY
A mother-daughter team runs this new-plus-vintage shop, known for reasonable prices on cute, youthful men's and women's clothing, Orla Kiely bags, and fun jewelry. *133 N. 3rd St. (btw. Arch & Race sts.).* ☎ 215/928-1311. *AE, DISC, MC, V. Bus: 5, 38, 48, 57. Subway: 2nd St. Map p 74.*

★ Smak Parlour OLD CITY
Adorable designers Abby Kessler and Katie Lofuts create each trendy skirt, flirty dress, and cool top in this girly shop, which also sells a smattering of shoes, jewelry, and gifts. *219 Market St. (btw. 2nd & 3rd sts.).* ☎ 215/625-4551. *www.smakparlour.com. AE, DISC, MC, V. Bus: 5, 17, 21, 33, 42, 48, 57. Subway: 2nd St. Map p 74.*

★★ Sugarcube OLD CITY
Up-and-coming labels are the not-inexpensive specialty of this shop, a must for the fashion set, men and women alike. *124 N. 3rd St. (btw. Arch and Race sts.).* ☎ 215/238-0825. *www.sugarcube.us. AE, MC, V. Bus: 5, 38, 48, 57. Subway: 2nd St. Map p 74.*

★★ Vagabond OLD CITY
This pioneering women's shop offers Uzi, LHOOQ, Ace & Jig, plus knits and dresses by the shop's stylish owners. *37 N. 3rd St. (btw. Market & Arch sts.).* ☎ 267/671-0737. *www.vagabondboutique.com. AE, DISC, MC, V. Bus: 5, 38, 48, 57. Subway: 2nd St. Map p 74.*

Trendsetting styles make Vagabond a stand-out on boutique-lined North 3rd Street.

Gifts

★★ Duross & Langel CENTER CITY A locavore's Lush—only better—this emporium of made-in-house body care products doesn't have shoppers, it has acolytes. Check out their bespoke soaps, fragrances, body washes, shampoos, scented candles, aromatic oils, and more. *117 S. 13th St. (at Sansom St.).* ☎ *215/834-7226. www.durossand langel.com. AE, DISC, MC, V. Bus: 4, 9, 12, 21, 23, 27, 31, 32, 33, 38, 42, 44, 45, 48, 62, 78, 124, 125. Subway: Walnut-Locust. Map p 74.*

★ Hello World WEST PHILLY Come here for restored vintage furnishings and great new shelter pieces, plus pretty jewelry and kids' clothes. *3610 Sansom St. (btw. 36th & 37th sts.).* ☎ *215/382-5207. www. shophelloworld.com. AE, DISC, MC, V. Bus: 30, 31, 40, LUCY. Map p 74.*

★★ Open House CENTER CITY Bright vases, clever pillows, pretty coffee cups, great kiddie goodies, and wonderful bath products make this one of the best spots for gift shopping—for yourself. *107 S. 13th St. (btw. Sansom & Chestnut sts.).* ☎ *215/922-1415. www.openhouse living.com. AE, MC, V. Bus: 4, 9, 12, 21, 23, 27, 31, 32, 33, 38, 42, 44, 45, 48, 62, 78, 124, 125. Subway: Walnut-Locust. Map p 74.*

★★ Scarlett Alley OLD CITY Here's the spot for fantastic, stylish souvenirs like Italian cordial glasses, hand-painted bowls, and great table linens. *241 Race St. (btw. 2nd & 3rd sts.).* ☎ *215/592-7898. www.scarlett-talley.com. AE, MC, V. Bus: 5, 38, 48, 57. Subway: 2nd St. Map p 74.*

Gourmet Food

★★ DiBruno Brothers SOUTH PHILLY Locals think this two-floor foodie mecca with its cheese cave and cafeteria is better than Dean & DeLuca. They're right. *930 S. 9th St.* ☎ *215/922-2876. www.dibruno. com. AE, DISC, MC, V. Bus: 2, 9 17, 21, 31, 32, 33, 33, 38, 42, 44, 48, 62, 78, 124, 125. Also at 1730 Chestnut St. (btw. 17th & 18th sts.),* ☎ *215/665-9220. Map p 74.*

★ Green Aisle Grocery SOUTH PHILLY The Erace brothers sell Philly faves—Zahav hummus, Fond meringues, Severino pasta, Momofuku cookies, Bing Bing dumplings—plus their own pickles and preserves and Lancaster farm produce out of this little Passyunk shop and its branch on Grays Ferry Ave. (at South & 23rd sts.). *1618 E. Passyunk Ave.* ☎ *215/465-1411. www.greenaislegrocery.com. AE, MC, V. Subway: Tasker-Morris. Bus: 4, 45. Map p 74.*

★★★ Reading Terminal Market CENTER CITY This charming 80-stall indoor market sells oysters, organic produce, ice cream, cookbooks, chocolates, sushi, tacos, gourmet cheeses, Pennsylvania

Cheese plays a starring role at the multi-level DiBruno Brothers.

Dutch pretzels, roast pork sandwiches, moon pies . . . *12th St. (btw. Arch & Filbert sts.).* ☎ *215/922-2317. www.readingterminalmarket. org. Some kiosks accept credit cards. Bus: 4, 23, 27, 45, 48, 61, 124, 125. Subway: 11th St. Train: Jefferson. Map p 74.*

Jewelry
★★★ **Halloween** ANTIQUE ROW   With only an orange business card in the window as signage, this boutique feels like a treasure trove, with pearls upon pearls, opals upon opals, silver upon

Hungry shoppers can stock up for a feast or two at indoor Reading Terminal Market.

silver—both vintage and custom pieces. *1329 Pine St. (at Juniper St.).* ☎ *215/732-7711. No credit cards. Bus: 4, 27, 32, 40, 45. Subway: Lombard South. Map p 74.*

★ **Lagos** RITTENHOUSE   Oprah is a fan of this local jeweler who made the big time (his line is now carried in all the chic department stores), known for its fashion-forward settings, colored gems, and beaded look. *1735 Walnut St. (btw. 17th & 18th sts.).* ☎ *215/567-0770. www.lagos.com. AE, MC, V. Bus: 2, 9, 12, 21, 42. Subway: 15th/16th & Locust St. Map p 74.*

★★ **TownHome** RITTENHOUSE   This pretty, extra-petite shop is known for amazing jewelry by the likes of Jennifer Meyer, Dana Rebecca, and Heather B. Moore. *1616 Walnut St.* ☎ *215/972-5100. www.townhomeonline.com. AE, MC, V. Bus: 2, 9, 12, 21, 42. Subway: 15th/16th & Locust St. Map p 74.*

Shoes
★ **Benjamin Lovell Shoes** OLD CITY   This locally based chain is best known for its comfort footwear from Merrell, Ugg, Ecco, Dansko, and Naot, plus fresh kicks from Camper and Cole Haan. *60 N. 3rd.*

Antiques Row/Jewelers Row

If you're browsing for high-end items, you'll often find top outlets clustered in a targeted area, allowing shoppers to compare like wares. The historic blocks of Pine Street between 9th and 12th streets have become known as **Antiques Row** (see listings above). Near Washington Square, Samson Street between 7th and 8th streets is **Jeweler's Row,** a couple blocks' worth of wholesale and retail merchants, whose vibe ranges from pawn shop to antiques shop. It's tailored to sellers of gold and buyers of engagement rings.

St. ☎ 215/238-1969. AE, DISC, MC, V. Bus: 5, 38, 48, 57. Subway: 2nd St. Bus: 2, 9 17, 21, 31, 32, 33, 33, 38, 42, 44, 48, 62, 78, 124, 125. www. blshoes.com. Also at 1728 Chestnut St. ☎ 215/564-4655. Map p 74.

★★ Bus Stop Boutique QUEEN VILLAGE Super-friendly British shopkeep Elena Brennan maintains a stylishly offbeat selection of women's and men's shoes, bags, and jewelry from cutting-edge European and local designers. 727 S. 4th St. (at Pemberton St.). ☎ 215/627-2357. www.busstopboutique.com. AE, DISC, MC, V. Bus: 47, 57. Map p 74.

The fashion choices at Bus Stop Boutique are stylishly offbeat.

Sporting Goods

★★ Mitchell & Ness Nostalgia Co. CENTER CITY Find authentic, licensed replicas of the jerseys, caps, and jackets of some of America's best-known athletes at this international chain's original flagship store. 1201 Chestnut St. (at 12th St.). ☎ 866/879-6485. www. mitchellandness.com. AE, DISC, MC, V. Bus: 4, 9, 12, 21, 23, 27, 31, 32, 33, 38, 42, 44, 45, 48, 62, 78, 124, 125. Subway: Walnut-Locust or 13th St. Map p 74.

★ I. Goldberg Army & Navy CENTER CITY Everything you need to spend the night outdoors is sold (cheap) at this classic army-navy outfitter. Camping gear bought here at age 11 saw me all the way through Eagle Scout. 718 Chestnut St. (btw. 7th & 8th St.). ☎ 215/925-9393. www.igoldberg. com. AE, DISC, MC, V. Bus: 9, 21, 33, 38, 42, 47, 47M, 124. Subway: Walnut-Locust or 13th St. Map p 74.

★ Philadelphia Runner RITTEN-HOUSE More than 250 styles of running and walking shoes are for sale at the retail home of the Philadelphia Running Club. 1601 Sansom St. (at 16th St.). ☎ 215/972-8333. www.philadelphiarunner.com. AE, DISC, MC, V. Bus: 2, 9, 12, 21, 42. Subway: 15th/16th & Locust St. Map p 74. ●

5

The Best of the
Outdoors

Fairmount Park by Bike

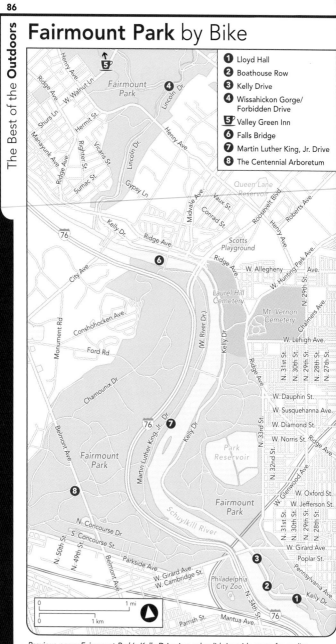

1. Lloyd Hall
2. Boathouse Row
3. Kelly Drive
4. Wissahickon Gorge/ Forbidden Drive
5. Valley Green Inn
6. Falls Bridge
7. Martin Luther King, Jr. Drive
8. The Centennial Arboretum

Previous page: Fairmount Park's Kelly Drive is a splendid riverside route for cyclists.

More than 215 miles of trails exist within the 9,200-plus acres that make Fairmount Park the world's largest landscaped city park (for comparison: NYC's Central Park is a mere 843 acres). This 18- to 22-mile route explores areas easiest accessed from Center City, via trails that are paved or gravel-covered, beginner-friendly, and bucolic. START: **Lloyd Hall, 1 Boathouse Row, behind the Philadelphia Museum of Art.**

① **Lloyd Hall.** This community boathouse has a bike-rental shack operated by Wheel Fun Rentals that's open whenever it's dry and over 50°F. ⏱ ¼ hr. 1 Boathouse Row. ☎ 215/232-7778. www.wheelfunrentals.com. Rentals from $10/hr.; $32/day. Late Mar–early May: daily 10am–sunset; Early May–early June and early Sept–mid-Nov: daily 9am–sunset; Early June–early Sept: daily 9am–10pm (see "Bike Rentals" on p 165 for other options).

② **★★ Boathouse Row.** You'll quickly whiz by these 10 Victorian-era crew-team clubhouses, so take some time to peep inside; note no. 13, Undine Barge Club, designed by Frank Furness (1839–1912); and perhaps see a college or high school athlete preparing to go sculling. ⏱ 10 min. See p 69.

③ **★★ Kelly Drive.** For about 4 miles, you'll ride between the Schuylkill ("Skoo-kill") River and this winding road peppered with sculptures and named after champion oarsman John B. "Jack" Kelly Sr. (1899–1960), three-time Olympic gold medalist and father to Princess Grace Kelly (and to John, Jr., himself a four-time Olympian). The Drive ends in a sharp left at Ridge Avenue, just after crossing Wissahickon Creek. The trail continues (after a harrowing mile along busy Main Street through trendy Manayunk) all the way to Valley Forge and beyond, but we're going to cross Ridge at the light and pick up a spur trail, the Wissahickon Bike Trail. ⏱ 45 min. See p 69.

④ **★★★ Wissahickon Gorge/ Forbidden Drive.** After following the trail along Lincoln Drive for 1.3 miles, you'll come to a small parking lot where you can turn left onto Forbidden Drive—a 1920s nickname that sounds portentous but

The 1,800-acre Wissahickon Gorge is one of the city's jewels.

really only means that cars were banned. This is the jewel of the park system, 1,800 acres of urban nature that we locals often call "Valley Green." The wide, gravelly, wooded trail rises and falls for 5.3 miles. Rocks rise on your left, the wide Wissahickon (Lenape Indian for "catfish creek") flows below to the right. Stop to spot owls, titmice, woodpeckers (five species nest here), bluebirds, cardinals, nuthatches, goldfinches, and plenty of mallards. Note the 19th-century stone bridges, 1930s-era WPA-built shelters, and the 1737 Thomas Mill Road covered bridge, which has its own mailbox for letters of appreciation for the bridge or Valley Green in general. There's no wading in the creek, and a permit is required to explore dirt trails by bike (both widely ignored ordinances). Cellphone service is spotty. ⏱ 2 hrs. Fairmount Park: ☎ 215/683-0200; www.fairmountpark.org. Call the Friends of the Wissahickon for park news and information): ☎ 215/247-0417; www.fow.org.

5⃣ ★ Valley Green Inn. About 3 miles up the trail, this charming, circa-1850 former roadhouse tavern (the last one left in the park) serves sit-down meals—chicken salad sandwiches, salmon clubs, and spinach salads—and has a walk-up stand for drinks and snacks. *Valley Green Rd. at Wissahickon.* ☎ 215/247-1730. www.valley greeninn.com. $$.

6⃣ Falls Bridge. Turn around to return the way you came—except once back on Kelly Drive, cross the river on this steel Pratt truss bridge built in 1894–95, a low tunnel of lacy steel struts, to head to Martin Luther King, Jr. Drive. (From the far end of Valley Green, about 7.3 miles.) ⏱ 1 hr.

The Valley Green Inn is a perfect place to stop and refuel.

7⃣ ★ Martin Luther King, Jr. Drive. On April–October weekends, this tree-lined thoroughfare (usually referred to as simply "West River Drive") is closed to vehicular traffic. Spread out, enjoy the smooth ride. (There's also a parallel bike trail for when the road's open to traffic, but frost heaves leave it eternally bumpy.) If you're tired, head back toward Center City, passing the **Philadelphia Zoo** on your right (see p 45), crossing over the river and in front of the Philadelphia Museum of Art (see p 13) then behind it past the Water Works (p 68), returning to Lloyd Hall. (Total from Falls Bridge: 5 miles.) If you're up for more scenery, take a right after 2.1 miles at the trail next to Montgomery Drive (just past the Columbia Railroad Bridge) for an uphill 0.6 miles, and turn left at Belmont Mansion Drive to the next stop. ⏱ ½ hr.

8⃣ ★★★ The Centennial Arboretum. To enjoy this park-within-a-park, hop off your bike and proceed on foot, exploring its 27 acres of elegant statuary, ponds, pools, tropical plants, fountains, gazebos, and butterflies. A

Fairmount Park by Other Means

By sneaker or skate: If the sun's out, so are the runners, walkers, and bladers along Kelly and MLK Jr. drives. From the Philadelphia Museum of Art, over Strawberry Mansion Bridge (at Ford Rd.) and back is 6.5 miles (10.4 km); go as far as the Falls Bridge (at Calumet St.), and you'll cover 8.5 miles (13.7km). Beware bikers—and resident Canada geese. **By kayak:** Get a river tour by kayak (including lesson, if needed) from **Hidden River Outfitters,** 25th and Walnut sts. (entrance at 25th and Locust sts.; ☎ 267/588-3512; www.hiddenriveroutfitters.com; tours $40–$50; various hours Jun–Sept: Sat–Sun and most Thurs), at Schuylkill Banks (www.schuylkillbanks.org)—or, for more advanced paddlers, a day trip to Bartram's Garden.

must-visit: **Shofuso,** a Japanese garden and teahouse (☎ 215/878-5097; japanphilly.org/shofuso; Apr–Oct Wed–Fri 10am–4pm, Sat–Sun 11am–5pm; Nov–Dec 9th Sat–Sun 10am–4pm; admission $12 adults, $8 seniors and students). Renowned architect Yoshimura Junzo (1908–1997) designed the Japanese house in 1953 in Nagoya. Five years later, it landed here, surrounded by lush moss, weeping cherry trees, and koi ponds. Inside are contemporary murals by Hiroshi Senju (b. 1958) and, occasionally, formal tea ceremonies. ⏱ *2 hrs. Belmont Ave. & Montgomery Dr. ☎ 215/685-0048 or 215/685-0096. www.fairmountpark.org. Free admission. Daily Nov–Mar 8am–5pm, Apr–Oct 8am–6pm.*

When you're through here, retrace your tracks back to MLK, Jr. Drive, where you'll take a right toward Center City and head back to Lloyd Hall, about 3½ miles.

The Shofusu Japanese garden is full of elegant ponds and fountains.

Park It: **Five Squares**

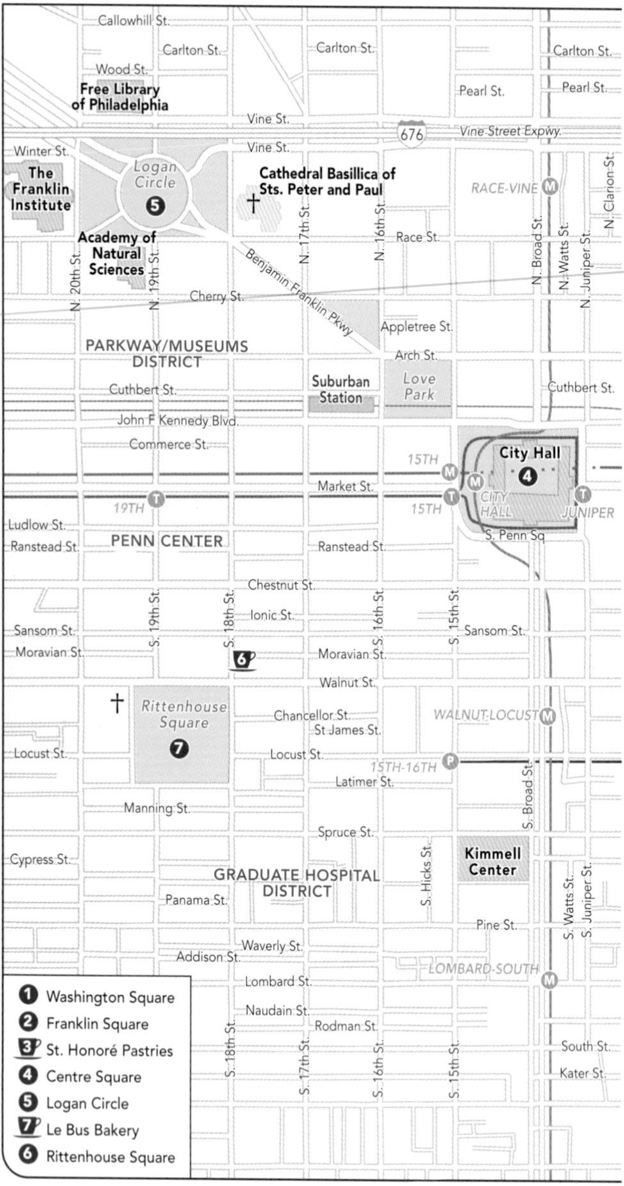

Map labels (reading across the map):

Callowhill St.
Carlton St. — Carlton St. — Carlton St.
Wood St.
Pearl St. — Pearl St.
Free Library of Philadelphia
Vine St.
Vine St. — 676 — Vine Street Expwy.
Winter St.
Logan Circle **5**
The Franklin Institute
Cathedral Basillica of Sts. Peter and Paul
RACE-VINE M
N. Clarion St.
Academy of Natural Sciences
Race St.
N. Broad St.
N. Watts St.
N. Juniper St.
N. 20th St.
N. 19th St.
N. 17th St.
N. 16th St.
Benjamin Franklin Pkwy
Cherry St.
Appletree St.
PARKWAY/MUSEUMS DISTRICT
Arch St.
Cuthbert St.
Suburban Station
Love Park
Cuthbert St.
John F Kennedy Blvd.
Commerce St.
15TH
City Hall **4**
Market St.
15TH M T
CITY HALL
JUNIPER T
19TH T
S. Penn Sq.
Ludlow St.
Ranstead St.
PENN CENTER
Ranstead St.
Chestnut St.
S. 19th St.
S. 18th St.
Ionic St.
S. 16th St.
S. 15th St.
Sansom St.
Moravian St
6
Moravian St.
Sansom St.
Walnut St.
WALNUT-LOCUST M
Rittenhouse Square **7**
Chancellor St.
St James St
Locust St.
15TH-16TH P
Locust St.
Latimer St.
Manning St.
S. Broad St.
Spruce St.
Cypress St.
GRADUATE HOSPITAL DISTRICT
Panama St.
S. Hicks St.
Kimmell Center
Pine St.
S. Watts St.
S. Juniper St.
Waverly St.
Addison St.
LOMBARD-SOUTH M
Lombard St.
Naudain St.
Rodman St.
S. 18th St.
S. 17th St.
S. 16th St.
S. 15th St.
South St.
Kater St.

Legend:
1 Washington Square
2 Franklin Square
3 St. Honoré Pastries
4 Centre Square
5 Logan Circle
7 Le Bus Bakery
6 Rittenhouse Square

In 1682, William Penn planned five green squares for his "Green Countrie Towne." True to his modest Quaker values, he simply named the spaces after their locations (Northwest Square, Centre Square, etc.). Today, Penn's parks (later given more evocative names) are the city's proudest al fresco showpieces. You can easily see them all in 1 day. START: **6th & Locust sts.**

❶ ★★ Washington Square.

The city's most historically significant park, 6½-acre "Southeast Square" was once pasture with a pair of fishable creeks. In 1704, a portion of these grounds became a potter's field—a burial ground for the city's unknown and poor. In 1776, troops who died fighting in the Revolutionary War were interred here; at the park's center, an eternal flame and bronze statue of Washington serve as the Tomb of the Unknown Revolutionary Soldier. In later years, Washington Square became the centerpiece of the city's publishing business, with the still-publishing *Farm Journal* in the southwest corner and **Curtis Publishing Company** (once home to the *Ladies' Home Journal* and the *Saturday Evening Post*) occupying Walnut St. between 6th and 7th sts. Stop in the Curtis Building (through the 7th St. entrance) and walk toward 6th Street to see the gorgeous 100,000-mosaic **Dream Garden mural,** a hidden gem by Maxfield Parrish (1870–1966) and Louis Comfort Tiffany (1848–19330). Also viewable (on weekdays) is the **Athenaeum** (219 S. 6th St.; ☎ 215/925-2688), an elegant collections library of rare books. ⏱ *1 hr. Btw. 6th & 7th, Spruce & Walnut sts.*

❷ ★★★ kids Franklin Square.

The most recently refreshed of the squares is the most kid-friendly, too. In 2006, after years of neglect, the city cleaned up the space and added 18 holes of Philadelphia-themed mini-golf, toddler-to-tween-friendly jungle gyms, a giant

Franklin Square is one of the most kid-friendly spaces in the city.

sand sculpture, a large and lovely carousel, benches for "Once Upon A Nation" performers, and fantastic Square Shack for better-than-average burgers, shakes, and fries. The best time to visit is spring through fall, when the amusements are up and running. In May and July, return after 6pm for the Chinese Lantern Festival. ⏱ *1 hr. See p 38.*

❸ ★★ Saint Honore Pastries.

Head west from Franklin Square through Chinatown, where you'll find this bakery's just-baked Hong Kong buns, stamped with lucky red characters and stuffed with sweet sesame, red bean, or azuki fillings. Other specialties of this walk-up shop include mango shakes, tiny cakes, and pastry-wrapped hot dogs. *935 Race St.* ☎ *215/925-5298. $.*

④ Centre Square. This least green of squares, once on the outskirts of the city, is today home to ornate City Hall (see p 15). The re-landscaped space of Dilworth Plaza (p 15) was named after beloved 1950s mayor Richardson Dilworth (1916–1997). ⏲ *15 min. Broad & Market sts.*

⑤ ★★ Logan Circle. The only square that became a circle, "Northwest" is the bucolic jewel of Ben Franklin Parkway, a boulevard that 20th-century architect Paul Philippe Cret modeled after Paris's Champs-Elysées to connect City Hall with the Art Museum. Logan's centerpiece is Alexander Stirling Calder's Swann Fountain (see p 32), with its sky-high arcs of water and three giant bronze horses surrounded by turtles, nymphs, and angels. The square is surrounded by cultural landmarks: the central branch of the **Free Library of Philadelphia** (p 67), the **Franklin Institute** (p 48), the **Academy of Natural Sciences** (p 67), and the 1846 **Cathedral Basilica of St. Peter and Paul** (pop in for refreshing cool darkness, and to peek at the dome's frescoes by Constantino Brumidi, famous for his paintings in the Capitol Building in D.C.;

☎ 215/561-1313; www.cathedral phila.org). ⏲ *½ hr. 19th & Race sts.*

⑥ ★ Le Bus Bakery. Grab a cold drink, a just-grilled panini (try the tuna or roast beef), or a chocolate chip cookie to enjoy on a bench in our next square, and you're all set. Just don't pronounce it "le boos"— it began as a bakery in an old school bus, so the name is pronounced American-style. *129 S. 18th St. (btw. Walnut & Sansom sts.).* ☎ *215/569-8299. lebusbakery.com. $.*

⑦ ★★ kids Rittenhouse Square. "Southwest Square," the best known in the group—a sublime urban landscape with tall sycamores, diagonal paths, reflecting pool, and scattered sculpture—is also the work of Paul Phillippe Cret (see above). If you plan to sit and people-watch anywhere on this list, do it here, paying special attention to the comings and goings around the Rittenhouse Hotel (p 141), the preferred overnight spot for movie stars in town for filming. On winter evenings, Rittenhouse's trees glitter with giant ornament lights. ⏲ *1 hr. Btw. 18th & 19th sts., Walnut & Rittenhouse sts.*

Rittenhouse Square is a prime spot to indulge in people-watching.

Penn's Landing

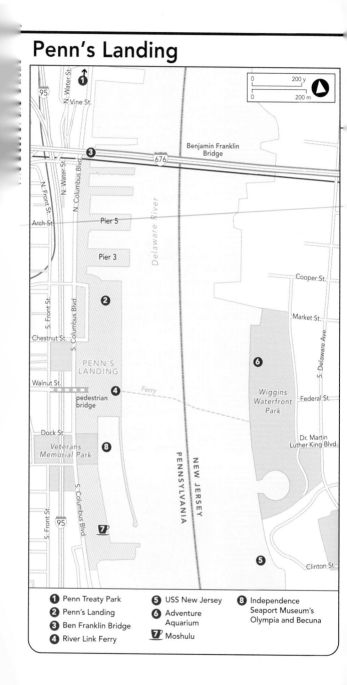

1. Penn Treaty Park
2. Penn's Landing
3. Ben Franklin Bridge
4. River Link Ferry
5. USS New Jersey
6. Adventure Aquarium
7. Moshulu
8. Independence Seaport Museum's Olympia and Becuna

Spanned by **Ben Franklin Bridge and bordered by tree and ship-lined shores,** the wide Delaware River has been the subject of much recent controversy regarding dredging and gambling (as for the latter: Philly is now the no. 2 gaming market in America, behind Vegas). For now, the riverfront retains a few nice stretches to explore, and even hop a ferry to Camden. START: **Penn Treaty Park.**

1 Penn Treaty Park. Formerly Shackamaxon, a village of the Native American Leni Lenape people, this riverside park hosted the 1683 meeting of William Penn and chief Tamanend, who stood under an elm to sign a peace treaty that endured 99 years. Today, the tranquil, loosely landscaped plot, bordered by industry, features a small obelisk where the elm once stood. Walk 3 blocks south, past Sugar-House Casino, to Frankford Avenue to catch the 25 bus down Delaware Avenue to Penn's Landing. ⏱ ½ hr. *Columbus Blvd & Beach St. (off of Delaware Ave.).* penntreatypark.org.

2 ★ Penn's Landing. Philadelphia began as a major freshwater port; as recently as 1945, 155 "finger" piers jutted out into the river. Today, 14 remain. Replacing some of them are the more visitor-centric circa-1976 **Great Plaza**, stretching from Spring Garden Street southward, with its multi-tiered, tree-lined amphitheater, space for summer festivals and concerts, and fantastic outdoor skating at RiverRink (ice skating in winter, roller skating in summer). South of Market Street, an esplanade with blue guardrails and charts identifies the New Jersey shoreline opposite. ⏱ ½ hr. *Columbus Blvd btw. Spring Garden & South sts., Visitor's Center at 301 S. Columbus Blvd.* ☎ *215/922-2386.* www.delaware riverwaterfrontcorp.com.

3 ★ Ben Franklin Bridge. Great cities have great bridges, and this 1926 suspension model is Philadelphia's. Paul Cret, architect of the

RiverRink at Penn's Landing offers summer roller skating and winter ice skating.

Ben Franklin Parkway and Rittenhouse Square, designed it. At night, each of its cables is lit and its span changes color. Pedestrians and cyclists can make the long climb across (it takes about an hour round-trip), but there's not much to do on the immediate other side (Camden, NJ) other than turn around and come back. ⏱ 15 min. *Entrance at 5th & Vine sts.* ☎ *856/968-2000.* www.drpa.org. *Daily 6am–dusk.*

4 ★★ kids River Link Ferry. Next to the Independence Seaport Museum (p 57), catch a ride across the Delaware to Camden, NJ's, riverfront. The scenic trip takes about 10 minutes and deposits you near the USS *New Jersey* and Adventure Aquarium (below). ⏱ 15 min. ☎ *856/541-7310.* www.riverlink ferry.org. *Memorial Day–Labor Day*

Mon–Fri 10am–6pm, Sat–Sun 10am–7pm. May and Sept weekends and BB&T Pavilion concert nights only. Round-trip $9 adults, $7 seniors & children 3–12.

⑤ ★ kids USS New Jersey. This giant, circa-1942 battleship, referred to as BB62, is the most decorated of its Iowa-class of "fast battleships." A tour involves climbing ladders, peering into 16-inch gun turrets, cramming into living quarters, and learning a history that stretches from tours in World War II to the Persian Gulf. ⏱ *2 hr. 100 Clinton St. (behind the BB&T Pavilion), Camden, NJ.* ☎ *866/877-6262. www.battleshipnewjersey.org. Admission $22 adults; $17 seniors, veterans & kids 5–11; free for children 4 & under, active military, WWII & BB-62 vets. May–Aug daily 9:30am–5pm; Mar–Apr & Sept–Dec daily 9:30am–3pm; Feb Sat–Sun 9:30am–3pm. Closed Jan.*

⑥ ★ kids Adventure Aquarium. Two million gallons of water fill this expansive museum of the life aquatic, where hippos bob for heads of lettuce; penguins and seals cavort at outdoor arenas; stingrays skim through open tanks; and jellyfish morph before your eyes. For one (stratospheric) price, you can feed sea turtles, party with penguins, or swim with the sharks. Among the must-see animals: alligators in the wild West Africa River Experience, rarely exhibited bluefin tuna in the 760,000-gallon Ocean Realm tank, and small sharks swimming in a petting tank for kids. ⏱ *2 hr. 1 Riverside Dr., Camden, NJ.* ☎ *844/474-3474. www.adventure aquarium.com. Admission $32 adults, $24 children 2–12. July–Aug daily 9:30am–5pm; late Mar–Jun & Sept–Dec Mon–Fri 9:30am–4pm, Sat–Sun 9:30am–5pm; Mar daily 10am–5pm.*

Adventure Aquarium lets you get up close to a wide array of aquatic creatures.

⑦ Moshulu. There are few places to grab much more than a hotdog along the waterfront, so head to the top deck of this four-masted ship for a burger and a piña colada. *401 S. Columbus Blvd. (btw. Pine & South sts.).* ☎ *215/923-2500. www.moshulu.com. $$.*

⑧ ★ kids Independence Seaport Museum's *Olympia* and *Becuna*. Just south of the Independence Seaport Museum's main building (p 57), this pair of historic ships offers a self-guided glimpse of the U.S. Navy of yore. The larger of the two is the *Olympia*, Admiral Dewey's circa-1892 steel flagship during the Spanish-American War, featuring a restored bridge and handsome, originally furnished examples of an officers' saloon and wardroom, flag officer's cabin, and junior officers' mess. Launched in 1944, the submarine *Becuna* served from World War II into the Cold War; it will impart a newfound appreciation for tight quarters. ⏱ *1 hr. See p 18.* ●

6 The Best **Dining**

Dining Best Bets

Best **Cheesesteak**
★ Cosmi's Deli, *1501 S. 8th St.
(p 104)*

Best for **Tapas**
★★★ Amada, *217-219 Chestnut
St. (p 102)*

Best for **Variety**
★★★ Reading Terminal Market,
51 N. 12th St. (p 110)

Best **Steakhouse**
★★ Butcher & Singer, *1500 Walnut
St. (p 103)*

Best for **Breakfast**
★★ Dutch Eating Place, *12th &
Arch Sts. (p 105)*

Best **Deli**
★ Famous Fourth Street Delicatessen, *700 S. 4th St. (p 106)*

Best for **Burgers**
★★★ Village Whiskey, *118 S. 20th
St. (p 112)*

Best **Date Spot**
★★★ Fork, *306 Market St. (p 106)*

Best for **Vegetarians**
★ HipCityVeg, *127 S. 18th St. (p 106)*

Best for **Seafood**
★★ The Oyster House, *1516
Sansom St. (p 108)*

Best for **Haute Japanese**
★★ Morimoto, *723 Chestnut St.
(p 108)*

Best for **Chinese**
★ Lee How Fook, *219 N. 11th St.
(p 107)*

Best for **Gourmet Italian**
★★★ Osteria, *640 N. Broad St.
(p 108)*

Best for ~~**Italian-American**~~
★ Villa di Roma, *936 S. 9th St.
(p 112)*

Best **Colonial vibe**
★★ City Tavern, *138 S. 2nd St.
(p 104)*

Best **Middle Eastern Fare**
★★★ Zahav, *237 St. James Pl.
(p 112)*

Best for **Pizza**
★ Marra's, *1734 E. Passyunk Ave.
(p 107)*

Best **Anniversary Dinner**
★★★ Vetri Cucina, *1312 Spruce
St. (p 112)*

Best for Lunch in **Old City**
★★ The Bourse, *111 S. Independence Mall E. (p 103)*

Ultra-fresh seafood shines at the Old City brasserie Fork. Previous page: Atop the Bellevue Hotel, stylish Nineteen serves formal teas, dressy dinners, and classic martinis.

South Philly Dining

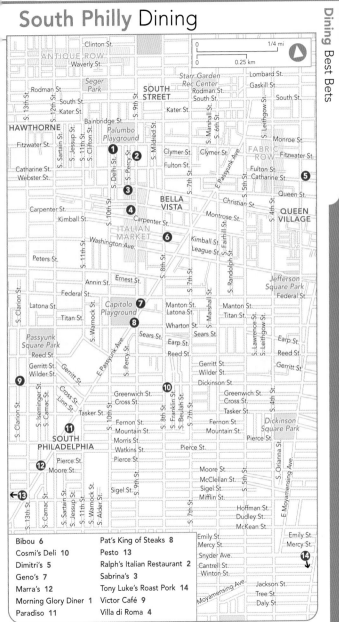

Bibou 6
Cosmi's Deli 10
Dimitri's 5
Geno's 7
Marra's 12
Morning Glory Diner 1
Paradiso 11
Pat's King of Steaks 8
Pesto 13
Ralph's Italian Restaurant 2
Sabrina's 3
Tony Luke's Roast Pork 14
Victor Café 9
Villa di Roma 4

Center City Dining

SEPTA Subway — M
PATCO Light Rail — P
Trolley — T
Church — †
Synagogue — ✡
Point of Interest — ■
Post Office — ✉

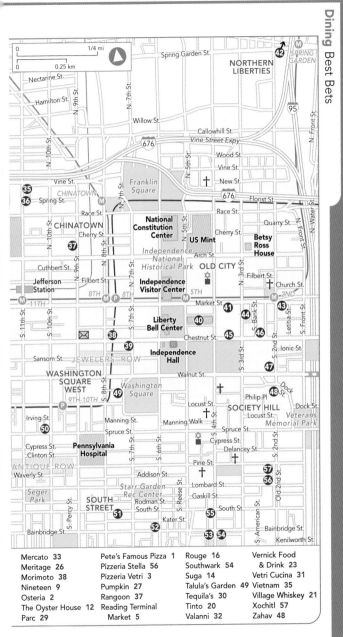

Mercato 33	Pete's Famous Pizza 1	Rouge 16	Vernick Food
Meritage 26	Pizzeria Stella 56	Southwark 54	& Drink 23
Morimoto 38	Pizzeria Vetri 3	Suga 14	Vetri Cucina 31
Nineteen 9	Pumpkin 27	Talula's Garden 49	Vietnam 35
Osteria 2	Rangoon 37	Tequila's 30	Village Whiskey 21
The Oyster House 12	Reading Terminal	Tinto 20	Xochitl 57
Parc 29	Market 5	Valanni 32	Zahav 48

Dining A to Z

★ **Alma de Cuba** RITTENHOUSE *CUBAN* Nuevo Latino cuisine—lobster ceviche, Kobe beef tacos, sugarcane tuna—in a Rockwell-designed decor makes for a glamorous night on the town. *1623 Walnut St.* ☎ *215/988-1799. www. almadecubarestaurant.com. Entrees $15–$35. AE, DC, DISC, MC, V. Dinner daily. Bus: 2, 9 17, 21, 31, 32, 33, 33, 38, 42, 44, 48, 62, 78, 124, 125. Subway: Walnut-Locust. Map p 100.*

★★★ **Amada** OLD CITY CONTEMPORARY TAPAS Chic and rustic Amada excels with Spanish cheeses and meats, plantain empanadas, and sangria. *217–219 Chestnut St. (btw. 2nd & 3rd sts.)* ☎ *215/625-2450. www.amada restaurant.com. Plates $9–$40. AE, DC, DISC, MC, V. Lunch & dinner daily. Bus: 9, 21, 38, 42, 57. Subway: 2nd St. Map p 100.*

★ **Audrey Claire** RITTENHOUSE *MEDITERRANEAN* Grilled Romaine salad, Gorgonzola-and-pear-topped flatbread, and pomegranate roast chicken are top choices at this stylish little village bistro. *276 S. 20th St. (at Spruce St.).*

☎ *215/731-1222. www.audreyclaire. com. Entrees $11–$28. No credit cards. BYOB. Dinner daily. Bus: 12, 17. Map p 100.*

★★ **Barclay Prime** RITTENHOUSE *STEAKS* Red meat with a boutique vibe: This low-lit emporium offers Gauchot & Gauchot beef, Kobe sliders, and a splurge-worthy $120 "cheesesteak." *237 S. 18th St. (btw. Locust & Spruce sts.).* ☎ *215/732-7560. www.barclay prime.com. Entrees $32–$195. AE, DC, MC, V. Dinner daily. Bus: 2, 9, 12, 21, 42. Subway: 15th/16th & Locust St. Map p 100.*

★ **Beau Monde** SOUTH STREET *FRENCH* Known for its crepes, this pretty, bustling Bretagne-inspired brasserie also serves lovely salads and romantic ambiance. *624 S. 6th St. (at Bainbridge St.).* ☎ *215/592-0656. www.creperie-beaumonde.com. Entrees $5–$26. AE, DC, MC, V. Lunch & dinner Tues–Sun. Bus: 40, 47. Map p 100.*

★★ **Bibou** BELLA VISTA *FRENCH* Chanterelles, foie gras, and escargots accent seven-course prix-fixe

Rustic-chic Amada has excellent Spanish cuisine.

menus at this petite bring-your-own-Bordeaux bistro just off the Italian Market. *1009 S. 8th St. (btw. Carpenter & Washington aves.).* ☎ *215/965-8290. www.biboubyob. com. Fixed-price menu $115. AE, MC, V. BYOB. Dinner Wed–Sat. Bus: 47, 47M. Map p 99.*

★ **The Blind Pig** NORTHERN LIBERTIES *MODERN AMERICAN* This unpretentious gastro-pub is famed for poutine (fries swimming in cheese curds and gravy), blue balls (breaded fried balls of beef, gorgonzola, and mashed potatoes), and dozens of canned beer options. *702 N. 2nd St. (at Fairmount Ave.).* ☎ *215/639-4565. www.blind pigphilly.com. Entrees $9–$17. AE, MC, V. Dinner daily; brunch Sun. Bus, 5, 25, 43. Subway: Spring Garden St. Map p 100.*

★★ **The Bourse** OLD CITY *FOOD HALL* America's oldest indoor mall (est. 1895) re-opened as a food hall in late 2018 with 29 vendors, restaurants, and stalls serving fare from Indian to Italian, Mexican to Ramen, sandwiches to oysters to ice cream—plus local distillers, chocolatiers, and florists. *111 S. Independence Mall E. (btw. Ranstead and Ludlow sts.). No central phone. www.theboursephilly. com. Prices vary. Daily 8am–7pm. Bus 9, 21, 42, 57. Map p 100.*

★ **Brauhaus Schmitz** SOUTH STREET *GERMAN* Schnitzel, wieners, brats, spätzle, strudel, and 122 kinds of hearty Belgian and German brews make this convivial *bierhalle* the best wurst place in town. *718 South St. (btw. 7th & 8th sts.).* ☎ *267/909-8814. www.brauhaus schmitz.com. Entrees $11–$38. Lunch & dinner daily. AE, DC, DISC, MC, V. Bus 40, 47, 47M. Map p 100.*

★ **Buddakan** OLD CITY *ASIAN FUSION* Trendy Buddakan dishes out lobster fried rice, edamame

An international selection of upscale food stands and cafes has transformed the elegant indoor mall of The Bourse.

ravioli, five-spice duck breast, and chocolate pagodas at a communal table beneath a giant gold Buddha. *325 Chestnut St. (btw. 3rd & 4th sts.)* ☎ *215/574-9440. www.buddakan. com. Entrees $11–$58. AE, DC, MC, V. Lunch Mon–Fri; dinner daily. Bus: 9, 21, 38, 42, 57. Subway: 2nd St. Map p 100.*

★ **Buena Onda** FAIRMOUNT *MEXICAN* Inspired by Bajan taquerias, chef Jose Garces combines fish or meat tacos and quesadillas with margaritas and locally brewed beers and sodas. *1901C Callowhill St.* ☎ *215/302-3530. buenaondatacos.com. Entrees: $3.75–$9. AE, MC, V. Lunch & dinner daily. Bus: 2, 7, 33, 48. Map p 100.*

★★ **Butcher & Singer** RITTEN-HOUSE *STEAKS* Beneath the soaring ceiling of an old bank, enormous servings of haute meat-and-potatoes satisfy expense-account diners. *1500 Walnut St. (at 15th St.)* ☎ *215/732-4444. www. butcherandsinger.com. Entrees $14–$75. AE, DC, MC, V. Lunch Mon–Fri; dinner daily. Bus: 2, 9, 12, 21, 42. Subway: Walnut-Locust. Map p 100.*

Costumed waiters add to the Colonial vibe of City Tavern, where the Founding Fathers dined during Continental Congresses.

★ **Caribou Café** CENTER CITY *FRENCH* This friendly brasserie is known for its steak frites, cassoulet, goat cheese salad, and wine list. *1126 Walnut St. (btw. 11th & 12th sts.)* ☎ *215/625-9535. www.caribou-cafe.com. Entrees $9–$26. AE, MC, V. Lunch & dinner daily. Bus: 9, 12, 21, 23, 42, 45. Map p 100.*

★★ **City Tavern** OLD CITY *AMERICAN* A replica of the pub where Washington and Adams enjoyed mead and pepper-pot soup features Colonial-garbed servers, Martha Washington's turkey potpie, and Jefferson's home brew. *138 S. 2nd St. (at Walnut St.).* ☎ *215/413-1443. www.citytavern. com. Entrees $16–$34. AE, DISC, MC, V. Lunch & dinner daily. Bus: 5, 9, 21, 42, 57. Subway: 2nd St. Map p 100.*

★ **kids Continental** OLD CITY *MODERN INTERNATIONAL* This stylish diner has something for everyone—from grilled cheese to Thai curry lobster and sugary martinis. (*138 Market St. (at 2nd St.).* ☎ *215/923-6069. www.continental martinibar.com. Entrees $10–$30.*

AE, DC, MC, V. Lunch & dinner daily. Bus: 5, 17, 21, 33, 42, 48, 57. Subway: 2nd St. Map p 100.

★ **kids Continental Mid-Town** RITTENHOUSE *MODERN INTERNATIONAL* At this buzzy three-story retro cocktail lounge (younger sib of Continental, above), menu faves include a big salad and Szechuan shoestring fries. *1801 Chestnut St. (at 18th St.).* ☎ *215/ 567-1800. www.continentalmidtown. com. Entrees $9–$34. AE, DC, MC, V. Lunch & dinner daily. Bus: 2, 9 17, 21, 31, 32, 33, 33, 38, 42, 44, 48, 62, 78, 124, 125. Map p 100.*

★ **Cosmi's Deli** SOUTH PHILLY *CHEESESTEAKS* Looks like a bodega, delivers like a champion: This neighbor to Pat's and Geno's beats the big guys in taste tests time after time. *1501 S. 8th St. (at Dickinson St.).* ☎ *215/468-6093. www.cosmideli.com. Sandwiches $7–$11. AE, DISC, MC, V. Lunch & dinner daily. Bus: 47, 47M. Map p 99.*

★ **kids Devil's Alley** RITTENHOUSE *AMERICAN* BBQ sliders, ribs, Cobb salad, creative burgers, and cold beers rule at this casual,

Continental has an exceptionally diverse menu.

Chinatown

The country's fourth-largest Chinatown (just north of the Convention Center, btw. 9th & 11th sts., Arch & Vine sts.) represents many more populations and cultures than just Chinese; these bustling blocks also boast residents from Vietnam, Burma, Thailand, Korea, Japan, Malaysia, and beyond. Check out the four suspended 1,500-lb. bronze dragons at 9th and Arch streets, the Friendship Arch at 10th and Arch streets, and (of course) a vibrant, morning-to-late-night dining scene. Among more than 100 restaurants are daytime dim sum palaces **Ocean Harbor** (1023 Race St.; ☎ 215/574-1398, www.ocean-harbor.com) and **Dim Sum Garden** (1020 Race St.; ☎ 215/873-0258, www.dimsumgardenphilly.com). For quick, inexpensive snacks like bubble tea, red bean buns, and mango shakes, seek out **Saint Honore** (935 Race St.; ☎ 215/925-5298) and **KC's Pastries** (109 N. 10th St.; ☎ 215/238-8808). It's definitely best to explore this central neighborhood on foot—the car traffic is always clogged.

popular grill. *1907 Chestnut St. (btw. 19th & 20th sts.).* ☎ *215/751-0707. www.devilsalleybarandgrill.com. $9–$19. AE, DISC, DC, MC, V. Lunch & dinner Mon–Fri; brunch & dinner Sat–Sun. Bus: 2, 9 17, 21, 31, 32, 33, 33, 38, 42, 44, 48, 62, 78, 124, 125. Map p 100.*

★★ Dimitri's QUEEN VILLAGE GREEK Seated elbow-to-elbow, locals dig into grilled squid, fresh bluefish, amazing hummus, and rice pudding; worth the first-come first-served wait. *795 S. 3rd St. (at Catharine St.).* ☎ *215/625-0556. www.dmitrisrestaurant.com. Entrees $10–$21. No credit cards. BYOB. Dinner daily. Bus: 57. Map p 99.*

★★ kids Distrito UNIVERSITY CITY MEXICAN Mexico City comes to Philly, with neon booths, lucha libre wrestling masks, and fancied-up taquería fare. *3945 Chestnut St. (at 40th St.).* ☎ *215/222-1657. www.distritorestaurant. com. Entrees $9–$24. AE, DISC, MC, V. Lunch & dinner daily. Bus: 21, 40. Subway: 40th St. Map p 100.*

★★ Dutch Eating Place CENTER CITY PENNSYLVANIA DUTCH Dig into the biggest, best breakfast in Philly—blueberry pancakes, apple toast, and oddly yummy scrapple (PA's meat-scrap specialty)—at this Mennonite-run luncheonette in Reading Terminal Market. For lunch, try chicken pot pie, a grilled Reuben, or a slice of shoo-fly pie. *12th & Arch sts.* ☎ *215/922-0425. Entrees $3.50–$7. AE, MC, V. Breakfast & lunch Tues–Sat. Bus: 4, 23, 27, 45, 48, 61, 124, 125. Subway: 11th St. Train: Jefferson. Map p 100.*

★ El Vez CENTER CITY MEXICAN Made-to-order guac and margaritas that rock keep this lounge-y Mexi-Vegas spot busy night after night. *121 S. 13th St. (at Sansom St.).* ☎ *215/928-9800. www. elvezrestaurant.com. Entrees $9–$25. AE, DISC, MC, V. Lunch & dinner daily. Bus: 4, 9, 12, 21, 23, 27, 31, 32, 33, 38, 42, 44, 45, 48, 62, 78, 124, 125. Subway: Walnut-Locust or 13th St. Map p 100.*

The Best Dining

★ **kids** **Famous Fourth Street Delicatessen** SOUTH STREET *DELI* Order pastrami sandwiches thick as phone books, matzo balls big as grapefruit, or marble cake that could double as a checkerboard. 700 S. 4th St. (at Bainbridge St.). ☎ 215/922-3274. www.famous4thstreetdelicatessen.com. Entrees $7–$24. AE, MC, V. Breakfast, lunch & dinner daily. Bus: 40, 57. Map p 100.

★ **FARMiCiA** OLD CITY MODERN AMERICAN This bakery-owned restaurant has super-fresh, sustainably grown fare. Great for brunch. 15 S. 3rd St. (btw. Market & Chestnut sts.) ☎ 215/627-6274. www.farmiciarestaurant.com. Entrees $16–$28. AE, MC, V. Lunch & dinner Tues–Fri; Breakfast, brunch & dinner Sat–Sun. Bus: 5, 17, 21, 33, 42, 48, 57. Subway: 2nd St. Map p 100.

★★★ **Fork** OLD CITY CONTINENTAL Fresh ingredients—Cape May fluke, house-made sausage, spring rhubarb—shine at this softly lit neighborhood brasserie. 306 Market St. ☎ 215/625-9425. www.forkrestaurant.com. Entrees $16–$55. AE, DC, DISC, MC, V. Dinner Mon–Sat; brunch & dinner Sun. Bus: 5, 17, 21, 33, 42, 48, 57. Subway: 2nd St. Map p 100.

Geno's SOUTH PHILLY CHEESE-STEAKS Pat's across-the-street rival is bigger, brighter, and more controversial, thanks to its "This is America—when ordering speak English" policy. 1219 S. 9th St. (at E. Passyunk Ave.) ☎ 215/389-0659. www.genosteaks.com. Cheesesteaks $8–$11. No credit cards. Open 24 hr. Bus: 45, 47, 47M. Map p 99.

★ **Good Dog** CENTER CITY PUB FARE Wooden booths, great microbrews, and a big-time juke-box are background to a blue-cheese-stuffed burger that's the bomb. 224 S. 15th St. (btw. Walnut

The burgers at Good Dog are legendary.

& Locust sts.). ☎ 215/985-9600. www.gooddogbar.com. Entrees $8–$26. AE, DC, DISC, MC, V. Lunch & dinner daily. Bus: 4, 9, 12, 21, 27, 32, 42. Subway: Walnut-Locust. Map p 100.

★★ **High Street on Market** OLD CITY CONTINENTAL Tasty salads, sandwiches, pastas, and grilled meats star at this rustic-chic cafe. 308 Market St. ☎ 215/625-0988. www.highstreetonmarket.com. Sandwiches & salads $11–$15; Entrees $4–$29. AE, DC, DISC, MC, V. Lunch & dinner daily. Bus: 5, 17, 21, 33, 42, 48, 57. Subway: 2nd St. Map p 100.

★ **HipCityVeg** RITTENHOUSE VEGAN At this excellent café, vegan burgers, wraps, soups, and salads are largely locally sourced. Try the signature Groothie, an apple-banana-kale smoothie. 127 S. 18th St. (btw. Sansom & Moravian sts.). ☎ 215/278-7605. www.hipcityveg.com. Entrees $8–$11. AE, DC, DISC, MC, V. Lunch & dinner daily. Bus: 2, 9 17, 21, 31, 32, 33, 33, 38, 42, 44, 48, 62, 78, 124, 125. Subway: Walnut-Locust. Map p 100.

★ **Jamonera** CENTER CITY SPANISH Classic and *nueva* tapas and *raciones* share the menu at this trendy Spanish-style wine bar—*jamon iberico* and *albondigas*, but also clam chorizo. 105 S. 13th St. (btw. Chestnut & Sansom sts.).

☎ 215/922-6061. www.jamonera restaurant.com. Tapas $6–$11; entrees $10–$27. AE, MC, V. Dinner daily. Bus: 4, 9, 21, 23, 27, 31, 32, 33, 38, 42, 44, 45, 48, 62, 78, 124, 125. Subway: Walnut-Locust or 13th St. Map p 100.

★ **Jim's Steaks** SOUTH STREET CHEESESTEAKS At this friendlier cousin to Pat's and Geno's, servers won't balk if you ask for lettuce and tomato. Plus: indoor seating—and beer. 400 South St. (at 4th St.) ☎ 215/928-1911. www.jimssouth street.com. Cheesesteaks $7–$10. No credit cards. Lunch & dinner daily. Bus: 40, 57. Map p 100.

kids Jones OLD CITY AMERICAN Mac and cheese, glazed carrots, meatloaf, and chicken nachos— you'll find all the comfort classics in this Brady Bunch–retro sunken dining room. 700 Chestnut St. (at 7th St.). ☎ 215/223-5663. www.jones restaurant.com. AE, DC, MC, V. Entrees $10–$20. Lunch & dinner daily; Brunch Sat–Sun. Bus: 9, 12, 21, 42, 47, 47M, 61. Subway: 8th St. & Market. Map p 100.

★ **Kanella** WASHINGTON SQUARE GREEK From the island of Cyprus, this place offers rustic (goat stew) and Mediterranean (pasta with capers and mint) fare. 1001 Spruce St. (at 10th St.). ☎ 215/928-2085. www.kanellagrill. com. Entrees $11–$14. DISC, MC, V. BYOB. Lunch & dinner Tues–Sun. Bus: 23, 45, 47M. Subway: 9th/10th & Locust. Map p 100.

★★★ **Lacroix** RITTENHOUSE MODERN INTERNATIONAL For gracious dining overlooking the Square, elegant LaCroix can't be beat. It's a la carte at lunch; dinners are 4- or 8-course tasting menus. The Rittenhouse Hotel, 210 W. Rittenhouse (btw. Locust & Walnut sts.). 215/790-2533. www.lacroixrestau rant.com. AE, DC, DISC, MC, V.

Entrees $12–$38; dinner menus $75– $120. Breakfast, lunch & dinner daily; brunch Sun. Bus: 2, 9, 12, 21, 42. Subway: 15th/16th & Locust St. Map p 100.

★ **Lee How Fook** CHINATOWN CHINESE Garlicky good-for-you greens, hearty duck noodle soup, and salt-baked squid pack this family place night after night. 219 N. 11th St. (btw. Race & Vine sts.). ☎ 215/925-7266. newleehowfook. com. Entrees $7–$19. MC, V. BYOB. Lunch & dinner daily. Bus: 23, 45, 61. Map p 100.

★★ **Lolita** CENTER CITY MEXICAN Classic dishes get dressed up for a night on the town at this funky little spot. Bring your own tequila for fresh-fruit margaritas. 106 S. 13th St. (btw. Sansom & Chestnut sts.). ☎ 215/546-7100. www.lolitabyob.com. Entrees $12– $26. No credit cards. BYOB. Lunch Mon-Sat; Dinner daily. Bus: 4, 9, 12, 21, 27, 32, 42. Subway: Walnut-Locust or 13th St. Map p 100.

★ **Marra's** SOUTH PHILLY ITALIAN/PIZZA One meal of sublimely simple pies and homemade escarole soup at this no-nonsense eatery—opened by Nonno Salvatore in the 1920s—and you'll never eat at Pizza Hut again. 1734 E. Passyunk Ave. (btw. Morris & Moore sts.). ☎ 215/463-9249. www.marrasone. com. Entrees $6.50–$25. DISC, MC, V. Lunch & dinner Tues–Sat; dinner Sun. Bus: 4, 45. Subway: Tasker-Morris. Map p 99.

★★ **Melograno** RITTENHOUSE ITALIAN House-cured pancetta, fig-and-walnut stuffing, homemade pappardelle: This ever-bustling bistro offers Roman fare for modern times. 2012 Sansom St. (btw. 20th & 21st sts.). ☎ 215/875-8116. www. melogranorestaurant.com. Entrees $16–$39. MC, V. BYOB. Dinner Tues– Sun. Bus: 2, 9, 12, 21, 42. Map p 100.

Midtown's Mercato has an inviting atmosphere alongside great food.

★★ **Mercato** CENTER CITY *ITALIAN* Every meal at this glittering bistro feels like a dinner party— only with better short ribs and risotto than you could ever pull off at home. *1216 Spruce St. (at Camac St., btw. 12th & 13th sts.).* ☎ *215/985-2962. www.mercato byob.com. Entrees $21–$32. No credit cards. BYOB. Dinner daily. Bus: 12, 23, 45. Subway: 12th/13th & Locust. Map p 100.*

★★ **Morimoto** OLD CITY *JAPANESE* Splurge on tableside-made tofu, luscious toro, and a sake martini at this futuristic showplace for the Iron Chef's signature flash. *723 Chestnut St. (btw. 7th & 8th sts.).* ☎ *215/413-9070. www.morimoto restaurant.com. Entrees $12–$58. AE, DC, MC, V. Lunch Mon–Fri; dinner daily. Bus: 9, 12, 21, 42, 47, 47M, 61. Subway: 8th St. Map p 100.*

★ **kids Morning Glory Diner** BELLA VISTA *AMERICAN* "Be nice or leave" is the motto of this corner luncheonette, where ketchup is homemade, coffee comes in steel mugs, and frittatas and pancakes are worth the wait. *735 S. 10th St. (at Fitzwater St.).* ☎ *215/413-3999. www.themorning glorydiner.com. $7–$12. No credit cards. Breakfast & lunch Mon–Fri; Brunch Sat–Sun. Bus: 40, 45, 47, 47M. Map p 99.*

★ **Nineteen** CENTER CITY *CONTINENTAL* On the Bellevue's 19th floor, formal tea, fresh oysters, and dress-up dinners are served in a sleekly elegant landmark setting. *Bellevue Hotel, 200 S. Broad St. (at Walnut St.).* ☎ *215/790-1919. www. nineteenrestaurant.com. Entrees $18–$38. AE, DC, DISC, MC, V. Breakfast, lunch & dinner daily. Bus: 4, 9, 12, 21, 27, 32, 42. Subway: Walnut-Locust. Map p 100.*

★★★ **Osteria** NORTH BROAD *ITALIAN* It's worth the trek to North Broad for Jeff Michaud's gourmet Italian fare, starring dishes such as egg-topped pizza and wild boar Bolognese. Book ahead. *640 N. Broad St. (at Wallace St.).* ☎ *215/763-0920. www.osteriaphilly. com. Entrees $15–$36. AE, DC, MC, V. Lunch Thurs–Fri; dinner daily. Bus: 4, 16, 23. Subway: Spring Garden St or Fairmount. Map p 100.*

★★ **The Oyster House** RITTENHOUSE *AMERICAN SEAFOOD* The raw bar is the star of this classic seafood spot; its shuckers have been at it for decades. *1516 Sansom St. (btw. 15th & 16th sts.).* ☎ *215/ 567-7683. www.oysterhousephilly. com. Entrees $12–$50. AE, DISC, MC, V. Lunch & dinner Mon–Sat. Bus: 2, 9, 12, 21, 42. Subway: 15th/16th & Locust St. Map p 100.*

★★ **Parc** RITTENHOUSE
FRENCH In this see-and-be-seen setting, the classic Parisian bistro fare includes moules frites, steak au poivre, and duck l'orange. *227 S. 18th St. (at Locust St.).* ☎ *215/545-2262. www.parc-restaurant.com. Entrees $11–$40. AE, DC, MC, V. Breakfast, lunch & dinner Mon–Fri; brunch, lunch, dinner Sat–Sun. Bus: 2, 9, 12, 21, 42. Subway: 15th/16th & Locust St. Map p 100.*

★★ **Paradiso** SOUTH PHILLY
ITALIAN Swanked-out South Philly neighbors nibble smoked trout salads and airy fried calamari before tucking into rabbit cacciatore and olive-dressed ahi tuna. *1627 E. Passyunk Ave. (btw. Tasker & Morris sts.).* ☎ *215/271-2066. www.paradisophilly.com. Entrees $10–$30. AE, MC, V. Lunch Tues–Fri; dinner Tues–Sun. Bus: 4, 45. Subway: Tasker-Morris. Map p 99.*

★ **Pat's King of Steaks** SOUTH PHILLY *CHEESESTEAKS* The originator, in all its roadside glory. Order one "wit" onions and/or (Cheez) Whiz. *1237 E. Passyunk Ave. (at 9th & Wharton sts.).* ☎ *215/468-1546. www.patskingofsteaks.com. Cheesesteaks $7–$10. No credit cards. Open 24 hr. Bus: 45, 47, 47M. Map p 99.*

Osteria's menu features gourmet Italian comfort food.

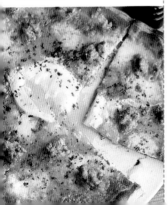

★ **Pesto** SOUTH PHILLY *ITALIAN* Giovanni and Concetta Varallo have run this beloved neighborhood trattoria since 2003, serving exquisite gnocchi, cavatelli, veal marsala, and other Italian staples. *1915 S. Broad St. (at Mifflin St.)* ☎ *215/336-8380. www.ristorantepesto.com. Entrees $17–$25. AE, MC, V. BYOB. Dinner Tues–Sun. Bus: 4, 45. Subway: Broad Street. Map p 99.*

Pete's Famous Pizza FAIRMOUNT *PIZZA & CHEESESTEAKS* In an area with limited dining options, this Fairmont classic has served delicious pizzas, cheesesteaks, hoagies, and burgers since 1980. *2328 Fairmount Ave. (btw. 23rd & 24th sts.)* ☎ *215/765-3040. www.petesfamouspizza.com. Sandwiches & entrees $6–$15. Lunch & dinner daily. Bus: 7, 32, 48. Map p 100.*

★★ **Pizzeria Stella** SOCIETY HILL *PIZZA* This place offers thin-crust pies, cleverly topped (guanciale, pistachios), plus juice glasses of Prosecco, egg-topped asparagus, and olive oil gelato. *420 S. 2nd St. (at Lombard St.).* ☎ *215/320-8000. www.pizzeriastella.net. Pizzas $11–$19. AE, DISC, MC, V. Lunch & dinner daily. Bus: 12, 40, 57. Map p 100.*

★★ **Pizzeria Vetri** FAIRMOUNT *PIZZA* The Museum Mile outpost of Marc Vetri's mini-empire serves brilliant gourmet pizzas topped with the finest ingredients. Start with a *rotolo*, a savory roll-up with mortadella, ricotta, and pistachio pesto. *1939 Callowhill St.* ☎ *215/600-2629. www.pizzeriavetri.com. Pizzas $12–$17. AE, MC, V. Lunch & dinner daily. Bus: 2, 7, 33, 48. Map p 100.*

★★ **Pumpkin** RITTENHOUSE *AMERICAN* Little and locavore, this neighborhood gem excels at seasonal cuisine, seafood, and steak. (Reservations highly recommended.) *1713 South St. (btw. 17th*

& 18th sts.). ☎ 215/545-4448. www.
pumpkinphilly.com. Entrees $15–$31.
No credit cards. BYOB. Dinner Tues–
Sun. Bus: 2, 17, 40. Map p 100.

Ralph's Italian Restaurant

BELLA VISTA *ITALIAN* Meatballs
and "red gravy" (marinara), chicken
Sorrento, and unpretentious service
are staples at this 5th-generation
family trattoria (est. 1900). *760 S. 9th
St. (btw. Fitzwater & Catharine sts.).*
☎ *215/627-6011. www.ralphsrestau
rant.com. Entrees $11–$32. No credit
cards. Lunch & dinner daily. Bus: 40,
45, 47, 47M. Map p 99.*

★ Rangoon CHINATOWN

BURMESE If you've never had the
pleasure of digging into a tealeaf
salad, coconut rice, or 1,000-layer
bread, do it at this casual, authentic
spot. *112 N. 9th St. (btw. Arch &
Cherry sts.).* ☎ *215/829-8939. www.
rangoonrestaurant.com. Entrees
$7–$19. MC, V. Lunch & dinner daily.
Bus: 47m, 48, 61. Map p 100.*

★★★ Reading Terminal
Market CENTER CITY *MARKET*

Opened in 1893, this farmers' market in the old train station has dozens of cafes and food stands
offering everything from Amish to
Indian, soul food to kebabs, cajun
to cheesesteaks . . . plus Bassett's
ice cream. *51 N. 12th St. (btw. Arch
& Filbert sts.).* ☎ *215/922-2317.
www.readingterminalmarket.org.*

Dishes $3–$25. Open daily 8am–6pm.
Some stalls accept credit cards. Bus:
4, 23, 27, 45, 48, 61, 124, 125. Subway: 11th St. Train: Jefferson. Map
p 100.

★★ Rouge RITTENHOUSE

AMERICAN-FRENCH In the mood
for a lavish burger, a teensy salad,
or a bottle of Dom for lunch?
This luxe little bistro understands.
If you want quiet conversation, better ask for an outdoor table. *205 S.
18th St. (btw. Walnut & Locust sts.).*
☎ *215/732-6622. www.rouge98.
com. Entrees $14–$35. AE, DISC,
MC, V. Lunch & dinner daily; brunch
Sat–Sun. Bus: 2, 9, 12, 21, 42. Subway: 15th/16th & Locust St. Map
p 100.*

Sabrina's BELLA VISTA *AMERI-

CAN* The reason folks wait hours
for a seat in this pink-and-blue-
hued eatery? Must be something in
the humongous French toast. *910
Christian St. (btw. 9th & 10th sts.).*
☎ *215/574-1599. www.sabrinascafe.
com. Entrees $6–$14. AE, MC, V.
BYOB. Breakfast, brunch & lunch
daily. Bus: 47, 47m. Map p 99.*

★★ Southwark SOUTH STREET

CONTINENTAL The ultimate spot
to eat is at the bar, from your first
Manhattan to your last bite of r
osemary panna cotta. Late-night
light menu, too. *701 S. 4th St (at
Bainbridge St.).* ☎ *215/930-8538.*

The menu at Southwark is as high-class as the surroundings.

www.southwarkrestaurant.com.
Entrees $13–$25. AE, MC, V. Dinner
Wed-Mon. Bus: 40, 57. Map p 100.

★ **Suga** RITTENHOUSE *CHI-
NESE* Philly fans of exquisite
modern Chinese rejoiced when
lauded chef Susanna Foo came out
of retirement in 2016 to help her
son, Gabriel, open this new spot
just north of Rittenhouse Square.
1720 Sansom Street. ☎ *215-717-
8968. www.sugabyfoo.com. Entrees
$15–$24. AE, MC, V. Lunch & dinner
daily. Bus: 2, 9, 12, 21, 42. Subway:
15th/16th & Locust St. Map p 100.*

★★ **Talula's Garden** WASHING-
TON SQUARE *AMERICAN
FUSION* Dinner in Talula's open-
air garden offers such delights as
agnolotti pasta pillows stuffed with
sweet corn and truffles; roasted
Scottish salmon with buttermilk
grits; and smoked pork belly served
with balsamic glazed peaches and
cornbread. *210 W. Washington Sq.*
☎ *215/572-7787. talulasgarden.
com. Entrees $20–$35. AE. MC, V.
Dinner daily, brunch Sun. Bus: 9, 12,
21, 42, 47, 47M, 61. Map p 100.*

★ **Tequila's** RITTENHOUSE *MEXI-
CAN* Classic fare, snappy delivery,
and smooth tequilas are served up
here in a mural-covered mansion.
*1602 Locust St. (btw. 16th & 17th
sts.).* ☎ *215/546-0181. www.tequilas
philly.com. Entrees $12–$30. AE, DC,
MC, V. Lunch Mon–Fri; dinner daily.
Bus: 2, 9, 12, 21, 42. Subway:
15th/16th & Locust St. Map p 100.*

★★ **Tinto** RITTENHOUSE
BASQUE TAPAS Chef Garces'
cozy lounge offers delicious snacks
like Serrano-wrapped figs and
cockle-studded sea bass. *114 S.
20th St. (btw. Sansom & Chestnut
sts.).* ☎ *215/665-9150. www.tinto
restaurant.com. Plates $7–$32.
AE, DC, MC, V. Dinner daily; brunch
Sun. Bus: 2, 9, 12, 21, 42. Subway:
15th/16th & Locust St. Map p 100.*

*Chefs at farm-to-table Talula's Garden
transform local, seasonal ingredients into
deep-flavored comfort food.*

★★ **Tony Luke's** SOUTH PHILLY
ITALIAN SANDWICHES Neon-lit,
two-handed dining: Have the roast
pork with garlicky broccoli rabe and
sharp provolone. *39 E. Oregon Ave.
(btw. I-95. & Front St.).* ☎ *215/551-
5725. www.tonylukes.com. Entrees
$6–$11. No credit cards. Lunch &
dinner daily; breakfast Mon–Sat. Bus:
G, 7, 25, 47M, 57. Map p 99.*

★ **Valanni** CENTER CITY *MEDI-
TERRANEAN-LATIN TAPAS* Enjoy
the modern lounge vibe, spicy-
sweet snacks (bacon-wrapped blue
cheese-stuffed figs, chickpea frites),
mezze, and paella meant for shar-
ing. Half-price mezze and cocktails
5–7pm. *1229 Spruce St. (btw. 12th &
13th sts.).* ☎ *215/790-9494. www.
valanni.com. Entrees $10–$26. AE,
DISC, MC, V. Dinner daily; brunch
Sun. Bus: 4, 12, 27, 32. Subway:
Walnut-Locust. Map p 100.*

★★ **Vernick Food & Drink** RIT-
TENHOUSE *AMERICAN* Greg
Vernick opened this seafood-for-
ward nouveau American bistro in
2012; in 2017, it earned him the
James Beard Award for Best Chef
in the Mid-Atlantic. *2031 Walnut St.*
☎ *267/639-6644. vernickphilly.com.
Entrees $14–$34. AE, MC, V. Dinner
Tues–Sun. Bus: 2, 9, 12, 21, 42.
Subway: 15th/16th & Locust St.
Map p 100.*

★★★ **Vetri Cucina** CENTER CITY *ITALIAN* Bon Appetit and Esquire have both christened chef Marc Vetri's handsome brownstone eatery the best Italian restaurant in the U.S. Tasting menus only. *1312 Spruce St. (btw. 13th & Juniper sts.).* ☎ *215/732-3478. www.vetricucina. com. Tasting menu $165. AE, MC, V. Dinner daily. Bus: 4, 12, 27, 32. Subway: Walnut-Locust. Map p 100.*

★ **Victor Café** SOUTH PHILLY *ITALIAN* Giant veal chops and homemade pastas compete for fame with this 1933 trattoria's opera-singing servers. It even appeared in a Rocky movie (see p 44)! *1303 Dickinson St. (btw. 13th & Broad sts.).* ☎ *215/468-3040. www.victor cafe.com. AE, MC, V. Main courses $17–$38. AE, MC, V. Dinner daily. Bus: 4, 45. Subway: Tasker-Morris. Map p 99.*

★ **Vietnam** CHINATOWN *VIETNAMESE* Peanut-dusted rice vermicelli, charbroiled pork, lime-glazed chicken, and handsome surroundings make this quietly exotic spot popular with locals (so does the $15 lunch special). *221 N. 11th St. (btw. Race & Vine sts.).* ☎ *215/ 592-1163. www.eatatvietnam.com. Entrees $10–$16. AE, DISC, MC, V. Lunch & dinner daily. Bus: 23, 45, 61. Map p 100.*

★ **Villa di Roma** ITALIAN MARKET *ITALIAN* Extra-casual Italian-American fare—classic meatballs, fried asparagus, homemade gnocchi—is served in a red-brick-tiled space. *936 S. 9th St. (btw. Montrose & Carpenter sts.).* ☎ *215/592-1295. www.villadiroma.com. Entrees $11–$32. No credit cards. Lunch & dinner Tues–Sun. Bus: 45, 47, 47M. Map p 99.*

★★★ **Village Whiskey** RITTEN-HOUSE *GOURMET PUB* You'll find Philly's longest whiskey list (and longer barstool wait) here,

along with a burger that'll knock you off that hard-won seat. *118 S. 20th St. (at Sansom St.).* ☎ *215/665-1088. www.villagewhiskey.com. Entrees $12–$26. AE, DISC, MC, V. Lunch & dinner daily, brunch Sat–Sun. Bus: 2, 9, 12, 21, 42. Subway: 15th/16th & Locust St. Map p 100.*

★★ **Xochitl** SOCIETY HILL *MEXICAN* Distinctive, refined, understated, and lounge-y, the fare and the vibe at sleek "So-cheet" are refreshingly sophisticated. *408 S. 2nd St. (btw. Pine & Lombard sts.).* ☎ *215/238-7280. www.xochitlphilly. com. Entrees $12–$25. AE, DISC, MC, V. Dinner daily. Bus: 12, 21, 42, 57. Map p 100.*

★★★ **Zahav** OLD CITY/SOCIETY HILL *MIDDLE EASTERN* Fans swear by the rich hummus and savory kebabs, and the James Beard Foundation must agree, awarding Michael Solomonov its 2017 title for Outstanding Chef. *237 St. James Place. (btw. 2nd & 3rd sts. at Dock St.).* ☎ *215/625-8800. www. zahavrestaurant.com. Plates $9–$28. AE, DISC, MC, V. Dinner daily. Bus: 12, 21, 42, 57. Subway: 2nd St. Map p 100.* ●

Even a simple dish like hummus on pita bread takes on new flavor dimensions at award-winning chef Michael Solomonov's Zahav.

Nightlife Best Bets

North Bowl's retro design includes 17 lanes and two bars. Previous page: The Wine Bar at Panorama offers more than 100 wines by the glass.

Best Beer List
★★ Monk's Café, *264 S. 16th St.*
(p 121)

Best Dive Bar
★ Dirty Frank's, *347 S. 13th St.*
(p 118)

Best for Local Brews
★★★ Standard Tap, *901 N. 2nd St. (p 122)*

Best for Canoodling
★ Friday Saturday Sunday, *261 S. 21st St. (p 118)*

Best for Eating
★★ Pub & Kitchen, *1946 Lombard St. (p 118)*

Best for Martinis
★★ Nineteen Bar, *200 S. Broad St. (p 120)*

Best for Bowling
★ North Bowl, *909 N. 2nd St. (p 115)*

Best for Salsa Dancing
Brasil's, *112 Chestnut St. (p 115)*

Best Irish Pub
★★ Fergie's, *1214 Sansom St. (p 121)*

Best Classic Gay Bar
★ Tavern on Camac, *243 S. Camac St. (p 119)*

Nightlife in Northern Liberties

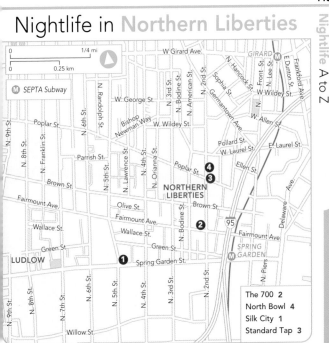

The 700 **2**
North Bowl **4**
Silk City **1**
Standard Tap **3**

Nightlife A to Z

Bowling

Lucky Strike Lanes CENTER CITY This swank, overpriced chain alley has 24 lanes, two floors, a low-slung lounge, cocktails, buckets of beers, and sliders galore. *1336 Chestnut St. (btw. 13th & Broad sts.).* ☎ *215/545-2471. www.bowllucky strike.com. $45–$55 per hr. lane. Shoe rental $4.50. Bus: 4, 9, 21, 23, 27, 31, 32, 33, 38, 42, 44, 48, 62, 78, 124, 125. Subway: Walnut-Locust or 13th St. Map p 116.*

★ **North Bowl** NORTHERN LIBERTIES This retro-chic, locally owned alley has 17 lanes, two bars (local brews), fun food (including an entire section for tater tots), and a major local following. *909 N. 2nd St.*

(btw. Poplar & N. Hancock sts.). ☎ *215/238-2695. www.northbowl philly.com. $3–$6 per person per game. Shoe rental $5. Bus: 5, 25, 43. Subway: Spring Garden St. Map above.*

Dance Clubs

★ **Brasil's** OLD CITY This compact upstairs club serves up the hottest Latin groove scene (and coolest caipirinhas) in town. Free salsa lessons from 9:30 to 10:30pm on Wednesday, Friday, and Saturday nights. *112 Chestnut St. (btw. Front & 2nd sts.).* ☎ *215/432-0031. www.brasilsnightclub-philly.com. Cover $5–$10. Bus: 5, 17, 21, 33, 42. Subway: 2nd St. Map p 116.*

Nightlife in Center City

Black Sheep **9**
Bob & Barbara's **8**
Brasil's **27**
Bridgid's **1**
Cavanaugh's **26**
D'Angelo's Lounge **4**
Dirty Frank's **23**
Drinker's Pub **2**
Fergie's **14**
Friday Saturday Sunday **5**
Jet Wine Bar **8**

Khyber Pass Pub **28**
L'Etage **25**
Lucky Strikes Lanes **12**
McGillin's Olde
  Ale House **13**
McGlinchey's **19**
Monk's Café **10**
Nineteen Bar **15**
Oscar's Tavern **11**
Pub & Kitchen **6**
Ray's Happy Birthday
  Bar **24**

Second District
  Brewing **7**
Tabu **21**
Tavern on Camac **20**
Toasted Walnut Bar **16**
The Trestle Inn **30**
Tria **3, 22**
Voyeur **18**
Wine Bar at Panorama **29**
Woody's **17**

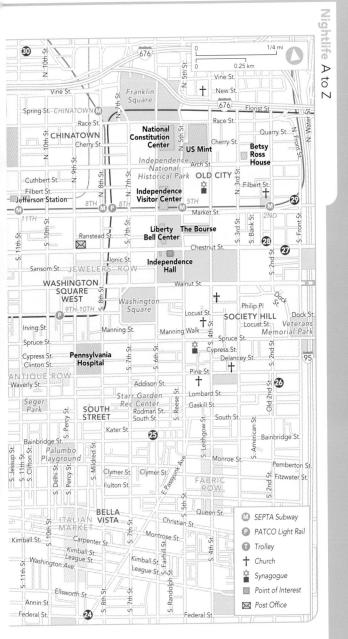

D'Angelo's Lounge RITTEN-HOUSE   Like a party scene from *The Sopranos*, this trattoria-with-a-dance-floor caters to a mature crowd who groove to Sinatra and Miami Sound Machine. *256 S. 20th St. (at Rittenhouse Square St. btw. Locust & Spruce sts.). ☎ 215/546-3935. www.dangeloristorante.com. No cover. Bus: 2, 9, 12, 21, 42. Subway: 15th/16th & Locust St. Map p 116.*

The Trestle Inn SPRING GAR-DEN   At this full-fledged retro Whiskey a Go-Go bar, mod dancers set the scene and a small dance floor of folks groove to 60s and 70s vinyl in between whiskey drinks and craft beers. *339 N. 11th St. (at Callowhill St.). ☎ 215/239-0290. www.thetrestleinn.com. $0–$5 cover. Bus: 23, 45. Map p 116.*

Dine-In Bars

★ Friday Saturday Sunday RIT-TENHOUSE   Brought back to life by new owners in 2015, this classic has a cocktail bar downstairs, a nouvelle American restaurant upstairs. (Note that, despite the name, it's open Tues–Sun.) *261 South 21st St. (at Rittenhouse Sq.). ☎ 215/546-4232. www.fridaysaturdaysunday.com. No cover. Bus: 7, 9, 12, 17, 21, 42. Map p 116.*

★★ Pub & Kitchen RITTEN-HOUSE   Rustic and refined, this corner spot has the menu of a bistro and the vibe of a stylish bar. Expect waits on weekends. *1946 Lombard St. (at 20th St.). ☎ 215/545-0350. www.thepubandkitchen.com. No cover. Bus: 17, 40. Map p 116.*

Dive Bars

★ Bob & Barbara's SOUTH STREET   This retro-style spot comes replete with vintage beer ads and lighting, a $4 Jim Beam-and-PBR special, and, on Thursday night, Philly's longest running drag performance. *1509 South St. (btw. 15th & 16th sts.). ☎ 215/545-4511. www.bobandbarbaras.com. $8 cover only for drag shows. Bus: 2, 4, 27, 32, 40. Subway: Lombard-South. Map p 116.*

★ Dirty Frank's CENTER CITY No sign, just a portrait mural of famous "Franks" announces this more-shabby-than-chic watering hole dating back to Prohibition. Locals play darts and sink into booths. Order a bottle, not a pint. *347 S. 13th St. (at Pine St.). ☎ 215/732-5010. www.dirtyfranksbar.com. No cover. Bus: 4, 27, 32, 40, 45. Map p 116.*

The sophisticated Pub & Kitchen welcomes drinkers and diners near Rittenhouse Square.

McGlinchey's RITTENHOUSE Ms. Pac Man tables, grumpy bartenders, cheap hotdogs, cheap shots, and even cheaper beer: No wonder this place is where the down-and-out chill and the glamorous slum. A proud exemption from Philly's smoke-free laws. *259 S. 15th St. (btw. Locust & Spruce sts.).* ☎ *215/735-1259. www.mcglincheys.com. No cover. Bus: 2, 9, 12, 21, 42. Subway: 15th/16th & Locust St. Map p 116.*

Oscar's Tavern RITTENHOUSE The textbook spot to hide from the boss, this dirt-cheap place dodged the smoking ban, allowing patrons to light up later into the night. Don't fear the roast beef. *1524 Sansom St. (btw. 15th & 16th sts.).* ☎ *215/972-9938. No cover. Bus: 2, 9, 12, 21, 42. Subway: 15th/16th & Locust St. Map p 116.*

★ Ray's Happy Birthday Bar SOUTH PHILLY Lou runs this corner joint (recently discovered by irony-dealing hipsters) and will be seriously bummed if you don't call ahead to tell him it's your b-day. Open at 7am(!), it's the best place to go for a brew after a cheesesteak at Pat's or Geno's. *1200 E. Passyunk Ave. (at Federal St.).* ☎ *215/365-1169. www.thehappybirthdaybar.com. No cover. Bus: 45, 47, 47M. Map p 116.*

Gay Bars

★ Tavern on Camac CENTER CITY This friendly, 60-year-old piano bar tucked on a side street is one of the oldest gay pubs in the U.S. There's something for any mood: Dining in the basement; piano bar on the ground floor; dance club upstairs. *243 S. Camac St. (btw. 12th & 13th sts., Locust & Spruce sts.).* ☎ *215/545-0900. www.tavernoncamac.com. No cover. Bus: 12, 23, 45. Subway: 12th/13th & Locust. Map p 116.*

Tabu CENTER CITY In 2018, the Gayborhood's favorite sports bar moved up the street into the old iCandy spot to expand into three floors of gay partying The ground floor will be the tried-and-true sports bar, with a dance club and stage on the second floor, and cabaret lounge on the top floor that spills onto the roof deck in summer. *254 S. 12th St. (btw. Locust & Spruce sts.).* ☎ *267/964-9675. www.tabuphilly.com. Cover $0–$10. Bus: 12, 23, 45. Subway: 12th/13th & Locust. Map p 116.*

Toasted Walnut Bar CENTER CITY The only lesbian bar in town covers 3,800 square feet to satisfy a diverse group that ranges from buzz-cut to glam. Best night: Thursday's karaoke. *1316 Walnut St. (btw. 13th & Broad sts.).* ☎ *215/546-8888. www.toastedwalnut.com. Cover $0–$20. Bus: 4, 9, 12, 21, 27, 32, 42. Subway: Walnut-Locust. Map p 116.*

★ Voyeur CENTER CITY There's room for 1,000 among the lavishly decorated floors (red leather, crystal spangles, faux fur), home to some of the East Coast's best DJs—and Philly's biggest circuit parties. One of Center City's few late-night spots, it attracts a mixed gay and straight crowd after 1am. *1221 St. James St. (btw. 12th & 13th sts.).* ☎ *215/735-5772. www.voyeurnightclub.com. Cover $10–$25. Bus: 9, 12, 21, 23, 42, 45. Subway: 12/13th & Locust. Map p 116.*

Woody's CENTER CITY This mega-bar has anchored the gayborhood since the '70s, sort of a community center with booze. Among the umpteen theme nights: Latin, country two-step, karaoke, and college. *202 S. 13th St. (btw. Walnut & Locust sts.).* ☎ *215/545-1893. www.woodysbar.com. Cover $0–$10. Bus: 4, 9, 12, 21, 27, 32, 42. Subway: Walnut-Locust. Map p 116.*

The tiny stage at L'Etage hosts everything from cabaret acts to poetry slams.

Lounges

★ L'Etage SOUTH STREET   Above Beau Monde (see p 102), this elegant spot offers banquette seating, a nice wine list, and entertainment from poetry slams to cabaret to weekend DJs. *624 S. 6th St. (at Bainbridge St.).* ☎ *215/592-0656. www.creperie-beaumonde. com. Cover $0–$15. Bus: 40, 47, 47M, 57. Map p 116.*

★★ Nineteen Bar CENTER CITY   Known for its fireside coziness, this see-and-be-seen 19th-floor lounge, bar, and restaurant draws an impeccable crowd—and martinis to match. *The Bellevue Hotel, 200 S. Broad St. (at Walnut St.).* ☎ *215/790-1919. www.nine teenrestaurant.com. No cover. Bus: 4, 9, 12, 21, 27, 32, 42. Subway: Walnut-Locust. Map p 116.*

The 700 NORTHERN LIBERTIES   Early on, the crowd at this two-floor spot is hipper-than-thou (in a nice way) artistic-types. Later, it's a mixed bag, adding in bachelorettes, frat bros, and yuppies. *700 N. 2nd St. (at Fairmount Ave.).* ☎ *215/413-3181. www.the700.org. No cover. Bus: 5, 25, 43. Subway: Spring Garden St. Map p 115.*

★ Silk City NORTHERN LIBERTIES   Attached to a silver-car diner and beer garden, this dimly lit lounge is known for its hipster clientele and DJs. *435 Spring Garden St. (btw. 4th & 5th sts.).* ☎ *215/592-8838. www.silkcityphilly.com. Cover $0–$10. Bus: 5, 25, 43, 57. Map p 115.*

Taprooms

Also check out "Popular Concert Venues" in Chapter 8 for bars with live music.

Black Sheep RITTENHOUSE   The suit-and-tie crowd flocks to this cozy Irish pub in a Colonial brick townhouse. The menu's worthy of staying past happy hour, too. *247 S. 17th St. (at Latimer St.).* ☎ *215/545-9473. www.theblacksheeppub.com. No cover. Bus: 2, 9, 12, 21, 42. Subway: 15th/16th & Locust St. Map p 116.*

★ Bridgid's FAIRMOUNT   Tiny and friendly, this horseshoe-shaped bar stocks an impressive array of Belgian beers—best accompanied by Italian dishes from the restaurant, which has improved under new owners. *726 N. 24th St. (btw. Fairmount Ave & Aspen St.).*

215/232-3232. www.bridgids.
com. No cover. Bus: 7, 32, 48. Map
p 116.

Cavanaugh's Headhouse SOCI-
ETY HILL If it's 4am and a World
Cup match is taking place, you can
probably catch it at this Brit-
inspired gastropub with lots of
rooms and snugs. Chef Ken McNa-
mara has been here from way back,
when this was "Dickens Inn". *421 S.
2nd St. (btw. Pine & Lombard sts.).*
215/928-9307. www.cavshead
house.com. No cover. Bus: 12, 40,
57. Map p 116.

Drinker's Pub RITTENHOUSE
At this aptly named bar, $1.50 tacos
and $3 PBRs draw a steady clien-
tele; a pool table and TVs tuned to
sports complete the picture. *1903
Chestnut St. (btw. 19th & 20th sts.);*
215/564-0914. www.drinkers
rittenhouse.com. No cover. Bus: 2, 9
17, 21, 31, 32, 33, 33, 38, 42, 44, 48,
62, 78, 124, 125. Map p 116.

★★ Fergie's CENTER CITY An
Irish pub actually owned by an Irish-
man, this find is cozy and candlelit,
and offers a large list of brews com-
plemented by some tasty pot pies,

*Silk City's beer garden is a must on warm
summer nights.*

burgers, and mussels and fries.
*1214 Sansom St. (btw. 12th & 13th
sts.).* 215/928-8118. www.fergies.
com. No cover. Bus: 9, 12, 21, 23, 27,
31, 32, 33, 38, 42, 44, 45, 124, 125.
Subway: 13th St. or City Hall. Map
p 116.

Khyber Pass Pub OLD CITY
Philly's oldest taproom—note the
carved gargoyles above the bar—
serves craft beers and Southern
and Cajun/Creole dishes in the
downstairs room; a small upstairs
room has a stage for up-and-coming local rock bands and DJs. *56 S.
2nd St. (btw. Market & Chestnut sts.).*
215/238-5888. www.thekhkhyber
passpubyber.com. Bus: 5, 17, 21, 33,
42, 48, 57. Subway: 2nd St. Map
p 116.

★ McGillin's Olde Ale House
CENTER CITY Hard to find—but
worth it—Philadelphia's oldest continuously operating tavern is as
popular now as it was in 1860, only
now there's karaoke (Wed and Sun)
with the pitchers of lager. *1310
Drury St. (btw. Chestnut & Sansom
sts., 13th & Juniper sts.).* 215/
735-5562. www.mcgillins.com. No
cover. Bus: 4, 9, 12, 21, 27, 32, 42.
Subway: Walnut-Locust or 13th &
Locust sts. Map p 116.

★★ Monk's Cafe RITTENHOUSE
The Penn crowd has adopted this
beer-connoisseur's spot—25 on
tap, another 200+ in bottles. Best
reason to come here: the house
special Flemish sour ale, served
with a bucket of mussels and the
house fries. *264 S. 16th St. (btw.
Locust & Spruce sts.).* 215/545-
7005. www.monkscafe.com. No
cover. Bus: 2, 9, 12, 21, 42. Subway:
15th/16th & Locust St. Map p 116.

★ Second District Brewing
SOUTH PHILLY For the ultimate
locavore drinker: A half-dozen truly
interesting beers brewed on prem-
ises, plus decent bar food. *1939*

Monk's Café has the city's best beer list.

Bancroft St. (btw. Mifflin & McKean sts.). ☎ 215/575-5900. www.second districtbrewing.com. No cover. Bus: 4, 45. Subway; Broad Street. Map p 116.

★★★ Standard Tap NORTH-
ERN LIBERTIES   Twenty local—and only local—beers daily, plus whatever other kind of drink you require, are served at this hip, handsome, vast, and justly popular gastro-pub. If it's nice out, ask for a table on the deck. 901 N. 2nd St. (at Poplar St.). ☎ 215/238-0630. www. standardtap.com. No cover. Bus: 5, 25, 43. Subway: Spring Garden St. Map p 115.

Wine Bars

Jet Wine Bar SOUTH STREET   Wines from across Europe are paired with classic meat and cheese platters and tasty small plates at this sleek little spot. 1525 South St. ☎ 215/735-1116. jetwine bar.com. No cover. Bus: 2, 4, 27, 32, 40. Map p 116.

★ The Wine Bar at Panorama
OLD CITY   Tucked into the ground floor of the Penn's View Hotel (see p 140) are some 150 wines by the glass, available by flights of five 1.5-ounce pours—all part of the hotel's Italian restaurant. 14 N. Front St. (btw. Market & Church sts.). ☎ 215/922-7800. www.penns-viewhotel.com/panorama. No cover. Bus: 5, 12, 17, 21, 33, 42, 48, 57. Subway: 2nd St. Map p 116.

★★ Tria RITTENHOUSE & WASH-
INGTON WEST   Spare and hand-some, this pair of narrow bars feel very Euro, what with their little savory plates and beginner-friendly selection of vino, categorized as bubbly, bold, zippy, and so on. Rittenhouse: 123 S. 18th St. (at Sansom St.); ☎ 215/972-8742. Bus: 2, 9, 12, 21, 42. Subway: 15th/16th & Locust St. Washington West: 1137 Spruce St. (at 12th St.); ☎ 215/629-9200. www.triaphilly.com. Bus: 12, 23, 45. Subway: 12th/13th & Locust. Map p 116. ●

The Euro-flavored Tria wine bars also offer lots of imported brews on tap.

Arts & Entertainment Best Bets

Best **Theater for Children's Performance**
★★ **kids** Arden Theatre Company, 40 S. 2nd St. (p 125)

Best for **Orchestra**
★★★ Kimmel Center for the Performing Arts, 300 S. Broad St. (p 129)

Best for **Local Productions**
★ **kids** Walnut Street Theater, 825 Walnut St. (p 128)

Best **Theater Facility, Period**
★★★ Academy of Music, 240 S. Broad St. (p 128)

Best **Hidden Gem**
★★ Academy of Vocal Arts, 1920 Spruce St. (p 128)

Best for **Outdoor Concerts**
★★ The Mann Center, 5201 Parkside Ave. (p 130)

Best for **Free Performances**
★★★ Curtis Institute of Music, 1726 Locust St. (p 129)

Best **Jazz Club**
★★ Ortlieb's Jazzhaus, 847 N. 3rd St. (p 130)

Best **Rock Club**
★ Johnny Brenda's, 1201 Frankford Ave. (p 131)

Best for **Broadway Productions**
★ The Forrest, 1114 Walnut St. (p 125)

Best for **Outdoor Concerts**
★ BB&T Pavilion, 1 Harbour Blvd., Camden (p 129)

Best for ~~Drama with an Edge~~
★ Wilma Theater, 265 S. Broad St. (p 128)

Best for **Cabaret**
★ L'Etage, 624 S. 6th St. (p 120)

Best for **Laid-Back Original Music**
★ The Locks at Sona, 4417 Main St. (p 131)

Best for **Family Concerts**
★★ World Café Live, 3025 Walnut St. (p 132)

The Kimmel Center for the Performing Arts is home to the Philadelphia Orchestra. Previous page: The Old Crow Medicine Show performs at the Franklin Music Hall, a Northern Liberties concert magnet.

Arts & Entertainment in
Northern Liberties

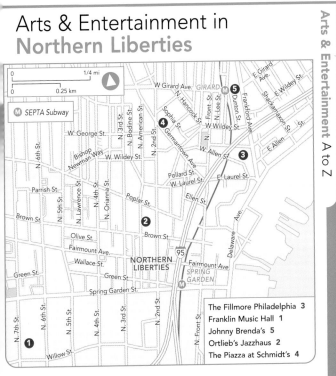

The Fillmore Philadelphia **3**
Franklin Music Hall **1**
Johnny Brenda's **5**
Ortlieb's Jazzhaus **2**
The Piazza at Schmidt's **4**

Arts & Entertainment A to Z

Theater

★★ kids Arden Theatre Company OLD CITY   Two intimate, contemporary performance spaces offer five popular productions each season—adaptations, premieres, and masterpieces—plus two excellent plays for families. *40 N. 2nd St. (btw. Market & Arch sts.).* ☎ *215/922-1122. www.arden theatre.org. Tickets $20–$55. Bus: 5, 17, 21, 33, 42, 48, 57. Subway: 2nd St. Map p 126.*

★ The Forrest Theatre WASHINGTON WEST   Best for big Broadway musicals, this spectacular venue was built for $2 million in 1927, when Gilbert & Sullivan launched productions here. *1114 Walnut St. (btw. 11th & 12th sts.).* ☎ *800/447-7400. www.forrest-theatre.com. Tickets $20–$150. Bus: 9, 12, 21, 23, 42, 45. Subway: 9th/10th & Locust. Map p 126.*

Merriam Theater CENTER CITY   This turn-of-the-20th-century Avenue of the Arts stunner welcomes top Broadway musicals as well as musical and other performances by everyone from Ira Glass to David Sedaris. *250 S. Broad St. (btw. Spruce & Locust sts.).*

Arts & Entertainment in
Center City

Academy of Music **13**
Academy of Vocal Arts **8**
Annenberg Center at the
 University of Pennsylvania **6**
Arden Theatre Company **23**
BB&T Pavilion **24**
Chris' Jazz Café **12**
Curtis Institute of Music **9**
The Forrest Theatre **18**
Helium Comedy Club **4**
Kimmel Center for the
 Performing Arts **16**
The Locks at Sona **1**
The Mann Center **2**

Merriam Theater **14**
Painted Bride Art Center **22**
Philly Improv Theater **5**
Plays & Players Theater **10**
Prince Music Theater **11**
Suzanne Roberts Theatre **17**
Theater of Living Arts **25**
Tower Theatre **3**
Trocadero **20**
Union Transfer **21**
Walnut Street Theater **19**
Wilma Theater **15**
World Café Live **7**

☎ *215/893-1999. www.kimmel center.org. Tickets $20–$165. Bus: 4, 12, 27, 32. Subway: Walnut-Locust. Map p 126.*

★ Plays & Players Theater

RITTENHOUSE   Charmingly rickety, this side-street landmark is home to the century-old amateur troupe of the same name, known for classic drama, works-in-progress, and interactive shows. *1714 Delancey St. (btw. 17th & 18th sts.).* ☎ *215/735-0630. www.playsand players.org. Tickets $10–$40. Bus: 2, 12, 17, 40. Map p 126.*

Prince Music Theater CENTER CITY   An old picture palace turned modern venue hosts live bands and comedy, filmed performances of the Royal Opera House and Royal Ballet, cabaret, and old and new movies. *1412 Chestnut St. (btw. Broad & 15th sts.).* ☎ *215/972-1000. www.princemusictheater.org. Tickets (to live performances) $15–$75. Bus: 4, 9, 21, 42, 124, 125. Subway: City Hall. Map p 126.*

Suzanne Roberts Theatre CENTER CITY   Universal access is the concept behind this newest and

The Academy of Vocal Arts is one of the world's most exclusive opera schools.

most iridescent of Broad Street's performing spaces, home base to both the Philadelphia Theatre and Koresh Dance companies. *480 S. Broad St. (at Lombard St.).* ☎ *215/985-1400. www.philadelphia theatrecompany.com. Philadelphia Theatre Co. tickets $15–$70. Bus: 4, 27, 32, 40. Subway: Lombard-South. Map p 126.*

★ kids Walnut Street Theater

WASHINGTON WEST   The country's oldest playhouse (ca. 1809) hosts locally produced Broadway-style productions and children's shows in its 1,100-seat theater, plus experimental works in adjoining studio spaces. *825 Walnut St. (at 9th St.).* ☎ *215/574-3550. www.walnut streettheatre.org. Tickets $15–$165. Bus: 9, 12, 21, 42, 47, 47M, 61. Map p 126.*

★ Wilma Theater CENTER

CITY   For drama buffs, this modern, 300-seat space offers modern works including premieres by playwrights such as Tom Stoppard. *265 S. Broad St. (at Spruce St.).* ☎ *215/546-7824. www.wilma theater.org. Tickets $33–$53. Bus: 4, 12, 27, 32. Subway: Walnut-Locust. Map p 126.*

Opera, Ballet, Classical

★★★ Academy of Music CEN-

TER CITY   The grandest performance hall in town—from its iconic gaslights to its gilded onstage columns—is home to the Pennsylvania Ballet, Philadelphia Opera Company, visiting performers, and traveling musical theater. *240 S. Broad St. (at Locust St.).* ☎ *215/893-1999. www.kimmelcenter.org. Tickets for ballet $29–$300. Bus: 4, 12, 27, 32. Subway: Walnut-Locust. Map p 126.*

★★ Academy of Vocal Arts

RITTENHOUSE   One of the world's most exclusive opera schools (only 30 students at a time)

The Walnut Street Theater hosts Broadway-style productions.

makes its home in—and gives marvelously intimate performances from—an ornate old townhouse. *1920 Spruce St. (btw. 19th & 20th sts.).* ☎ *215/735-1685. www.ava opera.org. Tickets $10–$103. Bus: 17. Map p 126.*

★★★ Curtis Institute of Music

RITTENHOUSE In a rambling limestone mansion, one of the world's finest music schools (Lang-Lang trained here) offers free student recitals (Oct–May Mon, Wed & Fri 8pm). Curtis students also perform full-scale opera at the Prince Music Theater (see p 128) and orchestral music at the Kimmel Center (see below). *1726 Locust St. (btw. 17th St. & Rittenhouse Sq.).* ☎ *215/893-7902. www.curtis.edu. Tickets free–$40. Bus: 2, 9, 12, 21, 42. Subway: 15th/16th & Locust St. Map p 126.*

Music/Performance Halls

★ Annenberg Center at the University of Pennsylvania

UNIVERSITY CITY A mixed bag of productions take place at this modern, double-stage space, from local jazz to dance to the International Children's Festival. *3680 Walnut St. (btw. 36th & 38th sts.).* ☎ *215/898-3900. www.pennpresents.org. Tickets $20–$78. Bus: 21, 31, 40. Trolley: 11, 13, 34, 36. Subway: 34th St. Map p 126.*

BB&T Pavilion CAMDEN,

NJ Just across the Delaware River, this 25,000-capacity summer amphiteater hosts major pop and rock acts, and festivals thereof, performing al fresco. *1 Harbour Blvd., Camden, NJ.* ☎ *856/365-1300. www.bbtpavilion.org. Tickets $17–$400. Bus (to ferry): 25. Map p 126.*

★ The Fillmore Philadelphia

FISHTOWN Live Nation converted this 25,000-square-foot warehouse into a concert venue for all sorts of performers—big acts in the 2,500-capacity main room and local artists in the 450-person The Foundry. *29 East Allen St.* ☎ *215/309-0150. www.thefillmore philly.org. Tickets $13–$200. Bus: 25. Trolley: 15. Subway: Girard. Map p 125.*

★★★ Kimmel Center for the Performing Arts CENTER

CITY This dramatic glass and steel vault includes the 2,500-seat cello-shaped Verizon Hall concert hall, built for the Philadelphia Orchestra (but used by all manner of musical acts), and a 650-seat space for chamber music, dance, and drama.

300 S. Broad St. (at Spruce St.).
☎ 215/893-1999. www.philorch.org.
Philadelphia Orchestra tickets $26–
$180. Bus: 4, 12, 27, 32. Subway:
Walnut-Locust. Map p 126.

★★ **The Mann Center** FAIR-
MOUNT PARK This summertime
amphitheater has covered seating
and picnicking on the grass for con-
certs by Yo-Yo Ma, the Indigo Girls,
John Legend, summer Philadelphia
Orchestra concerts, and more. 5201
Parkside Ave. (at Belmont Ave.).
☎ 215/546-7900. www.manncenter.
org. Tickets $15–$120. Bus: Mann
Center Loop bus (departs 19th &
Locust 70 min. before shows), 40, 52.
Trolley: 10. Map p 126.

Jazz & Blues Venues
★ **Chris' Jazz Café** CENTER
CITY Center City's only spot for
local jazz, this cozy, casual find has
a simple bar menu and a cool vibe.
Great for date night. 1421 Sansom
St. (btw. Broad & 15th sts.). ☎ 215/
568-3131. www.chrisjazzcafe.com.
Cover $10–$35. Bus: 4, 9, 12, 21, 27,
32, 42. Subway: Walnut-Locust. Map
p 126.

★★ **Ortlieb's Jazzhaus** NORTH-
ERN LIBERTIES Dimly lit and hard
to find, this joint gets smokin' when

the musicians start jamming. 847 N.
3rd St. (btw. Brown & Poplar sts.).
☎ 267/324-3348. www.ortliebs
philly.com. Cover $8–$22. Bus: 5, 25,
43, 57. Subway: Spring Garden St.
Map p 125.

★ **Painted Bride Art Center**
OLD CITY This effervescent, welcoming art gallery doubles as a
performance space for (often avant
garde) contemporary music, dance,
and theater—and Philadelphia's
longest-running jazz series.
230 Vine St. (btw. 2nd & 3rd sts.).
☎ 215/925-9914. www.painted
bride.org. Tickets $0–$25. Bus: 5, 57.
Map p 126.

Popular Concert Venues
Franklin Music Hall NORTHERN
LIBERTIES Formerly called the
Electric Factory, this storied indus-
trial setting may have changed its
name but it still hosts the same
type of acts: medium-large, all-ages
shows (Ani DiFranco, Thom Yorke,
Fall Out Boy, Rancid, Ja Rule,
Regina Spektor). 421 N. 7th St. (btw.
Callowhill & Spring Garden sts.).
☎ 215/627-1332. www.franklinmusic
hall.com. Tickets $20–$50. Bus: 43,
47, 47M. Map p 125.

Johnny Brenda's upstairs stage is a hip venue for live music.

Scoring Tickets

For week-of discounts, plus an up-to-date list of theatrical and artistic goings-on, visit the Greater Philadelphia Cultural Alliance's website at www.phillyfunguide.com, or call ☎ 215/399-3521. Tickets to the Philadelphia Orchestra, Pennsylvania Ballet, Academy of Music, and Merriam and Forrest Theaters can be had via Ticket Philadelphia (☎ 215/893-1999; www.ticketphiladelphia.org), or purchased directly from the Kimmel Center's box office open daily until 6pm, later on performance nights (see p 129). A lucky few can score a single $10 "community rush" ticket at 5:30pm the night of an evening performance or 11:30am for a matinee.

★ **Johnny Brenda's** NORTHERN LIBERTIES/FISHTOWN This dive-bar turned music venue/hipster gastro-pub has an upstairs stage for everything from indie folk groups to death metal acts. *1201 Frankford Ave. (at E. Girard Ave.).* ☎ 215/739-9684. www.johnny brendas.com. Tickets $0–$22. Bus: 5, 25. Trolley: 15. Subway: Girard Ave. Map p 125.

★ **The Locks at Sona** MANA-YUNK Singer-songwriters are the bread and butter of this subdued upstairs space, opened by the man who ran the (sadly defunct) Tin Angel. There's an Irish fusion gastropub downstairs, too. *4417 Main St. (at Conarroe St.).* ☎ 484/273-0481. www.sonapub.com. Tickets $10–$35. Bus: 35, 61, 62. Train: Manayunk. Map p 126.

The Piazza at Schmidt's NORTHERN LIBERTIES World music festivals, DJ'd dance parties (plus family movies and Phillies games on the big screen) are part of the scene at this al fresco courtyard of shops, bars, and condos. *2nd St. & Germantown Ave. (at Hancock St.).* ☎ 215/825-7552. www.livepiazza.com. Free admission. Bus: 5, 25. Trolley: 15. Subway: Girard Ave. Map p 125.

★ **Theater of Living Arts** SOUTH STREET Funk bands, French hip-hop acts, vintage Brit rockers, and all-American comedians fill the marquee of the TLA, a bare-bones, standing-room-only venue. Big-time local acts like The Roots sell out fast. *334 South St. (btw. 3rd & 4th sts.).* ☎ 215/922-1011. venue.tlaphilly.com. Tickets $18–$87. Bus: 40, 57. Map p 126.

★ **Tower Theatre** WEST PHILLY/UPPER DARBY All gilt and scrollwork, this shabby-majestic, 3,500-seat venue is a great spot to catch anyone from Weird Al to Joe Satriani to Neil Young. *19 S. 69th St. (at Ludlow St. off Market St.).* ☎ 610/352-2887. www.thetower philly.com. Tickets $23–$200. Bus: 21, 30, 65, 68, 101, 102, 103, 105, 106, 107, 108, 109, 110, 111, 112, 113, 120, 123, 126. Subway: 69th St. Map p 126.

★ **Trocadero** CHINA-TOWN Goth acts, punk bands, The Dandy Warhols, and 2 Live Crew have all performed beneath the timeworn vaulted ceilings of this 1870s vaudeville house. *1003 Arch St. (btw. 10th & 11th sts.).* ☎ 215/922-6888. www.thetroc.com. Tickets $5–$35. Bus: 23, 45, 61. Map p 126.

★ **Union Transfer** CALLOW-HILL Set in a converted railroad depot, Philly's independent large(ish) live music venue has reasonable prices (on both tickets and refreshments) and a wild variety of acts. *1026 Spring Garden St. (btw. 10th & 11th sts.).* ☎ *215/232-2100. utphilly.com. Tickets $15–$35. Bus: 23, 43. Map p 126.*

★★ **kids** **World Café Live** UNIVERSITY CITY Operated by Penn's indie music radio station, this multi-tasking venue offers a cafe stage and a two-level, 1,000-capacity space for concerts by They Might be Giants, Nick Lowe, Zap Mama, and kids' acts. *3025 Walnut St. (btw. 30th & 31st sts.).* ☎ *215/222-1400. www.world cafelive.com. Tickets $10–$55. Bus: 21, 42. Train: 30th St. Map p 126.*

The Meat Puppets perform at World Café Live.

Comedy

★ **Helium Comedy Club** RITTENHOUSE Knowns (John Oliver, Dave Attell, Kevin Pollack) and not-yet-knowns (Tues is $5 open-mic night) take the stage in front of a friendly, small, table-sitting crowd. *2031 Sansom St. (btw. 20th & 21st sts.).* ☎ *215/496-9001. www.helium comedy.com. Tickets $0–$40. Bus: 2, 9, 12, 21, 42. Subway: 15th/16th & Locust St. Map p 126.*

★ **Philly Improv Theater** RITTENHOUSE Long-form improvisational theater, sketches, and improv comedy entertain fans 7 nights a week, along with classes and free improv, sketch, and stand-up workshops. Lots of free shows. *2030 Sansom St. (btw. 20th & 21st sts.).* ☎ *267/233-1556. phillyimprov theater. Tickets $0–$15. Bus: 2, 9, 12, 21, 42. Subway: 15th/16th & Locust St. Map p 126.* ●

Helium is Philly go-to place for stand-up comedy.

Hotel Best Bets

Best at the Airport
★ Aloft $–$$ 4301 Island Ave.
(p 137)

Best for Kids
★ Sheraton Society Hill $$–$$$ 1
Dock St. (p 141)

Best for Pets
★ Loews Philadelphia Hotel $$
1200 Market St. (p 140)

Best for Beds
★★ Westin Philadelphia $$–$$$
99 S. 17th St. (p 142)

Best for a Splurge
★★★ Four Seasons $$$–$$$$ 1
N. 19th St. (p 138)

Best for Views
★ Hilton Philadelphia at Penn's
Landing $$–$$$ 201 S. Columbus
Blvd. (p 139)

Best Gym
★★ The Bellevue Hotel $$–$$$
200 S. Broad St. (p 137)

Best for a Long-Term Stay
★★ AKA Rittenhouse Square
$$–$$$$$ 135 S. 18th St. (p 137)

**Best Near the Convention
Center**
★★ Four Points by Sheraton
$$–$$$ 1201 Race St. (p 138)

Best for Celeb Spotting
★★★ Rittenhouse Hotel $$$–
$$$$$ 210 W. Rittenhouse Square
(p 141)

Best for Glamour
★★★ Ritz-Carlton Philadelphia
$$$–$$$$$ 10 S. Broad St. (p 141)

Best for Couples
★★ Penn's View Hotel $$–$$$
Front & Market sts. (p 140)

Best Historic Lodging
★★★ Thomas Bond House $$
129 S. 2nd St. (p 142)

Best for Bargain Rooms
★ Alexander Inn $$ 301 S. 12th St.
(p 137)

Best Bed & Breakfast
★★ La Reserve B&B $–$$ 1804–
1806 Pine St. (p 139)

*The boutique Morris House Hotel is located inside a former historic home. Previous
page: The Rittenhouse Hotel is an excellent place to spot celebs.*

East of Broad Lodging

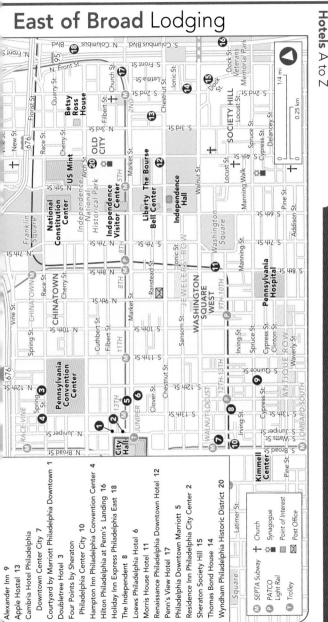

Alexander Inn 9
Apple Hostel 13
Cambria Hotel Philadelphia
Downtown Center City 7
Courtyard by Marriott Philadelphia Downtown 1
Doubletree Hotel 3
Four Points by Sheraton
Philadelphia Center City 10
Hampton Inn Philadelphia Convention Center 4
Hilton Philadelphia at Penn's Landing 16
Holiday Inn Express Philadelphia East 18
The Independent 8
Loews Philadelphia Hotel 6
Morris House Hotel 11
Penn's View Hotel 17
Philadelphia Downtown Marriott 5
Renaissance Philadelphia Downtown Hotel 12
Residence Inn Philadelphia City Center 2
Sheraton Society Hill 15
Thomas Bond House 14
Wyndham Philadelphia Historic District 20

M SEPTA Subway   + Church
P PATCO   ✡ Synagogue
  Light Rail   ▣ Point of Interest
T Trolley   ⊠ Post Office

West of Broad Lodging

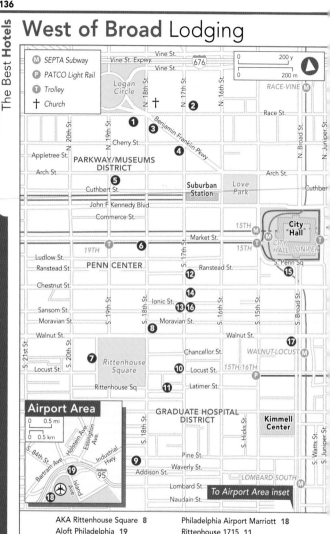

AKA Rittenhouse Square **8**
Aloft Philadelphia **19**
The Bellevue Hotel **17**
Club Quarters Philadelphia **14**
Embassy Suites Center City **3**
The Four Seasons **5**
The Logan Philadelphia **1**
Hotel Palomar **16**
La Reserve B&B **9**
Philadelphia 201 Hotel **2**

Philadelphia Airport Marriott **18**
Rittenhouse 1715 **11**
Rittenhouse Hotel **7**
Ritz-Carlton Philadelphia **15**
Sofitel Philadelphia **13**
Sonesta Philadelphia **6**
The Warwick Rittenhouse Square **10**
Westin Philadelphia **12**
Windsor Suites Philadelphia **4**

Hotels A to Z

★★ AKA Rittenhouse Square

RITTENHOUSE SQUARE Chic, just like its address, this all-suites spot is popular among discerning business travelers for week-long stays (although stays as brief as 2 nights are available). *135 S. 18th St. (btw. Walnut & Sansom sts.).* ☎ *888/252-0180 or 215/825-7000. www.stayaka.com. 78 units. Suites $194–$415. AE, DISC, MC, V. Bus: 2, 9, 12, 17, 21, 42. Map p 136.*

★ Alexander Inn WASHINGTON

WEST Simple little rooms—ask for a corner room; they're bigger—help make this boutique gayborhood spot affordable and popular. *301 S. 12th St. (at Spruce St.).* ☎ *877/253-9466 or 215/923-3535. www.alexanderinn.com. 48 units. Doubles from $125–$169 w/breakfast. AE, DC, DISC, MC, V. Bus: 23, 45. Map p 135.*

★ Aloft Philadelphia AIR-

PORT A modern, lower-priced, fast-paced version of the glitzy W, the Aloft features platform beds, Wi-Fi, and a 24-hour snack bar. *4301 Island Ave. (near I-95).* ☎ *877/462-5638 or 267/298-1700. www.marriott.com. 136 units. Doubles $149–$189. AE, DC, MC, V. Bus: 68. Train: Airport Line. Map p 136.*

Apple Hostel OLD CITY Dormstyle bunking, a TV lounge with billiards, shared baths, free pasta dinners (Wed), free beer, and pub crawls with strangers—this place is like college, only cheaper. *32 S. Bank St. (btw. 2nd & 3rd sts., Market & Chestnut sts.).* ☎ *877/275-1971 or 215/922-0222. www.applehostels. com. 70 beds. Dorm $35–$49; private room $124–$190. MC, V. Bus: 5, 9, 17, 21, 33, 42, 48, 57. Subway: 2nd St. Map p 135.*

Aloft Philadelphia is a stylish modern option near the airport.

★★ The Bellevue Hotel CEN-

TER CITY Once the country's most opulent hotel (in 1904), this Hyatt keeps up-to-date with spacious rooms, goose-down duvets, and a great gym. *200 South Broad St. (btw. Walnut & Locust sts.).* ☎ *215/893-1234. thebellevuehotel. hyatt.com. 172 units. Doubles $172–$524. AE, DC, DISC, MC, V. Bus: 4, 12, 27, 32. Subway: Walnut-Locust. Map p 136.*

★★ Cambria Hotel Philadelphia Downtown Center City

CENTER CITY Center City got a stylish new hotel in March 2018 with the custom-built Cambria, 15 stories of chic, modernist rooms, each with fridge and microwave. *219 South Broad St. (between Walnut and Locust sts.).* ☎ *215/732-5500. www. cambriaphiladelphia.com. 223 units. Doubles $135–$369. AE, DC, DISC, MC, V. Bus: 4, 23, 27, 32. Subway: Walnut-Locust. Map p 135.*

The sleek new Four Seasons Hotel overlooks Center City from the top floors of the Comcast Technology Center.

★ Club Quarters Philadelphia

RITTENHOUSE This handsome, business-savvy boutique chain also makes its sleek, modern, cozy rooms—many with kitchenette—available to non-members. *1628 Chestnut St. (at 17th St.).* ☎ *215/282-5000. www.clubquarters.com. Doubles $144–$244. AE, DC, DISC, MC, V. Bus: 2, 9, 21, 42. Map p 136.*

★★ Courtyard by Marriott Philadelphia Downtown

CONVENTION CENTER This is my favorite of the trio of Convention Center-ed Marriotts because of its circa-1926 setting and City Hall view. *21 N. Juniper St. (at Filbert St.).* ☎ *888/887-8130 or 215/496-3200. www.marriott.com. 498 units. Doubles $123–$389. AE, DC, DISC, MC, V. Bus: 27, 31, 32, 124, 125. Trolley: 10, 11, 13, 34, 36. Subway: 13th St. or City Hall. Map p 135.*

DoubleTree Hotel

CENTER CITY Location, location, location (and warm chocolate chip cookies): This business traveler's default across from the Academy of Music has views to the Delaware River from higher floors. *237 S. Broad St. (at Locust St.).* ☎ *800/222-8733 or 215/893-1600. www.doubletree hotels.com. 481 units. Doubles $149–$240. AE, DC, DISC, MC, V. Bus: 4, 12, 27, 32. Subway: Walnut-Locust. Map p 135.*

★ Embassy Suites Center City

LOGAN CIRCLE A cylindrical 1960s apartment building was converted to this all-suites hotel with balconies—it's nice for a longer stay. *1776 Ben Franklin Pkwy. (at 18th St.).* ☎ *800/362-2779 or 215/561-1776. embassysuites.hilton. com. 288 units. Suites $231–$380 w/ breakfast. AE, DC, DISC, MC, V. Bus: 2, 7, 27, 32, 33, 38. Map p 136.*

★★ Four Points by Sheraton Philadelphia Center City

CONVENTION CENTER The vibe, the bar, and the tiny rooms make it seem like a Manhattan boutique hotel, across the street from the Reading Terminal Market. *1201 Race St. (at 12th St.).* ☎ *215/496-2700. www.fourpointsphiladelphia citycenter.com. 92 units. Doubles $134–$260. AE, DC, MC, V. Bus: 2, 16, 23, 27, 45, 48, 61. Subway: Race Vine. Map p 135.*

★★★ Four Seasons Hotel

LOGAN CIRCLE The tallest hotel in the country opened in spring 2019 on the top 12 floors of Philly's brand new, Norman Foster–designed Comcast Technology Center (the tallest U.S. building outside of Chicago or New York). The chic Four Seasons has a spa, a penthouse restaurant, and killer views from elegant rooms. *1 N. 19th St (between Arch & Cuthbert Sts.).*

800/819-5053. www.fourseasons. com/philadelphia. 219 units. Rates not set at press time, but expect them to be the priciest in town. AE, DC, MC, V. Bus: 2, 7, 17, 27, 31, 32, 33, 38, 48. Map p 136.

Hampton Inn Philadelphia Convention Center CONVENTION CENTER This reliable chain offers straightforward lodging, friendly service, and an indoor pool. 1301 Race St. (at 13th St.). 800/ 426-7866 or 215/665-9100. www. hamptoninn.com. 250 units. Doubles $136–$269 w/breakfast. AE, DC, DISC, MC, V. Bus: 2, 16, 23, 27, 45, 48, 61. Subway: Race Vine. Map p 135.

★ kids **Hilton Philadelphia at Penn's Landing** PENN'S LANDING Your only truly waterfront option, this Art Deco–style complex boasts an indoor pool overlooking docked old ships and plenty of space for spreading out. 201 S. Columbus Blvd. (at Dock St.) 800/233-1234 or 215/521-6500. www.hilton.com. 348 units. Doubles $175–$361. AE, DC, MC, V. Bus: 12, 17, 25. Map p 135.

Holiday Inn Express Philadelphia Penn's Landing PENN'S LANDING Students and seniors frequent this cheap basic spot, a bit isolated from Old City but with great river views. 100 N. Columbus Blvd. (near the Ben Franklin Bridge.). 877/666-3243 or 215/627-7900. www.hiepennslanding.com. 184 units. Doubles $154–$247. AE, DC, DISC, MC, V. Bus: 17, 25. Map p 135.

★★ **Hotel Palomar** RITTENHOUSE Old Art Deco offices, now cozily contemporary and eco-minded, make up this boutique hotel from Kimpton. Most rooms have laptops. Many have great city views. 117 S. 17th St. (at Sansom St.). 888/725-1778 or 215/563-5006. www.hotelpalomar-philadelphia.com. 247 units. Doubles $175–$588. AE, DISC, MC, V. Bus: 2, 9, 21, 42. Map p 136.

★ **The Independent** CENTER CITY In the heart of the gayborhood, this Georgian Revival building has contemporary appointments, fireplaces in some rooms, and cathedral ceilings in others. 1234 Locust St. (btw. 12th & 13th sts.). 215/772-1440. www.theindepend enthotel.com. 24 units. Doubles $109–$379. AE, MC, V. Bus: 12, 45. Subway: Walnut-Locust. Map p 135.

★★ **La Reserve B&B** RITTENHOUSE In this elegant B&B in a pair of 1850s townhouses, half the rooms are studios or suites, for not much more than a double. Weekends, the Continental breakfast

Hotel Palomar's bar Square 1682 is a chic watering hole near Rittenhouse Square.

gives way to home-cooked. *1804–06 Pine St. (btw. 18th & 19th sts.).* ☎ *888/405-8567 or 215/735-1137. www.lareservebandb.com. 12 units. Doubles $99–$187 w/breakfast. AE, DISC, MC, V. Bus: 2, 17, 21, 40. Map p 136.*

★ kids Loews Philadelphia Hotel CENTER CITY

Beloved by aesthetes for its international style and Cartier wall clocks, this hotel is also adored by swimmers for its lap pool with a view, and by children (and traveling pets) for its toy cache. Rooms tend to be small. *1200 Market St. (at 12th St.).* ☎ *855/690-0313 or 215/627-1200. www.loewshotels.com. 581 units. Doubles $149–$339. AE, DC, DISC, MC, V. Bus: 23, 38, 44, 45, 62, 124, 125. Subway: 13th St. Map p 135.*

★ The Logan Philadelphia LOGAN CIRCLE

This Curio Collection hotel from Hilton occupies the former Four Seasons building with stylish rooms decorated by local artists, an Urban Farmer restaurant overlooking Logan Circle, and a rooftop lounge. *1 Logan Square (at 18th St. & Ben Franklin Pkwy.).* ☎ *215/963-1500. curiocollection3.hilton.com. 391 units. Doubles $205–$421. AE, DC, MC, V. Bus: 2, 7, 27, 32, 33, 38. Map p 136.*

★★ Morris House Hotel WASHINGTON SQUARE

Antique portrait paintings, uneven floorboards, and afternoon tea add to the charm of this 1787 house turned boutique hotel. Request a courtyard room to avoid street noise. *225 S. 8th St. (btw. Walnut & Locust sts.).* ☎ *215/922-2446. www.morrishousehotel.com. 15 units. Doubles $159–$229 w/breakfast. AE, MC, V. Bus: 9, 12, 21, 38, 42. Map p 135.*

★★ Penn's View Hotel OLD CITY

This hidden gem has European, family-run appeal—and a fantastic wine bar (see p 122). *14 N. Front St. (at Market St).* ☎ *800/331-7634 or 215/922-7600. www.pennsviewhotel.com. 51 units. Doubles $145–$399 w/breakfast. AE, MC, V. Bus: 5, 12, 17, 21, 33, 42, 48, 57. Subway: 2nd St. Map p 135.*

Philadelphia 201 Hotel LOGAN CIRCLE

As big as a city block, this cement behemoth feels like a cross between a convention center and a cruise ship. *201 N. 17th St. (at Race St.)* ☎ *800/325-3535 or 215/448-2000. www.marriott.com. 757 units. Doubles $139–$199. AE, DC, MC, V. Bus: 2, 27. Map p 136.*

★ Philadelphia Airport Marriott AIRPORT

If you're stuck at the airport and have just a few hours to sleep, this is the quiet, connected place to do it. *1 Arrivals Rd., Terminal B (via skywalk to PHL Airport).* ☎ *800/682-4087 or 215/492-9000. www.marriott.com. 419 units. Doubles $156–$329. AE, DC, DISC, MC, V. Bus: 37, 68. Train: Airport Line. Map p 136.*

Philadelphia Marriott Downtown CONVENTION CENTER

The biggest in town, this high-tech hotel is attached via skyway to the Pennsylvania Convention Center. It often books to capacity with business folk. *1201 Market St. (btw. 12th & 13th sts.).* ☎ *800/320-5744 or 215/625-2900. www.marriott.com. 1,408 units. Doubles $159–$389. AE, DC, MC, V. Bus: 27, 31, 32, 124, 125. Trolley: 10, 11, 13, 34, 36. Subway: 13th St. or City Hall. Map p 135.*

★ Renaissance Philadelphia Downtown Hotel OLD CITY

A primo location for history buffs, this polished, modernist hotel is across the street from Independence Park and has a staff known for its knowledge of the district. *401 Chestnut St. (at 4th St.).* ☎ *215/925-0000. renaissance-hotels.marriott.com.*

152 units. Doubles $189–$409. AE, DC, DISC, MC, V. Bus: 5, 9, 17, 21, 33, 38, 42, 48, 57. Subway: 5th St. Map p 135.

Residence Inn Philadelphia Center City
CENTER CITY This suites-only spot is surprisingly quiet, considering its location as the single most central hotel in town. City Hall views and a high-tech fitness center. *1 E. Penn Sq. (at Market St. & City Hall).* ☎ 800/331-3131 or 215/557-0005. www.marriott.com. *269 units. Suites $117–$359 w/ breakfast. AE, DC, MC, V. Bus: 27, 31, 32, 124, 125. Trolley: 10, 11, 13, 34, 36. Subway: 13th St. or City Hall. Map p 135.*

★★ Rittenhouse 1715
RITTEN-HOUSE In a city mansion on a leafy little street just off the southeast corner of Rittenhouse Square, this traditional, boutique-y spot has a European vibe. *1715 Rittenhouse Square St. (btw. 17th & 18th sts.).* ☎ 877/791-6500 or 215/546-6500. www.rittenhouse1715.com. *23 units. Doubles $160–$345 w/breakfast. AE, DC, MC, V. Bus: 2, 9, 12, 17, 21, 42. Map p 136.*

★★★ kids Rittenhouse Hotel
RITTENHOUSE This elegant, modern hotel has a restaurant overlooking the treetops of Rittenhouse Square, plus an amazing gym, salon, and spa. Jack Nicholson stays here when he's in town. *210 W. Rittenhouse Square (btw. Locust & Walnut sts.).* ☎ 800/635-1042 or 215/546-9000. www.rittenhousehotel.com. *98 units. Doubles $309–$659. AE, DC, MC, V. Bus: 2, 9, 12, 17, 21, 42. Map p 136.*

★★★ The Ritz-Carlton Philadelphia
CENTER CITY This all-marble former bank has butlered bath service and a lounge in the formidable colonnaded lobby. It's very posh. *10 Avenue of the Arts/S. Broad St. (btw. City Hall & Chestnut St.).* ☎ 215/523-8000. www.ritzcarlton.com. *299 units. Doubles $254–$599. AE, DC, DISC, MC, V. Bus: 4, 9, 27, 32, 38, 124, 125. Subway: City Hall. Map p 136.*

★ kids Sheraton Society Hill
OLD CITY On a curvy cobblestone street, this low, sprawling brick building offers traditional rooms, a lush atrium, and a splashy indoor pool. *1 Dock St. (at 2nd & Walnut sts.).* ☎ 800/325-3535 or 215/238-6000. www.sheraton.com/societyhill. *364 units. Doubles $161–$283. AE, DC, MC, V. Bus: 5, 9, 12, 17, 21, 42, 48, 57. Subway: 2nd St. Map p 135.*

The posh Ritz-Carlton Philadelphia.

★★ **Sofitel Philadelphia** RITTENHOUSE With low-key luxury, a "bonjour" at the door, and fresh croissants at breakfast, this French hotel is close to the city's poshest shopping and dining. *120 S. 17th St. (at Sansom St.).* ☎ *215/569-8300. www.sofitel-philadelphia.com. 306 units. Doubles $131–$467. AE, DC, MC, V. Bus: 2, 9, 12, 21, 42. Map p 136.*

Sonesta Philadelphia RITTENHOUSE Airline pilots and conventioneers come for the large rooms and easy city access in a nonsense-free setting. *1800 Market St. (at 18th St.).* ☎ *215/561-7500. www.sonesta. com. 445 units. Doubles $239–$359. AE, DC, MC, V. Bus: 2, 9, 12, 17, 21, 42. Trolley: 10, 11, 13, 34, 36. Subway: 15th St. Map p 136.*

★★★ **Thomas Bond House** OLD CITY Named for its first occupant, Thomas Bond (1712–1784 and co-founder of Pennsylvania Hospital), this cheerful, colonial B&B is as historic as a Philly overnight gets. *129 S. 2nd St. (btw. Chestnut & Samson sts.).* ☎ *800/845-2663 or 215/923-8523. www.thomasbondhousebandb.com.*

The historic Thomas Bond House is a cheerful B&B.

12 units. Doubles $145–$215 w/ breakfast. AE, DISC, MC, V. Bus: 5, 9, 12, 17, 21, 42, 48, 57. Subway: 2nd St. Map p 135.*

★ **The Warwick Rittenhouse Square** RITTENHOUSE Inside this 1928 landmark hotel, where Ava Gardner honeymooned, you'll find surprisingly edgy, sleek design, as well as a retro steakhouse. *220 S. 17th St. (at Chancellor St.).* ☎ *800/ 967-9033 or 215/735-6000. www.war wickrittenhouse.com. 301 units. Doubles $115–$374. AE, DC, DISC, MC, V. Bus: 2, 9, 12, 21, 42. Map p 136.*

★★ **Westin Philadelphia** RITTENHOUSE Handsomely clubby atmosphere—with the best beds in town—is tucked into one of Philadelphia's iconic skyscrapers. *99 S. 17th St. (btw. Market & Chestnut sts.).* ☎ *215/563-1600. www.westin philadelphiahotel.com. 294 units. Doubles $161–$411. AE, DISC, MC, V. Bus: 2, 9, 12, 17, 21, 42. Map p 136.*

kids Windsor Suites Philadelphia LOGAN CIRCLE Great for families whose kids don't mind sleeping on a pullout sofa, this bargain-priced all-suites offering isn't super fancy, but it's really close to the museums. *1700 Benjamin Franklin Pkwy. (at 17th St.).* ☎ *877/784-8379 or 215/981-5678. www. thewindsorsuites.com. Suites from $123–$302. AE, DC, DISC, MC, V. Bus: 2, 7, 27, 32, 33, 38. Map p 136.*

Wyndham Philadelphia Historic District OLD CITY Nothing fancy: Just an easy-to-access eight-floor hotel with nice rooms that's convenient to historical sites, galleries, and shopping. There's a rooftop pool, too. *400 Arch St. (at 4th St.).* ☎ *215/923-8660. www.philly downtownhotel.com. 364 units. Doubles $127–$249. AE, DC, DISC, MC, V. Bus: 5, 9, 17, 33, 48, 57. Map p 135.* ●

The Best of Brandywine Valley

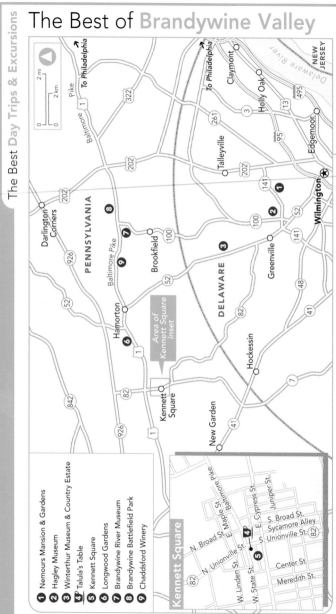

1 Nemours Mansion & Gardens
2 Hagley Museum
3 Winterthur Museum & Country Estate
4 Talula's Table
5 Kennett Square
6 Longwood Gardens
7 Brandywine River Museum
8 Brandywine Battlefield Park
9 Chaddsford Winery

Previous page: The opulent Nemours Mansion is one of several DuPont family estates in the Brandywine Valley.

The bucolic, historic countryside around the Brandywine River in Delaware has largely been defined by two famous families: First the entrepreneurial, elegant, and munificent du Ponts, then the earthy, cerebral, prolific, and certainly artistic Wyeths. *Tip:* Get the Brandywine Treasure Trail Passport (www.visit wilmingtonde.com) for admission to 11 area attractions, including all of those mentioned below, for $35 (May 25–Sept 2 only). START: I-95 S for about 23 miles to Wilmington, then 82 to Kennett Sq., then Baltimore Pike (Rte. 1) to Longwood & Chadds Ford; the drive takes approx. 1 hr.

❶ Nemours Mansion & Gardens. Come here to experience the opulence of Alfred I. du Pont's circa-1910 Louis XVI-style chateau and Petit Trianon–modeled garden, with its 23K gold statuary. ⏱ 3 hrs. 850 Alapocas Dr., Wilmington, DE. ☎ 302/651-6912. www.nemours mansion.org. Admission $18 adults, $16 seniors & students, $8 ages 5–16. May–Dec, Tues–Sat 10am–5pm, Sun noon–5pm.

❷ ★★ Hagley Museum. More du Pont acreage, the Hagley combines a Georgian manse and gardens, restored gunpowder mills, a historic workers' community, and an interactive science exhibit highlighting DuPont materials (try on a space suit; sit in Jeff Gordon's NASCAR racer). ⏱ 1 hr. Rte. 141 (200 Hagley Rd.), Wilmington, DE.

☎ 302/658-2400. www.hagley.org. Admission $15 adults, $11 seniors & students, $6 children 6–14. Daily 10am–5pm (closes 4pm early Nov–mid-Mar).

❸ ★★★ kids Winterthur Museum & Country Estate. The best of the du Pont estates has the country's foremost collection of American decorative arts, including gems of interior architecture salvaged from a variety of historic buildings from every Eastern seaboard colony, carefully removed and reassembled here: a Montmorenci stair hall, Shaker rooms, and a grand dining hall. In spring, extensive gardens bloom with azaleas. Kids can explore a 3-acre "enchanted woods." Christmastime is busiest, with splendid holiday trimmings. The gift shops are

Winterthur Museum & Country Estate has America's foremost collection of decorative arts.

fabulous. Weather permitting, tram tours are offered March to Christmas. ⏱ *1 hr. 5105 Kennett Pike (Rte. 52), Winterthur, DE* ☎ *800/448-3883. www.winterthur. org. Admission $20 adults, $18 seniors & students, $6 children 2–11. Tues–Sun 10am–5pm.*

4 ★★★ **Talula's Table.** This charming country market sells artisan cheeses, homemade soups, petite sandwiches, awesome fruit tarts, and coffee. (Come for lunch; scoring the sole dinner table is next to impossible.) 102 W. State St., Kennett Square, PA. ☎ 610/444-8255. www.talulastable.com. $–$$.

5 ★★ **Kennett Square.** Originally a Lenape Native American settlement, this village became a stopover during the Revolutionary War, then home to free Quakers who established safe havens along the Underground Railroad. A short walk around the historic borough—from State Street to Union, then Mulberry, then back up Broad Street—reveals Queen Anne, Gothic Revival, Italianate, and Tudor architecture. There are plenty of shops. If you dine here, order anything with mushrooms; Kennett Square is the "mushroom capital of the world." Local farmers produce more than 400 million delicious pounds of fungi each year. ⏱ *1 hr. Historic Kennett Square Visitors Center, 106 W. State St., Kennett Square, PA.* ☎ *610/444-8188. www.historickennettsquare.com.*

6 ★★★ kids **Longwood Gardens.** One of the world's greatest gardens owes its existence to Pierre S.—you guessed it—du Pont, who devoted his life to horticulture and turned a 19th-century arboretum into the ultimate 1,077-acre green estate. Among its must-see attractions: The main garden fountain puts on water shows June to September (daily at 11:15am, 1:15pm, 3;15pm, and 5;15pm, plus half-hour illuminated shows Fri–Sat evenings). A topiary garden surrounds a 37-foot sundial. Ponds are filled with massive lily pads. Four acres of bronze and glass conservatories include the Orangery, practically overflowing with African violets, century-old bonsai trees, tropicals, seasonal plants, and visiting collections. A children's garden features 17 splash fountains, two mazes, a grotto, and kid-friendly plants. Du Pont's lovely country residence offers a "heritage" collection that includes 2,000-year-old Native American spear points. Spring is a prime time to visit, but winter

The estate at Longwood Gardens covers more than 1,000 acres.

The Brandywine River Museum displays art from the Wyeth family collection.

holidays are marvelous too, with strolling carolers and (naturally) decorated trees galore. ⏱ 1½ hrs. 1001 Longwood Rd. (at Rte. 1), Kennett Square, PA. ☎ 800/737-5500 or 610/388-1000. www.longwoodgardens.org. Admission $23 adults, $20 seniors & students, $12 ages 5–18. Mid-Mar–late Nov daily 9am–6pm (Thurs–Sat until 10pm early May–Sept, until 9pm Oct); late Nov–mid-Jan daily 9am–10pm; Jan–mid-Mar daily 9am–5pm.

7 ★★ Brandywine River Museum.

If you've read a Scribner Classic like *Treasure Island, Robin Hood, Robinson Crusoe,* or *Last of the Mohicans,* you already know the amazing illustrations of early 20th-century artist N.C. Wyeth, who settled in Chadds Ford. This 19th-century gristmill showcases the art of three generations of Wyeths—N.C., his famous children Andrew and Carolyn, and grandson Jamie. Illustrations and landscape paintings by other American artists are also displayed. April through mid-November, off-site tours (via shuttle bus) visit N.C.'s house and studio, Andrew's studio, and the Kuerner Farm where Andrew found so much inspiration; tours cost $8. ⏱ 1 hr. 1 Hoffman's Mill Rd,, Chadds Ford, PA. ☎ 610/388-2700. www.brandywine museum.org. Admission $18 adults,

$15 seniors, $6 students and ages 6–18. Daily 9:30am–5pm.

8 ★ Brandywine Battlefield Park.

Great for a hike, this site witnessed a rare full-army clash between Continental and British troops in September 1777. You can also visit the houses Washington and Lafayette commandeered as their battle headquarters. ⏱ ½ hr. 1491 Baltimore Pike (Rte. 1), Chadds Ford, PA. ☎ 610/459-3342. www. brandywinebattlefield.org. Free admission to grounds; museum $3; museum plus house tours $8 adults, $7 seniors & veterans, $5 children 6–17. Tues–Sat 9am–4pm, Sun noon–4pm (Wed–Sun only May & Sept–Oct; Thurs–Sun only Apr & Nov; Fri–Sun only late Mar and Dec; Christmas week Wed–Sun). Closed Jan–mid-Mar.

9 Chaddsford Winery.

This 17th-century barn, surrounded by 300 mineral-rich acres, is the closest Pennsylvania gets to Napa. The friendly vintners offer tastings and cellar tours, and host al fresco blues bands and BBQs in summer. ⏱ 1 hr. 632 Baltimore Pike (Rte. 1), Chadds Ford, PA. ☎ 610/388-6221. www.chaddsford.com. Tastings $10–$15; weekend tour and tasting $25. Daily 11am–5:30pm; Sat–Sun tastings every half hour.

The Best of Lancaster County

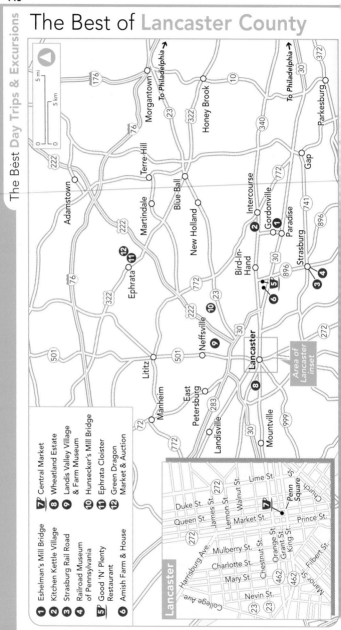

1. Eshelman's Mill Bridge
2. Kitchen Kettle Village
3. Strasburg Rail Road
4. Railroad Museum of Pennsylvania
5. Good 'N' Plenty Restaurant
6. Amish Farm & House
7. Central Market
8. Wheatland Estate
9. Landis Valley Village & Farm Museum
10. Hunsecker's Mill Bridge
11. Ephrata Cloister
12. Green Dragon Market & Auction

Though less than 60 miles from Philadelphia, farm-rich Lancaster County feels worlds away. Thousands of Old Order Amish and Mennonite residents live off the land in a devout fashion, shunning modern ways, choosing horse-and-buggies over cars, nature over technology, plain over fancy. *Tips for visiting:* Please do not take photographs of Amish people, do not trespass on their land, and try not to stare, though a wave and a friendly smile are appreciated. START: **PA Turnpike (76-W) to Rte. 30; the drive should take approx. 1 hr. during non-rush-hour times.**

❶ ★ Eshleman's Mill Bridge.
Also known as Paradise Bridge or Leaman's Place Bridge, this red-painted covered wooden bridge from 1893 stands amid cornfields and farms, a pastoral introduction to a pastoral region. Drive slowly: There's only one lane. ⏱ ¼ hr. *N. Belmont Rd., ½ mile north of Rte. 30 just east of Paradise.*

❷ kids Kitchen Kettle Village.
Friendly, countrified, and, yes, kitschy, this outdoor mall has a few dozen vendors of quilts, crafts, homemade jams, relishes, and ice creams. ⏱ 1/2 hr. *3529 Old Philadelphia Pike (Rte. 340), Intercourse.* ☎ 800/732-3538 or 717/768-8261. www.kitchenkettle.com. May–Oct Mon–Sat 9am–6pm; Mar–Apr and Nov–Dec Mon–Sat 9am–5pm; Jan–Feb hours vary by shop.

❸ ★ kids Strasburg Rail Road.
Book a ticket for a 45-minute ride on America's oldest short-line train. Other train-themed amusements include a working vintage pump car, a miniature "pufferbelly" steam train, and hand-propelled 1930s "cranky cars." Check the website's schedule for holiday-themed rides (Santa, Easter Bunny, and Halloween) and dates when a full-size Thomas-brand tank engine shows up to offer rides to young fans. ⏱ 1½ hr. *301 Gap Rd (Rte. 741-East), Ronks.* ☎ 866/725-9666. www.strasburgrailroad.com. Admission $15.50–$26. Open daily; hours vary wildly—check the website.

❹ kids Railroad Museum of Pennsylvania.
Want more trains? Cross the street to this history-rich display, where dozens of stationary engines tell the tale of America's locomotive era. ⏱ ½ hr. *300 Gap Rd. (Rte. 741-East), Ronks.* ☎ 717/687-8628. www.rrmuseumpa.org. Admission $10 adults, $9 seniors, $8 children 3–11. Mon–Sat 9am–5pm, Sun noon–5pm (Nov–Mar closed Mon).

❺
Stick-to-yer-ribs country fare is the name of the game in these parts. Diners sit at tables for 10 or 12 to dig into family-style fried chicken, chow chow, and shoofly pie at ★ **Good 'N' Plenty Restaurant.** *150 Eastbrook Rd/Rte. 896 (btw. Rtes. 340 and 30), Smoketown.* ☎ 717/394-7111. www.goodnplenty.com. $$.

The Strasburg Rail Road departs from a circa-1832 station.

Hershey Park Happy

The "sweetest place on Earth" is just a 30-minute drive from downtown Lancaster. At the turn of the 20th century, chocolate-bar-maker Milton Hershey became Pennsylvania's Walt Disney. His eponymous town features chocolate kiss lampposts, a **Chocolate World** for tastings and factory tours (251 Park Blvd.; ☎ 717/534-4900; www.hersheyschocolateworld.com), and 110-acre ★★ **kids Hersheypark** (Rtes. 743 and 422; ☎ 800/HERSHEY [800/437-7439]; www.hersheypark.com), a family-friendly amusement park featuring a dozen roller coasters, a full-fledged zoo (www.zooamerica.com), a water-play area, and al fresco concerts. Hersheypark is open daily late May through August and again in December, weekends only Apr–late May and Sept–Nov). Admission costs $69 adults, $47 ages 3–8 and 55–69, $29 ages 70 and over. For overnights, book a room at the elegant and historic ★★★ **Hotel Hershey** (100 Hotel Rd., Hershey; ☎ 844/330-1711; www.thehotelhershey.com; 278 units; doubles from $299; AE, DC, DISC, MC, V).

6 ★ **kids** **Amish Farm & House.** Outsiders (or "English") are, respectfully, unwelcome upon Amish farms or inside Amish homes or schoolhouses. The next best thing is to visit this facsimile. Tune

The replica Amish Farm & House feels sublimely authentic.

out the suburban surroundings, and the experience feels sublimely authentic. Basic admission includes a 40-minute tour of a 204-year-old, 10-room house, a newer one-room schoolhouse, old covered bridge, and 15-acre farm with live animals. ⏱ 1½ hr. 2395 Lincoln Hwy. at Witmer Rd., east of Lancaster. ☎ 717/394-6185. www.amishfarmandhouse.com. Admission $10 adults, $9 seniors, $7 children 5–11. Daily 9:45am–4:45pm.

7 ★★ **Central Market.** In the heart of Lancaster, the nation's oldest farmer's market—est. 1730 and housed in a stunning Romanesque Revival building—offers 60+ stalls of local delicacies, from sweet bologna and shoofly pie to scrapple, schnitzel, and whoopie pies. 23 N. Market St., Lancaster. ☎ 717/735-6890. www.centralmarketlancaster.com. $–$$. Open Tues & Fri 6am–4pm, Sat 6am–2pm.

8 ★ Wheatland Estate. Two miles west of Lancaster, costumed guides offer hour-long tours of the gracious Federal mansion and arboretum of James Buchanan, the 15th U.S. president. ⏲ *1 hr. 230 N. President Ave (at Marietta Ave./Rte. 23) Lancaster.* ☎ *717/392-4633. www.lancasterhistory.org. Admission $15 adults, $13 seniors, $8 students 11–17, free 10 and under. Mon–Sat 10am–5pm.*

9 ★★ Landis Valley Village & Farm Museum. Costumed re-enactors scattered amid 40 historic structures bring traditional, old-time Dutch country living authentically to life in this complex just 2½ miles northeast of Lancaster. Displays and demonstrations highlight what everyday life was like for PA's rural German communities from 1740 to 1940. Once or twice a month, Hands-on History Days let the family try their hands at ye olde chores, from churning butter to punching tin to cooking on an open hearth. ⏲ *1½ hr. 2451 Kissel Hill Road, Lancaster.* ☎ *717/569-0401. www.landisvalleymuseum.org. Admission $12 adults, $10 seniors, $8 ages 2–11. Mar 11–Dec Tues–Sat 9am–5pm, Sun noon–5pm; Jan–Mar 10 Wed–Sat 9am–5pm, Sun noon–5pm.*

10 Hunsecker's Mill Bridge. Photo op! The country's longest single-span covered bridge (180 ft) divides two townships and turns Hunsecker Road into Hunsicker Road. Think of it as Lancaster's version of the equator. ⏲ *¼ hr. Hunsicker Rd. just west of Mondale Rd. (1 mile southeast of Rte. 222; 1/2 mile north of Rte. 23), Upper Leacock & Manheim townships.*

11 ★ Ephrata Cloister. In the 1720s, Conrad Beissel moved from Germany to Pennsylvania to establish a monastic version of Christianity. His rules about celibacy made it difficult to attract members, and after he died in 1768, the cloister's residents became German Seventh Day Adventists. See how these folks lived, alone and apart. Pay special detail to their beautiful *frakturschriften* (calligraphy used in printmaking), pottery, and book binding. ⏲ *1½ hr. 632 W. Main St., Ephrata (near jct of rtes. 272 & 322).* ☎ *717/733-6600. www.ephratacloister.org. Admission $10 adults, $9 seniors, $6 ages 3–11. Mon–Sat 9am–5pm, Sun noon–5pm.*

12 ★★★ Green Dragon Market & Auction. If it's Friday, make sure you stop at this giant spread of 400 stalls manned by growers, merchants, and artisans; an auction house for hay and small animals, and (weather permitting) an outdoor flea market and arcade. It's a true taste of rural America, Pennsylvania Dutch–style. ⏲ *1 hr. 955 N. State St., Ephrata.* ☎ *717/738-1117. www.greendragonmarket.com. Fri 9am–9pm.*

Landis Valley Village & Farm offers a glimpse of rural life from 1740 to 1940.

The Best of Bucks County

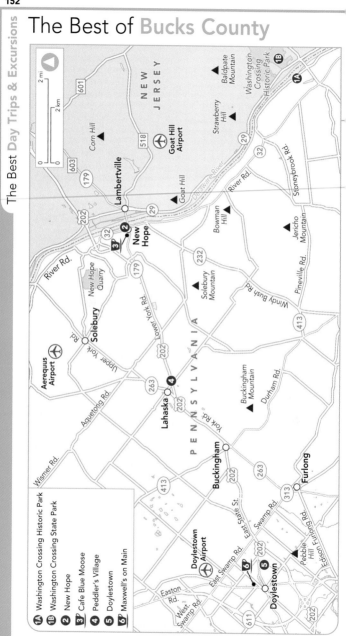

The county north of Philly is full of weekend pleasures: the historic site where Washington crossed the Delaware; hip, riverside New Hope; the bustling streets of Doylestown; and the quaint shops of Peddler's Village. START: Take I-95/295 north from Philadelphia, and just after crossing the Delaware into New Jersey, take exit 76 onto River Rd (Rte. 29) and drive north 3 miles to the Washington Crossing Bridge.

❶ ★ Washington's Crossing.

Following a string of defeats, the Patriot cause was at its lowest ebb in December 1776. Most army contracts were up, the weary troops ready to go home—until George Washington entreated them to stick it out for one last campaign. On a frigid Christmas Eve, under cover of darkness, Washington and 2,400 troops silently crossed the ice-choked Delaware River in Durham Boats from Pennsylvania to Johnson's Ferry, NJ. They marched to Trenton, surprising the Hessian troops stationed there. After a brief battle—in which the Americans lost just two men (among the 5 wounded: future president James Monroe)—the Hessians surrendered. Turning the tide, this victory boosted morale and led to a string of Patriot victories at the Second Battle of Trenton (Jan 2), Princeton (Jan 3), and Cowpens (Jan 17).

There are interpretive parks on both sides of the river. On the PA side, the 500-acre ❶A Washington Crossing Historic Park includes McConkey's Ferry Inn, where Washington dined and made the final plans for the daring crossing. On the NJ side, 3,575-acre ❶B Washington Crossing State Park has 15 miles of hiking trails, a museum and visitor center, the historic Johnson Ferry House, and an open-air theater for summer plays and Monday-night movies. ⏱ 1½ hr. Washington Crossing Historic Park, PA: 1112 River Rd., Washington Crossing, PA. ☎ 215/493-4076. www.ushistory.

org/washingtoncrossing. Historic buildings $7 each; outdoor park free. Daily 10am–4pm. Washington Crossing State Park, NJ: 355 Washington Crossing-Pennington Road, Titusville, NJ. ☎ 609/737-0623. www.state.nj.us. Free except vehicle charge Memorial Day–Labor Day of $7 ($5 NJ residents). Daily 8am–7pm (Visitors Center Museum: 9am–4pm).

❷ ★★ New Hope. This pre-Revolutionary ferry depot on the Delaware River (once home to Colonial hothead Aaron Burr) became an art colony in the early 1900s, a gay Mecca in the 1950s, and a thriving summer-home spot and tourist destination today. The **Bucks County Playhouse** (www.bcptheater.org) boasts a surprising pedigree of A-listers (Sigourney Weaver and

Broadway-bound plays often start out at the prestigious Bucks County Playhouse in New Hope.

David Hyde Pierce recently trod its boards) and premieres from the likes of Neil Simon and Terrence McNally fine-tuning Broadway-bound productions. The town also anchors the **Ivyland Railroad** (32 W. Bridge St., ☎ 215/862-2332, www.newhoperailroad.com), a 45-minute round-trip steam train loop to Lahaska (see bullet ➎) made famous in the 1914 *Perils of Pauline* cliffhanger serials (picture: a villain twirling his mustache; a damsel tied to the tracks; will our hero save her in time?). ⏱ *2 hrs. General info: www.visitnewhope.com and www.newhopehs.org. Ivyland R&R: From $22 adults, $20 ages 3–11, $5 under age 3. Hourly runs daily late May–Oct and late Nov–Dec, weekends in winter.*

➌ ★ **Cafe Blue Moose.** Innovative BYOB started by local teens—though the owner is now a seasoned chef in his mid-20s—with French-inflected European prix-fixe menus ($27 for 2 courses, $35 for 3). 9 W. Mechanic St., New Hope. ☎ *215/862-6800. www.cafeblue moose.com. Wed–Sun dinner; Sat–Sun brunch. AE, M, V. $–$$.*

➍ **Peddler's Village.** Ye olde strip mall, a conglomeration of 70 shops—heavy on the gifts and crafts—and a half-dozen restaurants in a brick-paved country-town setting. ⏱ *1 hr. At Rtes. 202 and 263, Lahaska.* ☎ *215/794-4000. www. peddlersvillage.com. Mon–Wed 10am–6pm, Thurs–Sat 10am–8pm, Sun 11am–6pm (late Nov–Dec open until 9pm Mon–Sat, until 7 Sun; Jan–Mar closes 5pm Sun–Thurs).*

➎ ★★★ **Doylestown.** Bucks' county seat—a lovely collection of Victorian homes, shops, and restaurants—has been home to notables from Margaret Mead and Oscar

The Mercer Museum is packed with 40,000 pre-industrial objects.

Hammerstein to Pearl S. Buck and P!nk. Prolific author James Michener (1907–1997) left his mark with downtown's **James A. Michener Art Museum** (138 S. Pine St., ☎ 215/340-9800, www.michen erartmuseum.org) celebrating local artists. Just across the street. Henry Mercer (1856–1930), founder of the Moravian Tile Works, left his mark with the **Mercer Museum** (84 S. Pine St., ☎ 215/345-0210; www. mercermuseum.org), a treasure trove of everyday Americana—think: Grandma's attic re-imagined by M.C. Escher, six stories of hidden rooms, meandering halls, and secret staircases zigzagging around an open atrium, all packed with 40,000 pre-industrial objects from Franklin stoves to cider presses to Conestoga wagons. On the edge of town, Mercer's colorful tiles decorate the wacky poured-cement **Fonthill Castle** (525 E. Court St., ☎ 215/348-9461, www.fonthill museum.org); book ahead for the required tour. ⏱ *3½ hrs. www.*

doylestownborough.net. *Michener:* Admission $15 adults, $13 seniors, $8 students, $5 ages 6–18; Tues–Fri 10am–4:30pm, Sat 10am–5pm, Sun noon–5pm. *Mercer Museum:* $15 adults, $13 seniors, $8 ages 6–17; Mon–Sat 10am–5pm, Sun noon–5pm. *Fonthill:* $15 adults, $13 seniors, $8 ages 6–17; tours Mon–Fri 11am–4pm, Sat 11:30am–4pm, Sun noon–4pm.

6 ★ **Maxwell's on Main.** This family-run restaurant in the center of town serves fabulous French toast and Eggs Bayou (Cajun-style "Benedict") at brunch; burgers, sandwiches, and pizza-like flat-breads at lunch. *37 N. Main St., Doylestown.* ☎ 215/340-1880. www. momsmaxwellsonmain.com. $–$$.

The Best of Chestnut Hill & Montgomery County

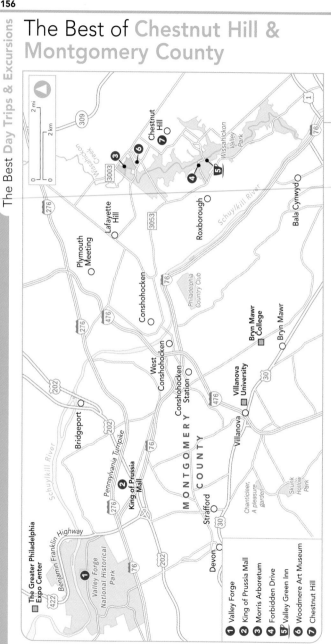

- ① Valley Forge
- ② King of Prussia Mall
- ③ Morris Arboretum
- ④ Forbidden Drive
- ⑤ Valley Green Inn
- ⑥ Woodmere Art Museum
- ⑦ Chestnut Hill

■ The Greater Philadelphia Expo Center

Valley Forge National Historical Park

Benjamin Franklin Highway

Bridgeport

Pennsylvania Turnpike

King of Prussia Mall

Devon

Strafford

Chanticleer, A pleasure garden

Skunk Hollow Park

Villanova

Villanova University

Bryn Mawr College

Bryn Mawr

Bala Cynwyd

Conshohocken Station

West Conshohocken

Conshohocken

Philadelphia Country Club

Plymouth Meeting

Lafayette Hill

Roxborough

Schuylkill River

Wissahickon Valley Park

Chestnut Hill

MONTGOMERY COUNTY

Schuylkill River

2 mi

2 km

At Philadelphia's border with suburban Montgomery County, you'll find contrasts galore: The Revolutionary war history of Valley Forge, the gardens and sculptures of Morris Arboretum, the leafy streets of Philly's Chestnut Hill neighborhood, and the largest mall in America. START: **Take I-76 21 miles north to Valley Forge (or city buses 125 & 139); there are also two SEPTA train lines to Chestnut Hill).**

❶ ★★ Valley Forge National Historic Park. In 1893, Pennsylvania's first state park was created around the trim stone house where General George Washington rode out the bitter winter of 1777–78, keeping an eye on supply lines from Reading and Lancaster—and on the British-occupied capital of Philadelphia down the road. Today it's a national park covering 3,500 acres, dotted with replicas of the crude cabins that housed Washington's ragtag troops, a coalition of state militias, each with its own uniforms and loyalties. After 6 months of drills in modern military techniques under Prussian officer Friedrich von Steuben, the troops emerged as a unified fighting machine: the U.S. Continental Army. ⏱ *2 hrs. 1400 N. Outer Line Dr., King of Prussia. (where Rte. 422 crosses the PA Turnpike).* ☎ *610/783-1000. www.nps.gov/vafo. Free admission. Daily 7am–sunset (Visitor Center 9am–5pm).*

Valley Forge National Historic Park was built around Washington's stone house.

❷ King of Prussia Mall. Only 3 miles southeast of Valley Forge, re-enter modern consumer culture at this mega-mall, with 40 restaurants and 450+ stores. ⏱ *½ hr. 160 N. Guelph Rd. (where I-76, PA 202 & the PA Turnpike cross).* ☎ *610/265-5727. www.kingofprussiamall.com. Mon–Sat 10am–9pm, Sun 11am–6pm.*

❸ ★★ Morris Arboretum. Originally the showpiece of the Morris family's 1887 estate, these manicured gardens, now owned by the University of Pennsylvania, display more than 12,000 labeled plants from 34 countries—massive examples of Engler beech, Bender oak, Blue Atlas Cedar, and katsura along with an English rose garden and a canopy walk offering a squirrel-eye's view of the trees. Don't miss the outdoor model railroad tracks that trundle past tiny replicas of Philly-area landmark houses. ⏱ *1 hr. 100 E. Northwestern Ave. (btw. Stenton & Germantown Aves.).* ☎ *215/247-5777. www.morrisarboretum.org. Admission $19 adults, $17 over 65, $10 ages 3–17 and students. Mon–Fri 10am–4pm, Sat–Sun 10am–5pm.*

❹ ★ Forbidden Drive. Join joggers, bikers, parents with strollers, and the occasional horseback rider on this wide path along Wissahickon Creek in Fairmount Park (see p 86). ⏱ *½–2 hr.* ☎ *215/683-0200; www.fairmountpark.org. The Friends of the Wissahickon (a good resource):* ☎ *215/247-0417; www.fow.org.*

The Sky's the Limit

Incorporated into a modern Friends meeting house just off Germantown Avenue in Chestnut Hill, ★ **Chestnut Hill Skyspace** (20 E. Mermaid Lane, ☎ 215/247-3553, www.chestnuthillskyspace.org) is a mesmerizing 50-minute artistic "experience" designed by famed Quaker light artist James Turrell. Participants observe the sky—at dusk or dawn—through a large roof opening while subtly shifting colored lights play across the rim. There's also a 20-minute version for cold or rainy weather. There's a suggested donation of $5. Hours and days vary—check the website—and remember to bring a sweatshirt, because lying still for an hour can get chilly!

5 ★ **Valley Green Inn.** At this charming former tavern you can walk up for a drink or snack or sit down for a meal. *Valley Green Rd. at Wissahickon.* ☎ *215/247-1730. www.valleygreeninn.com. $$.*

6 ★ **Woodmere Art Museum.** Dedicated to Philadelphia arts and artists, this museum sits in a 19th-century stone mansion just north of the Chestnut Hill shopping district. Contemporary sculptures are set around its 6-acre grounds; the galleries inside split between the historic collections (paintings by Benjamin West, Rembrandt Peale, Frederic Edwin Church) and galleries showcasing modern works. ① ½ *hr. 9201 Germantown Ave. (at Bells Mill Rd.).* ☎ *215/247-0476. www.woodmereartmuseum.org. Admission $10 adults (free Sun), free for children and students. Tues–Thurs 10am–5pm, Fri 10am–8pm, Sat 10am–6pm, Sun 10am–5pm.*

7 ★★★ **Chestnut Hill.** Cobblestoned Germantown Avenue, the main street of this leafy northwest Philly neighborhood, is paradise for strollers and window-shoppers, lined by restaurants and record stores, bakeries and boutiques, cafes and cheese shops—not to mention ice cream parlors, microbreweries, and little farmers markets. Drive the side streets—especially those west of Germantown—to see some lovely, often magnificent houses. ① *2 hr. Germantown Ave.* ☎ *215/247-6696. www.chestnuthillpa.com. Also handy: www.chestnuthilllocal.com.* ●

Families celebrate Independence Day in Chestnut Hill with a decorated bicycle parade for kids.

Before You Go

Official Tourist Information

The centrally located **Independence Visitor Center** is at 1 Independence Mall West, at 6th & Market sts. (☎ 800/537-7676; www.phlvisitorcenter.com and www.uwishunu.com). Other tourist offices are in **Sister Cities Park,** N. 18th St. at the Benjamin Franklin Parkway; in **City Hall,** Broad & Market sts. (☎ 215/686-2840); in the **Convention Center,** 1101 Arch St.; and in **Love Park,** 1599 JFK Blvd. at 16th St. (☎ 215/683-0246).

The Best Time to Go

Summer is the height of tourism season, especially around historic attractions. Late July through August, be prepared to swelter in line for Independence Hall. (On the other hand, summer is the best time to score a table at a trendy restaurant.) Fall and winter offer the lowest prices on hotel rooms. Spring weather is often peculiar—hot one day, chilly the next—but late May and early June are usually best for garden buffs. Times to avoid: During the University of Pennsylvania's graduation in mid-May.

Festivals and Special Events

JAN. New Year's Day means the odd, debauched, daylong **Mummer's Parade** (☎ 215/336-3050; www.phillymummers.com) along Broad Street.

FEB. Mid-to-late month, Chinatown pops and sparkles with a **Chinese New Year celebration** (☎ 215/922-2156; chinatown-pcdc. org) on its streets and in its restaurants.

Previous page: Travelers come and go through 30th Street Station, a hub for Amtrak, subway, and regional SEPTA trains.

MAR. The **Philadelphia Flower Show** (☎ 215/988-8800; www.the flowershow.com) is the largest indoor exhibit of its kind. Go early for the freshest displays. Expect crowds.

APR. For 3 days, 22,000 of the best college, high school, and track club runners from 60 countries (and 100,000 spectators) descend upon Franklin Field for the exuberant **Penn Relays** (☎ 215/898-6154; www.thepennrelays.com), the country's largest and oldest (est. 1895) track-and-field meet with some 425 races over 35 hours.

MAY On a (hopefully) sunny Saturday, some 50,000 celebrants turn out for the **Rittenhouse Row Spring Festival** (www.rittenhouse row.org), a block party gone chic, thanks to dozens of outdoor kiosks offering haute cuisine and sublime shopping.

JUNE Early in the month, bars and breweries host beer-centric events for **Philly Beer Week** (www.philly lovesbeer.org), showcasing suds both local and exotic. Every June evening, Franklin Square turns into a Little China with a **Chinese Lantern Festival** of traditional foods, artist exhibitions, and of course fanciful lights (historicphiladelphia. org). There's no better place to celebrate **Flag Day** (June 14) than Old City's Betsy Ross House (☎ 215/629-4026; www.betsyross house.org).

JULY The city where the Declaration of Independence was written celebrates **Independence Week** (the week of July 4) at just about every venue—notably, of course, at the historic sights around Independence Mall—with re-enactments, outdoor movies, ice cream socials, and concerts and performances

Useful Websites

www.phlvisitorcenter.com The city's official portal for visitors, also the place to reserve tickets to Independence Hall and for the basics for a short visit.

www.visitphilly.com A comprehensive guide to Philadelphia and the surrounding Pennsylvania counties, created by the region's premier promoters—also great for hotel discounts. Check out their blog www.uwishunu.com.

www.discoverphl.com The site for Philadelphia Conventions & Visitors Bureau, packed with useful info.

www.phila.gov Straight from local government, this less-frequently updated website has useful info nonetheless.

www.philly.com Run by the city's two major newspapers, the *Philadelphia Inquirer* and the *Philadelphia Daily News*, the best and fastest sources for local news and events.

www.phillyfunguide.com An arts and events site maintained by the Greater Philadelphia Cultural Alliance.

www.phillymag.com The website of monthly *Philadelphia* magazine, offering local insider stories and editorials on shopping, dining, and events.

www.visitpa.com The official Pennsylvania state tourism site.

galore, culminating in fireworks over Penn's Landing and the Philadelphia Museum of Art.

AUG. On a sunny Sunday in early August, the **2nd Street Festival** (www.2ndstfestival.org) fills seven long blocks from Spring Garden to Chestnut St. with food trucks and live bands jamming late into the night.

SEPT. Inspired by the cutting-edge Scottish arts extravaganza of the same name, the **Philly Fringe Arts Festival** (☎ 215/413-9006; www.fringearts.com.org) fills 2 weeks in early September with experimental theater and more in and beyond Old City.

OCT. All manner of fine artists let the public into their workspaces during 2 weekends of **Philadelphia Open Studio Tours** (☎ 215/546-7775; www.philaopenstudios.org).

NOV. **Philadelphia Museum of Art Craft Show** (☎ 215/684-7930; pmacraftshow.org) shows off the work of local and international artisans in the Convention Center.

DEC. The biggest, most historic of military sporting events, the **Army-Navy game** (☎ 215/463-5500; armynavygame.com) is a grand tradition come early December. So is the **holiday light and music show**—a rite of passage among local kids—at Macy's in the old John Wanamaker Building (☎ 215/241-9000; www.macys.com)—as well as its postmodern cousin, the **Comcast Centers Holiday Spectacular audio-visual extravaganza** at 1701 JFK Blvd.

Weather

Philadelphia's mid-Atlantic climate produces cold and often gray winters, cool and sometimes rainy springs, hot and typically humid summers, and mild and crisp falls. Just like the seasons in kids' books.

Restaurant and Theater Reservations

Though a few notable BYOB restaurants are first-come, first-served, most larger restaurants accept reservations by phone or via the Internet at **Open Table** (www.open table.com). For performances by the Philadelphia Orchestra, the Pennsylvania Ballet, Philadelphia Chamber Music Society, and at the Kimmel Center for the Performing Arts, Academy of Music, Mann, Merriam, and others, the telephone box office is **Ticket Philadelphia** (☎ 215/893-1999; www.ticketphila delphia.org). The official site www. phillyfunguide.com offers last-minute half-price tickets and other discounts.

Car Rentals

Most major renters maintain offices at Philadelphia International Airport, and there are a small number of cars available from 30th Street Station and at Center City kiosks. Check out www.rentalcars.com—or any number of travel websites—for car-rental discounts.

Getting **There**

By Plane

Philadelphia International Airport (PHL; ☎ 800/745-4283 or 215/937-6937; www.phl.org) is the city's major airport, on I-95 about 10 miles southwest of Center City. A **SEPTA train** (☎ 215/580-7800; www.septa.com) runs every 30 minutes to town ($8 adults one-way). A taxi costs about $30, including tip.

By Car

I-95 runs north and south along the city's eastern edge. The Pennsylvania Turnpike (**I-276**) cuts east-west through the city's northern suburbs. **I-76** (aka the Schuylkill Expwy.) runs southeast to northwest, connecting to Center City via the Vine Street Expressway (**I-676**). **I-476** (aka the Blue Route) connects all of the above via western suburbs, about 15 miles west of town, linking I-276 and I-76 at the north, and I-95 to the south.

By Train

Amtrak (☎ 800/872-7245; www. amtrak.com) runs to 30th Street Station (at Market St., in West Philly just over the Schuylkill River from Center City), where you can pick up a cab to your hotel, or connect to subways or regional rail (SEPTA) lines.

By Bus

Greyhound/Peter Pan buses arrive at the **Greyhound Bus Terminal** (10th and Filbert sts.; ☎ 800/231-2222; www.greyhound.com).

　　BoltBus (www.boltbus.com) connects Philly with NYC, Boston, Baltimore, Newark, and Washington, DC. **Megabus** (www.megabus.com) goes to and from a dozen destinations—including NYC, Boston, Washington, Baltimore, Pittsburgh, and Toronto. Both budget buses have their main Philly stop on JFK Blvd. about 150 yards west of 30th Street Station (Megabus also has a second stop, for NYC service only, off Independence Mall).

Getting **Around**

On Foot
Center City measures 25 blocks (2 miles) from east to west and 12 blocks (1 mile) north to south. A pedestrian should be able to cross town in about an hour and cross Old City in 15 minutes.

By Car
Two-thirds of all visitors to Philadelphia arrive by car. Traffic into town can be congested, especially during rush hours. The majority of Center City's streets are one-way, and some open up to three lanes during rush hour, so pay close attention to street signs. For info on garages, lots, and parking meters, check out the official www.philapark.org.

By Taxi
Base fare for cabs is $2.70, adding 23¢ for every ⅒ mile traveled. A cross-town trip should cost about $11. Two good operators are **Olde City Taxi** (☎ 215/338-0838) and **Quaker City** (☎ 215/728-8000), although hailing from a street corner is usually fastest. Or use **Uber** or **Lyft.**

By Public Transportation
SEPTA (☎ 215/580-7800; www.septa.com) operates all public transit, including buses that run along most major streets; trolleys; and subways that run beneath Market and Broad streets (use the Broad Street Line if you're headed to a sporting event or concert at a stadium in South Philadelphia; it's much faster and cheaper than driving).

Note that SEPTA is in the midst of overhauling all of its bus routes, so take any bus numbers printed in this book with a grain of salt. Also, SEPTA has been (slowly) rolling out a ticketless NPT system, using pre-paid tap-and-go Key Cards to pay fares. Fares on buses, trolley, and the subway are $2 on the Key Card, or $2.50 in cash (exact change required). A one-day $13 Independence Pass ($30 for the Family Pass for up to 5 family members, of which no more than 2 are over 18) is valid for unlimited rides on any SEPTA bus, subway, trolley, Phlash bus, the Airport line, and regional rail arriving in Center City after 9:30am. A $9 One Day Convenience Pass is valid for trips on buses, subways, and trolleys (not valid for regional rail), and can be loaded only onto a Key Card.

By Tourist Bus
The purple, daytime-only **Phlash Bus** (☎ 215/389-8687; www.phillyphlash.com) loops around 19 attractions every 15 minutes. It runs daily from May through early Sept and again late Nov through Dec; Fri–Sun in Apr and early Sept–mid-Nov. Fare is $2 per ride, or $5 for an all-day pass (online only, get a 2-day pass for $7).

Philadelphia Trolley Works (☎ 215/389-8687; www.phillytour.com) operates double-decker hop-on/hop-off bus and Victorian-style trolley tours with 27 stops. An all-day pass is $35 adults, $12 children 4–12.

Philadelphia Neighborhoods

CENTER CITY The Schuylkill and Delaware rivers bind this city section between Vine Street and South Street. (Confusingly, "Center City" is also sometimes used to refer to just the grid of streets right around City Hall). Center City's neighborhoods include:

OLD CITY In the shadow of the Benjamin Franklin Bridge, just north of Independence National Historical Park, an eclectic blend of 18th-century row houses, 19th-century warehouses, and 20th-century rehabs is now the city's hottest neighborhood, with chic restaurants, bars, and boutiques set in historic buildings and storefronts.

RITTENHOUSE SQUARE This beautifully landscaped park—ringed by elegant 1930s condos and historic mansions—exemplifies Philadelphia's elegance, wealth, and culture.

SOCIETY HILL In this fashionable heart of reclaimed 18th-century Philadelphia, loosely defined by Walnut and Lombard streets and Front and 7th streets, you can stroll among restored Federal, Colonial, and Georgian homes.

WASHINGTON WEST AND MIDTOWN VILLAGE The area just west of Washington Square shades into Midtown Village (between 11th and Broad sts. from Market to Spruce sts.), aka the "Gayborhood."

SOUTH STREET The southern border of Society Hill, the city limit in William Penn's day, is quiet by day and cruised by night: A colorful spot for casual dining, drinking, shopping, gallery-hopping, and getting pierced (or tattooed). Check out www.south street.com.

FAIRMOUNT Also known as "the Art Museum area," this neighborhood stretches north from the Benjamin Franklin Parkway to Girard Avenue.

SOUTH PHILADELPHIA / PASSYUNK Rocky Balboa meets artist lofts and authentic *taquerías* in this colorful and ethnically diverse neighborhood, with 300 years of immigration history.

UNIVERSITY CITY Wander through Penn's west Philadelphia campus for Ivy League architecture that includes an 1895 college green modeled on Oxford and Cambridge.

Fast **Facts**

APARTMENT RENTALS Short-term: Try www.airbnb.com, www.vrbo. com, or www.rentalo.com. **Long-term:** try www.craigslist.org or the alt weekly newspaper, *Philadelphia Weekly* (www.philadelphiaweekly. com).

AREA CODES In Philadelphia: 215 and 267. In the Pennsylvania suburbs: 610 and 484. In southern New Jersey: 856 and 609.

ATMS Throughout the city, most banks and convenience stores have 24-hour ATMs, most charging $2–$4 fee per use if the machine does not belong to your own bank. *Tip:* Call it a "Mac machine" and they'll think you're a local.

BABYSITTING Hotel concierges are your best source.

BANKING HOURS Most banks are open weekdays 6am to 5pm.

B&BS Try **Bed & Breakfast Connections of Philadelphia** (☎ 800/448-3619; www.bnbphila delphia.com), or visit www.bedand breakfast.com, www.booking.com, or www.airbnb.com.

BIKE RENTALS Philly now has a bike share program called **Indego** (www.rideindego.com). The $10 Day Pass—which you can buy at any of the 100+ bike stations— allows unlimited free 30-minute rides all day ($4 per half hour if you go over). **Wheel Fun Rentals** (www. wheelfunrentals.com) rents bikes ($10–$13/hour or $32–$38/day) and surreys at several locations whenever it's sunny and over 50°F: 1 Boathouse Row behind the Art Museum (☎ 215/232-7778).

BUSINESS HOURS Most shops and restaurants are open Monday to Saturday 10am to 6 or 7pm, Sunday noon to 6pm. Offices are usually open weekdays 9am to 5pm.

CONSULATES AND EMBASSIES Austria, France, Denmark, Germany, Malta, Mexico, Panama, Poland, Israel, Italy, Spain, and Sweden all have consulates in Philadelphia. The closest locations for most other foreign consulates are Washington, D.C. or New York City. Find yours: www.embassyworld.com.

DENTISTS For dental emergencies, call ☎ 855/352-6790 (www.emer gencydentist247.com).

DOCTORS See Emergencies.

EMERGENCIES For fire, police, and medical emergencies, dial ☎ 911. The non-emergency number for the police is ☎ 311. For poison control, dial ☎ 800/222-1222.

EVENT LISTINGS Check out the daily newspapers the *Philadelphia Inquirer* and the *Philadelphia Daily News,* and their joint website **www. philly.com**. The *Philadelphia Weekly,* available free from corner boxes, publishes on Wednesday (www.philadelphiaweekly.com). Monthly *Philadelphia Magazine* and its website (www.phillymag.com) are also a great source of info. The events websites run by official tourism bodies are www.phillyfunguide. com and www.uwishunu.com.

FAMILY TRAVEL For family travel info, visit the **Greater Philadelphia Tourism Marketing Corporation** (www.visitphilly.com); don't miss The Philadelphia Pass for family discounts on admission (www.phila delphiapass.com).

GAY & LESBIAN TRAVELERS Center City is welcoming to LGBTQ residents and visitors. The neighborhoods of Midtown and Washington West, a.k.a. the "Gayborhood" (especially between Broad and 12th sts., Walnut and Spruce sts.), have a concentration of gay-owned,

How to Speak Like a Philadelphian in 10 Terms

Philly. Use only if you're a native. Otherwise, use "Philadelphia."

Broad Street. The north-south boulevard bisecting Center City is what would be 14th Street. But never call Broad Street "14th Street." The new tourist-friendly designation of its section just south of City Hall as "Avenue of the Arts" is a little suspicious, too. But "Broad" is good.

Second Street. In South Philadelphia, call it "Two Street."

Front Street. Really 1st Street. Call it "Front."

Schuylkill. Pronounced "Skoo-kill," the river that flows by the Philadelphia Museum of Art between Martin Luther King, Jr. and Kelly drives is the local name for I-76, the eternally clogged northwest-southeast interstate expressway running along the city's western edge.

Blue Route. I-476 connects the suburbs and exurbs west of Philadelphia from I-95 near the airport to the Pennsylvania Turnpike (confusingly numbered I-76 if you head west toward Pittsburgh, but I-276 headed east to New Jersey).

Passyunk Avenue. Pronounced "Pass-yunk," this one-way avenue runs diagonally from Broad Street to South Street through South Philadelphia.

Sansom Street. "San-som," not "Samp-son." Although, if you're going to make a mistake, this is the one to make.

The Boulevard. The Roosevelt Boulevard, Route 1 North, is a high-speed thoroughfare running through Northeast Philadelphia, connecting the Schuylkill Expressway (I-76) to the Pennsylvania Turnpike, which leads to the New Jersey Turnpike.

Cheesesteak. One word. Not "cheese steak." Definitely not "Philly cheese steak."

-operated, and -friendly businesses. The *Philadelphia Gay News* (www.epgn.com) is available from sidewalk boxes. Also handy: **phillygay calendar.com** and **www.facebook.com/VisitGayPhilly**. For support groups and events, contact the **William Way Community Center,** 1315 Spruce St. (☎ 215/732-2220, www.waygay.org).

HEALTH CLUBS **Philadelphia Sports Clubs** (www.mysportsclubs.com) offers day passes for $15 at 250 S. 5th St. (☎ 215/592-8900); 1735 Market St. (☎ 215/564-5353); and 2000 Hamilton Pl. (☎ 215/568-9555). **Sweat Gym** (www.sweatfitness.com) offers day passes for $25 at locations including 1 S. Broad St. (☎ 215/564-0303); 200 S. 24th St. (☎ 215/351-0100); 45 N. 3rd St. (☎ 215/923-8763); 1509 E.

Passyunk Ave. (☎ 215/271-0303), and 700 Passyunk Ave. (☎ 215/627-5600).

HOLIDAYS Public and observed: January 1 (New Year's Day), Martin Luther King, Jr. Day (3rd Mon in Jan), Presidents Day (3rd Mon in Feb), Memorial Day (last Mon in May), July 4 (Independence Day), Labor Day (1st Mon in Sept), November 11 (Veteran's Day), Thanksgiving (4th Thurs in Nov), December 25 (Christmas).

HOSPITALS Centrally located hospitals include **Philadelphia Children's Hospital,** 34th Street and Civic Center Boulevard (☎ 215/590-2178; www.chop.edu); **University of Pennsylvania Hospital,** 3400 Spruce St. (☎ 800/789-7366; www.pennhealth.com); **Pennsylvania Hospital,** 8th and Spruce streets (☎ 215/829-3000; www.pennhealth.com/pahosp); **Thomas Jefferson University Hospital,** 11th and Walnut streets (☎ 215/955-6000; www.jefferson hospital.org).

INSURANCE Check your existing policies (and credit cards) before purchasing insurance to cover trip cancellation, lost luggage, medical expenses, medical evacuation, or car rental. There are more than two-dozen travel insurance specialists, so the best way to comparison shop policies is to use an aggregator that specializes in comparing all available policies at the same time: www.insuremytrip.com or www.squaremouth.com.

INTERNET Most coffee shops offer free wireless Internet access, as do some public spaces like the Kimmel Center. As we went to press, civic authorities were installing hundreds of high-speed free Wi-Fi kiosks through the **LinkPHL** initiative. For computer terminals, try branches of the **Free Library of Philadelphia** (☎ 215/686-5322; www.freelibrary. org).

LAUNDROMATS Two handy Center City options are **U-Do-It Laundry & Dry Cleaning** (1513 Spruce St.; ☎ 215/735-1255; www.udoitlaun dry.com; open daily 7am–10pm) and **Quick & Clean Coin Laundry** (320 S. 10th St., btw Spruce and Pine sts.; no phone; open daily 8am–8pm).

LIMOS Try **Dave's Best Limousine** (☎ 215/288-1000; www.daves bestlimoservice.com) or **Executive Towncar** (☎ 215/485-7265; www. philly-sedan.com).

LOST CREDIT CARDS For **American Express,** call ☎ 800/950-5114. For **MasterCard,** call ☎ 800/627-8372. For **Visa,** call ☎ 800/847-2911. For other credit cards, call this directory: ☎ 800/555-1212.

LOST PROPERTY At the airport: Check with the Communications Center at the Philadelphia International Airport, Departures Roadway, between Terminals C and D (☎ 215/937-6888; www.phl.org). **On public transit:** If you've lost an item on a SEPTA bus, subway, trolley, or train call ☎ 215/580-7800.

MAIL & POSTAGE At press time, domestic postage rates were 35¢ for a postcard, 50¢ for a letter. Find post offices and international rates at www.usps.gov.

PARKING On-street parking is notoriously complicated in Philly, with zoned neighborhood permits, regulations that change according to day and hour, and fewer and fewer coin-operated parking meters. The city is slowly moving toward a block-by-block payment system using automated ticket kiosks. Parking garages abound, but are not cheap: Expect to pay around $24 to $30 per day. More info: www.philapark.org.

PASSES Philadelphia Citypass (www.citypass.com), valid for 9 days, offers admission to your choice of three ($49 adults, $37 ages 2–12), four ($65/$47), or five ($77/$57) of a dozen top sights, including the Franklin Institute, Adventure Aquarium, Philadelphia Zoo, National Constitution Center, The Barnes Foundation, Museum of the American Revolution, and the Academy of Natural Sciences. The **Philadelphia Pass** (www.philadelphiapass.com) gives free entry to 36 attractions and tours—from the Art Museum to the Franklin Institute—plus a few shopping and dining discounts for 1 day ($59 adults, $44 ages 2–12), 2 days ($84/$59), 3 days ($99/$69), or 5 days ($119/$89).

PASSPORTS Virtually every traveler entering the U.S. must show a passport. U.S. and Canadian citizens traveling by land or sea from within the Western Hemisphere may present government-issued proof of citizenship (Enhanced Driver's License/Enhanced Identification Card or NEXUS card), although a passport is recommended.

PHARMACIES For 24-hour service, go to **CVS** (www.cvs.com) at 1826 Chestnut St. at 19th St. (☎ 215/972-0909) or 1500 Spruce St. at 15th St (☎ 215/790-3290); **Rite Aid** (www.riteaid.com) at 2301 Walnut St. at 23rd St. (☎ 215/636-9634), 1638 Chestnut St. at 16th St. (☎ 215/972-0234), or 1900 Arch St. at 19th St. (☎ 215/587-2101); or **Walgreens** (www.walgreens.com) at 1 S. Broad St. (☎ 215/330-0290).

SAFETY Center City is generally quite safe, but it is not without its muggings and purse-snatchings. The northerly neighborhoods of Northern Liberties, Fishtown, and Fairmount are still in the artists' lofts/hipster bars phase of gentrification—which means, outside of a few busy blocks lined with bars and restaurants, many streets feel rather dicey after dark. No matter where you are, do not leave belongings unattended, especially in a cafe or restaurant, and be especially

vigilant during holiday times. Use common city sense and be aware of your surroundings.

SENIOR TRAVELERS A compact downtown, vibrant cultural life, and widely available senior discounts at museums, events, and attractions make Philadelphia attractive to an increasing population of retirees and empty nesters.

SMOKING Philadelphia's smoking ban prohibits smoking on public transit and inside restaurants, cafes, shops, offices, hotels and hotel rooms, and the vast majority of bars (a handful of places, mostly dive bars, were granted exemptions). Smoking is permitted at outside tables and in most public spaces (i.e., on sidewalks, in parks). You must be 18 years old to purchase tobacco products.

SPECTATOR SPORTS All of Philadelphia's professional sports teams play at the stadiums at the south end of Broad Street (the AT&T stop on SEPTA's Broad Street Line—though locals, disgusted by runaway branding, still call it the "Pattison Ave." station). Early April through early October, the **Phillies** play baseball at Citizens Bank Park (www.mlb.com/phillies). Mid-September through early January, the **Eagles** play football at Lincoln Financial Field (www.philadelphiaeagles.com). October through April, the **Flyers** play ice hockey at the Wells Fargo Center (www.nhl.com/flyers). Late October through mid-April, the **76ers** play basketball at the Wells Fargo Center (www.nba.com/sixers).

STUDENT TRAVEL There are more colleges and universities in and around Philadelphia than in any other city in the country (depending on how you define "area," there are between 50 and 80—easily double that of Boston), so students will find a warm reception

What Things Cost in Philadelphia

A cup of coffee from La Colombe	$1.75
Subway, bus, or trolley fare	$2–$2.50
A pint of Yards ale at Standard Tap	$4–$5
Cheesesteak at Pat's King of Steaks	$11
Adult admission to the Philadelphia Museum of Art	$20
Nosebleed-seat Phillies tickets	$18–$38
Taxi ride from airport to Center City, with tip	$30
Train ride from airport to Center City	$8
Dinner for two at Parc Restaurant	$90
Average double hotel room, 1 night (before tax)	$149

from local vendors. A valid student ID will get you reduced rates on cultural sites, accommodations, car rentals, and more. You'll also earn a deep discount at **Apple Hostel**, 32 S. Bank St. (☎ 877/275-1971), right in the center of Old City nightlife—oh, and the history, too. For listings, pick up student papers such as the *Daily Pennsylvanian* (www.thedp.com) at the University of Pennsylvania, 34th and Walnut sts. (☎ 215/898-5000; www.upenn.edu); *The Temple News* (www.temple-news.com) at Temple University, N. Broad St.(☎ 215/204-7000; www.temple.edu); or *The Triangle* (www.thetriangle.org) at Drexel University, 32nd and Chestnut sts. (☎ 215/895-2000; www.drexel.edu).

TAXES At press time, Philadelphia's total retail sales tax is 8% on everything except clothing and groceries (prepared foods, such as restaurant meals, are taxed). Tax on liquor is 10%. The hotel tax is 8.5%. (**Note:** Outside the city limits, the retail sales tax drops to the state level of 6%.) Most other taxes (parking, etc.) are already folded into the prices and rates quoted to the public.

TAXIS See Getting Around, By Taxi.

TELEPHONES Public telephones are few and far between these days; a few remain at transportation hubs (train stations or the airport) and civic buildings. The cost for local calls varies with provider, but is usually 50¢. International calls start around $1 for 4 minutes. Some phones accept coins; others take credit cards.

TICKETS See Chapter 8, p 131.

TIPPING For restaurant servers and spa employees, tip 18% to 20% of the bill; taxi drivers 15% of fare. Tip hotel chamber staff $2 to $3 per day; coat check $1; valet parking $1 per ride. Remember that in many U.S. service industry jobs, employers expect their workers to receive tips and pay them less accordingly—if you don't tip, these low-paid workers will really feel the shortfall.

TOILETS Like most American cities, Philadelphia has few public toilets. Most attractions have facilities, however, as do restaurants and cafes. The latter often have a "customers only" usage policy, though you can often saunter into those at fast food establishments and chain cafes.

TOURIST OFFICES See Official Tourist Information, p 160.

TOURS See Getting Around: By Tourist Bus (p 163) for hop-on/hop-off trolley and bus tours.

Free and Friendly Tours (☎ 877/558-9671; freeandfriendly-tours.com) is exactly what it sounds like: the tours are free; you tip what you like.

Philly is the hometown of the world's top scholar-led walking tour company, **Context Travel** (☎ 800/691-6036; www.context-travel.com), which offers a dozen or so thematic walks—from art and history to South Philly food and African-American sites—led by PhDs and other academics. They come highly regarded, but they don't come cheap ($85). For a variety of less-expensive city walks ($14–$65) from multiple local companies, consult **www.viator.com**.

The non-profit **Historic Philadelphia,** 150 S. Independence Mall W. (☎ 215/629-4026; www.historicphiladelphia.org)—the estimable organization that provides the costumed storytellers and re-enactors peppered around Old City (and runs the Betsy Ross House and Franklin Square)—also offers a number of fun paid evening walks, including Independence After Hours ($85, includes dinner at City Tavern and a night visit to Independence Hall) and the Tippler's Tour Colonial Pub Crawl ($50).

Horse-and-buggies gather along the south end of Independence Mall East for tours of Society Hill and Old City; prices start at $30 for 1 to 4 people; $7 per additional person (buggy seats up to 6).

Philadelphia Segway Tours, in the visitors center at 1 N. Independence Mall W. (☎ 215/607-2851; philadelphiasegwaytours.com) offers a 1-hour tour ($55), and 2-hour tours of general sights, murals, or cheesesteaks (each $85).

TRAVELERS WITH DISABILITIES Most attractions—although not all National Historic Landmarks—offer ADA-approved access to their facilities. For basic Philadelphia information, contact the **Mayor's Commission on People with Disabilities** (☎ 215/686-2798; www.phila.gov/mcpd). SEPTA buses are lift-equipped, and all major train stations have elevator access. **ArtReach** (☎ 215/568-2115; www.art-reach.org), a not-for-profit organization, maintains a list of more than 140 area facilities that offer access to persons with disabilities. The **Philadelphia International Airport hotline** for travelers with disabilities is ☎ 215/937-6937 (TDD ☎ 215/937-6755). The Independence Visitor Center publishes *Accessibilities,* a brochure detailing accessible parking spots. The **America the Beautiful pass** (nps.gov) gives visually impaired or permanently disabled persons free lifetime entrance to federal recreation sites administered by the National Park Service, which includes Independence Mall.

A Brief **History**

1701 Penn issues a charter establishing Philadelphia as a city.

1731 Benjamin Franklin (1706–1790) creates America's first lending library.

1749 Benjamin Franklin creates the University of Pennsylvania.

1751 Benjamin Franklin invents the lightning rod.

1751 Benjamin Franklin and Thomas Bond (1712–1784) create the Colonies' first hospital.

1760 Benjamin Franklin invents the bifocal.

1774 At Carpenters' Hall (p 26), the First Continental Congress petitions King George for redress of colonists' grievances

1775 Delegates from all 13 Colonies meet for the Second Continental Congress, after the first battles of the American Revolutionary War.

1776 The Congress signs the United States Declaration of Independence, declaring colonies to be states separated from England.

1783 The American Revolution ends.

1790 Philadelphia becomes the capital of the new United States of America.

1800 The newly built Washington, D.C., becomes the capital of the U.S.

1816 Philadelphia's free black community founds the African Methodist Episcopal Church (AME), the U.S.'s first independent black denomination.

1835 German and Irish immigrant workers in Philadelphia mount North America's first general strike, in which workers win a ten-hour workday.

1876 The Centennial Exposition of 1876—the first world's fair—takes place in Fairmount Park and establishes the Philadelphia Museum of Art.

1901–1908 Philadelphia City Hall is the tallest habitable building in the world.

1912 Albert Barnes (1872–1951) meets Pablo Picasso and Henri Matisse in Paris, and begins to collect art. S

1917 Benjamin Franklin Parkway construction begins, creating a future home for the city's most important museums.

1930 A hot-dog vendor named Pat Olivieri slaps some steak and cheese on a bun. The cheesesteak is born.

1946 A Penn professor and a lab assistant build ENIAC, the world's first computer.

1970 French chef Georges Perrier opens Le Bec-Fin, starting a Philadelphia restaurant renaissance.

1971 Kenny Gamble and Leon Huff found Philadelphia International Records and establish The Sound of Philadelphia, Motown's biggest competitor.

1975 Elton John's *Philadelphia Freedom* hits number one on the American pop charts, teeing up Philly's role in the U.S. Bicentennial celebrations.

1976 *Rocky* hits it big in the box office, then wins the Best Picture Oscar, sealing Philly's hardscrabble rep.

1980 Philly makes sports history as the only American city to reach the championships of all four major pro sports in the same year. The Sixers lose the NBA Finals to the Lakers, the Flyers lose the Stanley Cup to the

Islanders, the Eagles lose Super Bowl XV to the Raiders—but the Phillies win the World Series!

1985 Mayor Wilson Goode authorizes the dropping of a bomb on a home belonging to radical black roots group MOVE, killing 11 MOVE members and destroying 62 homes.

1991 Future Pennsylvania governor Edward Rendell wins the mayor's race and spurs on the rebirth of Center City as a destination for dining, shopping, and bar-hopping.

1999 Suburban local M. Night Shyamalan releases *The Sixth Sense* and puts Philadelphia back on the filmmaking map.

2005 The FX sitcom *It's Always Sunny in Philadelphia* debuts, detailing the antics of a gang of

politically incorrect misfits running a bar in South Philly.

2008 The Phillies win the World Series again.

2012 The Barnes Foundation moves to the Parkway and the nearby Rodin Museum reopens, revitalizing Philly's Museum Row.

2016 Philly hosts the Democratic National Convention, which nominates Hillary Clinton as the first female major party candidate for President.

2017 Merriam-Webster adds to its dictionary an entry for "Jawn: the Philadelphia all-purpose noun."

2018 The Eagles win the Super Bowl for the first time ever. Fans barely manage not to burn down the city in celebration.

Philadelphia **Architecture**

Like the city itself, Philadelphia's architecture is a melting pot of schools and styles. Walk down most any Center City street, and you'll encounter Art Deco facades, Victorian townhouses, Colonial brick buildings, freshly painted murals, and glass-and-steel skyscrapers. Philadelphia's very first buildings, simple log cabins, are now all but lost to time. The city's second architectural wave was more enduring: 17th-century denizens often built their meeting houses and worship sites in brick, using a mix of architectural styles from their diverse backgrounds. (Check out the Old Swedes' Church, p 23, built around 1700). Examples of **Georgian architecture**—typified by symmetry and simplicity, paned windows and rectangular transoms—include plainly elegant Christ Church (p 11), Carpenters' Hall (p 26), Powel House (p 55), and Independence Hall (p 9).

A half a century later, the next wave of building design married Greek Palladian and Georgian styles in so-called **Federal style**, which dominated until the mid-1800s.

Examples can be found in four-pilastered American Philosophical Society Library and the Pine Street side of Pennsylvania Hospital (p 56), in addition to dozens of houses in

Society Hill: Look for a front door surrounded by glass panes and topped by an arched window. Another sure sign of a Federal building: the presence of a bald eagle.

The next several decades subtracted the Georgian leanings from Federal architecture and revived the classically Greek. Not surprisingly, this early-19th-century architectural style is called **Greek Revival**—or, if you prefer, neoclassical. Architects known for this style included William Strickland (1788–1854), who designed the dramatically domed Second Bank of the United States (p 17); Old City's imposing Merchants' Exchange at 2nd and Walnut streets; and the National Mechanic Bank, 22 S. 3rd St. (btw. Market and Chestnut sts.), now a restaurant and bar. Similarly, architect William Haviland (1792–1852) did some of his most important work in Center City, including the Walnut Street Theater (p 128), the University of the Arts building at Broad and Pine streets, and Eastern State Penitentiary (p 68).

Frank Furness (1839–1912), another native son, designed distinctively ornamental **Victorian Gothic** buildings featuring polychromatic masonry (multicolored bricked laid in an icing-type fashion), including the elegant Pennsylvania Academy of the Fine Arts (p 30) and Fischer Fine Arts Library at the University of Pennsylvania (p 71). Scotsman John McArthur, Jr. designed the all-masonry City Hall (p 15) in Second Empire style.

Philadelphia's earliest skyscrapers would not be considered so by modern standards. Upon their building, the **Ben Franklin House** on Chestnut Street, between 8th and 9th streets; **30th Street Station** (p 71); and the **Franklin Institute** (p 48) were considered tall. The first modern-looking skyscraper was the steel-and-glass 1932 **PSFS building** (now a Loews Hotel, p 140), designed by William Lescaze and George Howe, considered the world's first International Style building. Native son Louis I. Kahn (1901–1974) served as architect for **Richards Medical Library** at the University of Pennsylvania, while I.M. Pei designed **Society Hill Towers** (p 18) and the shining **National Constitution Center** (p 10).

In the 1980s, chess piece–like **Liberty One** (1650 Market St.) and **Liberty Two** (1601 Chestnut St.) were the first buildings to rise above the brim of William Penn's hat atop City Hall—formerly the unofficial cap on local building height. More skyscrapers quickly sprouted. In 2008, cable giant Comcast put its name on the city's tallest building to date, the USB-stick-looking **Comcast Center** at 17th Street and JFK Boulevard (p 63), and then upped the ante in 2018 with the even taller **Comcast Technology Center**—at 1,121 feet (342 m) and 60 stories, the tallest in the U.S. outside of New York or Chicago.

Index

See also Accommodations and Restaurant indexes, below.

A

Academy of Music, 61, 124, 128
Academy of Natural Sciences, 67, 93
Academy of Vocal Arts, 124, 128–129
Accommodations. See also Accommodations Index
best bets, 134
Adams, John, 24, 55, 57
Adventure Aquarium, 96
African Methodist Episcopal Church, Mother Bethel, 24
Aibel, Bob, 53
Air travel, 162
American Philosophical Society, 17
Amish Farm & House (near Lancaster), 150
Amish people, 149
Amtrak, 162
Annenberg Center at the University of Pennsylvania, 129
Anthony's Chocolate House, 19
Antiques Row, 84
Antiques/vintage, 77
Apartment rentals, 165
Arader Galleries, 77
Architecture, 172–173
Arch Street Meeting House, 27
Arden Theatre Company, 124, 125
Area codes, 165
Army-Navy game, 161
Art galleries, 32, 77–79
Arts and entertainment, best bets, 124
Art Star, 79
ATMs, 165
Audubon, John J., 17
Avenue of the Arts, 59

B

Babysitting, 165
Ballet, 128
Banking hours, 165
Barnes, Albert, 4, 15
Barnes Foundation, 15, 32, 33, 67

Bartram's Garden, 89
Barye, Antoine-Louis, 64
BB&T Pavilion, 124, 129
Becuna, USS, 18, 57, 96
Bed & breakfasts (B&Bs), 165
Ben Franklin Bridge, 95
Benjamin Franklin Life & Legacy Museum, 39
Benjamin Lovell Shoes, 83
Betsy Ross House, 11, 27, 40, 51, 160
Bike rentals, 165
Biking, 87–89
Bishop White House, 25, 55
Black Sheep, 120
Blendo, 77
Blue Route, 166
B'nai Abraham, 24
Boathouse Row, 14, 69, 87
Bob & Barbara's, 118
Bond, Thomas, 56–57
Bookstores, 79
Booth, John Wilkes, 64
Born Yesterday, 79
The Boulevard, 166
Bowling, 115
Boyd's, 81
Brancusi, 30
Brancusi, Constantin, 14
Brandywine Battlefield Park (Chadds Ford, PA), 147
Brandywine River Museum (Chadds Ford, PA), 147
Brandywine Treasure Trail Passport, 145
Brandywine Valley, 145
Brasil's, 114, 115
Bridgid's, 120–121
Broad Street, 166
Brumidi, Constantino, 93
Buchanan, James, 151
Bucks County, 153–155
Bucks County Playhouse, 153–154
Business hours, 165
Bus Stop Boutique, 84
Bus travel, 162, 163

C

Calder, Alexander, 14
Calder, Alexander Milne, 15, 32
Calder, Alexander Stirling, 15, 32, 93
Camden, NJ, 95
Card Players (Cézanne), 33
Carpenter's Hall, 26
Car rentals, 162
Car travel, 162, 163
Cassatt, Mary, 14

Cathedral Basilica of St. Peter and Paul, 93
Cavanaugh's Headhouse, 121
The Centennial Arboretum, 88
Center City, 163, 164
Center for Architecture + Design, 59
Central Market (Lancaster), 150
Centre Square, 93
Cézanne, Paul, 4, 13–15, 33, 35, 67
Chaddsford Winery (Chadds Ford, PA), 147
Chapterhouse, 18
Cheesesteak, 6, 166
Chestnut Hill, 158
Chestnut Hill Skyspace, 158
Chinatown, 105, 160
Chinese Lantern Festival, 160
Chinese New Year, 160
Chocolate World (Hershey), 150
Chris' Jazz Café, 130
Christ Church, 11, 27, 51
Christ Church Burial Ground, 10
Citizens Bank Park, 4
City Hall, 15, 59, 60
Citypass, 167–168
Claudio's, 19
The Clay Studio, 52, 80
Cleveland, Grover, 63–64
Climate, 162
Clothespin (Oldenburg), 30
Comcast Center, 63
Comcast Centers Holiday Spectacular, 161
Comedy, 132
Common Threads (Saligman), 34
Computer terminals, 167
Consulates, 165
Context Travel, 170
Cowboy (Remington), 69
Credit cards, lost, 167
Cret, Paul Phillippe, 15, 64, 93, 95
Curie, Marie, 17
Curtis Institute of Music, 124, 129
Curtis Publishing Company, 92

D

Dallas, George Mifflin, 24
Dance clubs, 115, 118
The Dance II (Matisse), 33
D'Angelo's Lounge, 118

Photo **Credits**

Notes